DEVELOPMENT

This book details the history of the idea of psychological development over the past two millennia. The developmental idea played a major part in the shift from religious ways of explaining human nature to secular, modern ones. In this shift, the 'elect' (chosen by God) became the 'normal' and grace was replaced by cognitive ability as the essentially human quality. A theory of psychological development was derived from theories of bodily development, leading scholars to describe human beings as passing through necessary 'stages of development' over the lifespan. By exploring the historical and religious roots of modern psychological concepts and theories, this book demonstrates that history is a method for standing outside psychology and thereby evaluating its fundamental premises. It will spark new interest in the history, sociology and philosophy of the mind sciences, as well as in the rights of children and developmentally disabled people.

CHRISTOPHER GOODEY is a former lecturer in the Faculty of Arts and Social Science at the Open University and the author of *A History of Intelligence and 'Intellectual Disability': The Shaping of Psychology in Early Modern Europe* (2011).

DEVELOPMENT
The History of a Psychological Concept

CHRISTOPHER GOODEY

Shaftesbury Road, Cambridge CB2 8EA, United Kingdom

One Liberty Plaza, 20th Floor, New York, NY 10006, USA

477 Williamstown Road, Port Melbourne, VIC 3207, Australia

314–321, 3rd Floor, Plot 3, Splendor Forum, Jasola District Centre, New Delhi – 110025, India

103 Penang Road, #05–06/07, Visioncrest Commercial, Singapore 238467

Cambridge University Press is part of Cambridge University Press & Assessment, a department of the University of Cambridge.

We share the University's mission to contribute to society through the pursuit of education, learning and research at the highest international levels of excellence.

www.cambridge.org
Information on this title: www.cambridge.org/9781108970501

DOI: 10.1017/9781108980845

© Christopher Goodey 2021

This publication is in copyright. Subject to statutory exception and to the provisions of relevant collective licensing agreements, no reproduction of any part may take place without the written permission of Cambridge University Press & Assessment.

First published 2021
First paperback edition 2023

A catalogue record for this publication is available from the British Library

ISBN 978-1-108-83347-9 Hardback
ISBN 978-1-108-97050-1 Paperback

Cambridge University Press & Assessment has no responsibility for the persistence or accuracy of URLs for external or third-party internet websites referred to in this publication and does not guarantee that any content on such websites is, or will remain, accurate or appropriate.

Contents

Acknowledgements		*page* vi
	Introduction	1
1	Development and the Origin of Psychological Concepts	9
2	The History of Christianity and the First Principles of Development: Linear Time, Interiority, Structure	22
3	The History of Education: Rearing the Elect Child	69
4	Pascal on the Ordering of Human Time	85
5	The Normalization of the Elect: Locke to Montesquieu	105
6	The Coining of a Developmental Theory: Leibniz to Bonnet	137
7	*Emile*: Rousseau's Well-Ordered Developer	166
8	Nature versus Nurture and Cognitive Ability Testing: Historical Sketches	186
	Postscript: Further Targets for Historical Research	205
Index		208

Acknowledgements

As this ought to be my final assault on topics that have occupied many years, I would like to thank three people who have been important for much of that time. When I try to think what they have had in common, my gratitude is for the fact that they have all been hard to please. When a long time ago I started to look for ways in which young children might be able to participate directly in social policy research, Priscilla Alderson was already doing it. Where the only thing I had was intuition, she already had a clear view of the moral and intellectual path, and generously set me on the road by involving me in parts of her research. Her large output is an essential starting point for any understanding of childhood today. Roger Smith has waded through quite a few premature drafts of mine, including those for the present book. It is not just that no one knows more about the history of psychology; I have been influenced by his deeper insight, namely that the history of psychology is as much a force in our lives as our own individual 'psychologies'. At a more personal level, and despite his intellectual interests lying elsewhere, Istvan Hont usually knew what next step I thought I needed to take. Along with his merciless eye for the reading of historical texts, he knew that a modicum of self-understanding is 'all' that is additionally necessary if we are to understand the difference between salvaging history and merely rearranging its deckchairs. The friendship and modesty of this remarkable person sometimes kept me going when I felt despair. Of course I should have said so at the time, and it is sad that I can no longer acknowledge it to him.

Thanks are also due to Delphine Antoine-Mahut, Nicola Grove, Simon Jarrett and Michael Sonenscher for reading all or parts of the script; Julie Brumberg-Chaumont provided me with an essential opportunity to synthesize some of the arguments found in Chapter 2. Finally, I would like to thank the six anonymous reviewers of my original manuscript, as well as my copyeditor Andrew Kerr-Jarrett for his meticulous reading of the final version.

Introduction

Development is one of psychology's given components. Psychologists and consequently the lay public in Western cultures see childhood as well as adult character in terms of what I call here 'the developmental idea', describing a scientific category that exists 'out there' in nature. The human interior, it seems, passes through a necessary series of stages that play out over time. And so the youngest of us are only potential human beings; we do not start to display signs of 'empathy', say, until we are three, or 'logical reasoning' until we are six: or so we are told. Adult character and conduct are the desired outcome of those stages (though a few of us, it appears, never reach them even when we arrive at adulthood by calendar age).

In any science, however, it is axiomatic that starting assumptions be kept under close observation. The existence of 'development' may be taken for granted, but is it truly a fact of nature? This book approaches the question by a historical route. After all, without knowing how the idea of development arrived we can hardly know what the thing itself really is. Historians of psychology often proceed by taking an obvious category like this and searching past literature for an early, primitive awareness of it. They assume that it is what the philosophy of science calls a 'natural kind': something that has been and always will be around, only awaiting an accurate scientific description. Critics of this approach call it 'presentism'. Rather than skip the stage of submitting their starting premises to scrutiny, they have found instead that psychological categories assumed to be natural kinds often turn out to be human creations, arising from the midstream of historical contingencies. Rather than ask where historical concepts are heading, they ask where modern concepts come from. Categories as basic to the discipline as memory, intelligence, emotion, depression and inhibition have been looked at afresh in this way.[1] This book adds development to the list.

---

[1] Kurt Danziger, *Marking the Mind: A History of Memory* (Cambridge: Cambridge University Press, 2008); C. F. Goodey, *A History of Intelligence and 'Intellectual Disability': The Shaping of Psychology in*

To see the developmental idea and even the thing itself as historical creations is to say that there were once and may in future be totally different ways of understanding what it is to be human. Few sociologists have questioned the natural status of development;[2] its social critics in general, by focusing on the power relationships for which the concept has been used, also tend thereby to leave its core premise intact.[3] And it is the historical perspective, more so than any other, that enables us to stand fully outside the formative conceptual ingredients of psychology and make an external assessment of them.

The practical implications of this are vast: for the specific social out-groups it has created such as those deemed to be not yet developed (children), for those who by the same criterion will never develop (developmentally disabled) and ultimately for all of us. However, this book is neither a social nor an ethical critique. Here, if there are judgements to be passed, it is history itself that will be doing the job. It tells us that once upon a time, people did not develop. If this seems for the moment implausible, at least it might be agreed that there was no *developmental idea*: no sense of human individuals being cognitively complete or incomplete, emotionally mature or immature, no sense that full humanity is either merely potential or actual and achieved. The fact that children grow physically did not prompt parallel thoughts about interior growth. Only at a certain point in history did the developmental idea arrive. It belongs to a particular era with a beginning and, who knows, an end.[4]

That era is not just the last century or so, during which developmental and child psychology have become a formal scientific discipline, but also the many previous centuries on which the discipline drew for its content. Seeds of the developmental idea were sown during the first centuries of Christianity and monotheism generally. Later, towards the sixteenth and early seventeenth centuries, came the notion of a *structured* interior timeline. This notion was modelled on a small number of people: not just the

---

Early Modern Europe (Farnham: Ashgate, 2011); Daniel Gross, *The Secret History of Emotion: From Aristotle's Rhetoric to Modern Brain Science* (Chicago: University of Chicago Press, 2006); Matthew Bell, *Melancholia: The Western Malady* (Cambridge: Cambridge University Press, 2014); Roger Smith, *Inhibition: History and Meaning in the Sciences of Mind and Brain* (Berkeley: University of California Press, 1992).

[2] For the rare exception, see Priscilla Alderson, *Childhoods Real and Imagined: An Introduction to Critical Realism and Childhood Studies*, vol. 1 (London: Routledge, 2013); also *Young Children's Rights: Exploring Beliefs, Principles and Practice* (London: Jessica Kingsley, 2008), especially chapter 4.

[3] See, for example, Erica Burman, *Deconstructing Developmental Psychology* (London: Routledge, 2016); John Morss, *The Biologizing of Childhood: Developmental Psychology and the Darwinian Myth* (London: Routledge, 1990).

[4] For an acknowledgement from within the discipline concerning the possibility of an end, see William Kessen, *The Rise and Fall of Development* (Worcester MA: Clark University Press, 1990).

social elite but even more importantly the 'elect' – that is, those few whom God had predestined to be saved from damnation. It was this elect minority that would later transition into the 'normal' majority familiar to the modern outlook. The developmental idea, as it emerges in the texts of early modern thought, is part of this shift from explaining human nature in terms of religion to a modern, secular-looking psychology. This book focuses chiefly on the religious beliefs of major historical thinkers in the century prior to the arrival of the word 'development' itself in the mid-eighteenth century.

Early Christian thinkers broke with cyclical ways of reckoning time in human lives. They prescribed for the human individual the sense that time is linear and heading towards an identifiable destination. They structured this linear time into a necessary series of stages. And they shifted the main criterion for division among human beings from their external status and worldly power, or lack of it, to their interior status and their salvation, or damnation. By the late sixteenth century, there was a widespread theory that God had determined everyone's afterlife destination (and therefore their interior status while on earth) before birth. The efficacy of individual effort was thereby marginalized: you could do nothing to alter your destiny. And because in the case of the damned this situation did not seem just, religious writers were forced to look for excuses. It was no longer enough just to quote the Bible. They started to try and defend God's actions by means of a rational theory.

Meanwhile, God was becoming an indwelling power within nature that sustained the universe in its becoming rather than as a spatially hierarchical structure. He was seen as prolonging its motion towards a goal, at the same time as religion set itself to discovering causes for prospective, linear time within the individual. This conception of God would peak in eighteenth-century theories of a rationally explicable or 'natural' religion, from which direct lines to the modern mind sciences can be traced. If, in external nature, being was increasingly studied in terms of its becoming, the human being was increasingly studied as a human becoming. And from this rational religion arose large chunks of modern psychological theory, of modern human sciences and political philosophy.

I have mentioned the contingent character of our history. If modern psychological categories have since gone on to acquire an observable reality of their own, it is because they were not quite fabricated out of thin air. They built on previous conceptual categories which now seem obsolete but which we cannot escape because their previous continual accumulation decided who we would become along the way and who we are now. The developmental idea had a two thousand years' gestation, its roots roughly coinciding with the start of monotheistic religion and the expansion of empire around the Mediterranean. The study of human interiority – at first in theological and then in psychological terms – began from that point on to assemble its theories and conceptual armoury, and ultimately the labels that now clutter journalistic trivia and everyday talk. Out of that long historical framework, the mind sciences have come to dominate both the staking out of separate group identities and the overall notion of what it is to be human.

Without such historical preconditions the developmental idea would not exist in its present form today. Nor would its own particular way of dividing human beings off from each other, especially through concepts of childhood and developmental disability. What the long-term conceptual history shows us is that 'development' is less a scientific and natural category, than a temporary way of seeing each other. More specifically it is a dummy term for normality. To develop is to be normal, to be normal is to develop. For the adult thus conceptualized, *to have developed* is to be normal, and so for the child, *to be developing* is to be on the way to being normal. But simply *to be a child* is to be not normal, or not fully. Both childhood (in general) and developmental disability (in adults) come under a single rubric. They denote absence in the kinds of ability which humankind in current Western cultures sets for itself as its supreme identifying characteristic.

As a conceptual history the book inevitably follows a rough historical sequence, but it also involves thematic similarities between different periods. It cannot be a matter of choosing between a chronological and a thematic approach; the more one confines oneself to one or the other, the more one distorts. The reader will be following a course that forms *overall* a historical sequence; but they will find at times that I dwell on the structural similarities between one period and another quite distant one within the long period covered overall.

Persevering with the intellectual challenge is a necessity because here is the stuff of which the modern psychological disciplines were made. We cannot understand the mind sciences and the human sciences more generally unless we know what their raw materials were and are. The reader must be prepared to accept, at least as a hypothesis, that human beings – and that includes children – do not develop: they change, of course, but there is no necessary reason why change should be represented as development. A moral acceptance of this hypothesis will make it easier to grasp texts and explanations of texts that will sometimes lie beyond the reader's usual experience.

Chapter 1 provides an introduction to two general points which may seem unusual to the modern reader and which therefore need to be understood, especially given the historical remoteness of some of the historical texts discussed later: first, that the basic ideas forming developmental psychology proper, educational and child psychology, and cognitive psychology more generally, are the outcomes of historical contingency; and secondly, that they are a modern continuation not only of the social functions of religion but also of the actual content of theological arguments.

Chapter 2 outlines the interdependent first principles underpinning the developmental idea: namely, linear time, interiority and structure. Concerning the first of these I describe 'development' as just one particular way, confined to one historical era, of conceptualizing the more fundamental category of *change*. Its historical specificity means we can compare it, as an anthropologist would, with other ways of conceptualizing change. Developmental change defines the individual in terms of a permanent interiority structured according to stages of linear time and oriented towards a final goal. Christianity was distinctive among monotheistic religions in conceiving 'redemption' as that goal, an idea that would later transition into that of the earthly perfectibility of man. Early Christian theologians already conceived of time as an irreversible arrow, seeing the linear trajectory of the human lifespan as a potentially successful 'recapitulation' of Adam's initial failure. Medieval historians would then begin to draw parallels between individual interior growth and the forward trajectory (later, 'progress') of the species on earth.

The next section in this chapter looks at the principle of interiority. In pre-Christian cultures interiority was conceived in terms of temporary visitation or possession. Monotheistic religion emphasized the *permanence* of the interior status. Augustine defined time itself as a 'distention' of the soul or mind, a necessary deviation from and prelude to being with God. Then, in what became known as the 'faculty psychology' of the late medieval era, labelled subcategories of interiority began to proliferate: for example, abstraction, attention, consciousness, logical reasoning. The detailed description of these cognitive categories was modelled on the professional activities of the era's elite literate administrators and bureaucrats. The increasingly temporal emphases in faculty psychology also accompanied monastic and religious notions of selfhood, as well as humanist ones of the individual.

The final section of this chapter looks at the principle of structure. Augustine's theory of the 'six ages' of man gave the focus on the lifespan a fixed structural dimension. The burgeoning idea of structured interior growth following the Reformation and Counter-Reformation drew on Augustine's once esoteric theory of predestination. The structure of interiority in the elect minority was seen as following a predetermined stadial sequence, with a built-in destination (salvation). When secular notions of interiority started to arrive, still using the language of medieval faculty psychology, they drew on debates about the stages by which 'saving' grace arrives in the elect.

Chapters 3–7 then focus in more detail on the crucial century up to the arrival of an explicit theory of psychological development in Rousseau; the texts under discussion are largely though not exclusively French ones.

Chapter 3 looks at the principles behind the experimental primary schools established by the Jansenist wing of French Catholicism. There had once been no clear distinction between the child's interiority and the adult's, since 'saving grace' could arrive at any point in the lifespan; nevertheless, the rudimentary developmental idea was already suggesting a more sharply defined category of childhood. The Jansenist schools aimed at preserving the purity of the children of the elect from contamination by the surrounding mass of reprobates in thrall to the Devil. The prophylactic was precisely *not* religious instruction but a secular, humanist curriculum based on reason.

Chapter 4 deals with the scientist and philosopher Blaise Pascal, whose hints at a temporal concept of soul, mind and human interiority stand on the cusp of the shift from a spatial to a temporal view of human existence, and were deeply influential on subsequent pioneers of the developmental idea. On the one hand, using spatial analogies drawn from geometry, he considered the most important aspect of the individual's interiority to be 'Order'. On the other, Order was a temporal phenomenon because it had to control the movements of interiority over time, which otherwise had a 'lunatic' unpredictability. Pascal believed it was possible even for the predestined elect to lapse, and elements of a modern, forward-moving and quasi-developmental interiority can be seen in his search for a 'counterweight' that might push back against the likelihood of this.

Chapter 5 looks at the transition from 'elect' to what would eventually become 'normal' in a cluster of key texts around 1700. It is clear that when influential philosophers immediately prior to the Enlightenment such as Leibniz and Malebranche speculate about the interior life of 'Man' they presuppose the *elect*, saved man. These shadows cast by predestinarian thinking can still be detected even in Locke and Montesquieu, regarded as the founding figures of the Enlightenment. The concept of election would retain a subliminal presence in the nascent human sciences of the eighteenth century. So too would their increasing preoccupation with determinism, first divine then biological, which was attached to the causes of election and reprobation and later of developmental normality and abnormality.

Chapter 6 describes how the normalization of the elect acquired a corresponding theoretical framework. From the late seventeenth century the preferred explanation for physical growth had been 'preformation': that all living organisms have pre-existed from the Creation and are born as miniature versions which 'unfold' through predetermined stages (e.g. caterpillar – chrysalis – butterfly). Leibniz suggested applying this model of staged development to the human mind. It was in this context that the word itself, development (whose first appearances are better translated as 'unfolding'), was first employed. The pioneering naturalist Charles Bonnet went on to apply preformationism to what he now expressly termed 'psychology'. He assimilated it with the stages of regeneration in the elect; this in turn reflected the idea of social progress as the unfolding of Revelation, which is gradual rather than instantaneous.

In Chapter 7 we arrive at the application of the word 'development' to a clear, fully formulated principle of temporal 'Order'. This happens in Rousseau's *Emile*, and is modelled by the childhood of its young central character. The biologist Buffon, the psychologist Condillac and particularly Bonnet all influenced this seminal treatise. But where they had used 'development' only occasionally and in an abstract sense, with Rousseau it becomes ubiquitous and the main descriptor of the structured lifespan of the individual. In the need for human lives to adhere strictly to an ordered temporal structure, the developmental idea finally reaches its own maturity. Man is born free and everywhere he is in the wrong kind of chains; instead, he should be ordered by the temporal determinism of 'stages'. Rousseau retains the older sense of development as the 'unfolding' of an already existing, preformed structure; nevertheless, he also reveals in outline the modern human sciences' presupposition that the child is an incomplete being. Emile is both the last holy child and the first normal child.

Chapter 8 shows briefly how the book's themes launched nineteenth- and twentieth-century debates about child development, and about freedom and necessity, that are still central in education and psychology today. From the mid-eighteenth century onwards not only the more 'psychological' work of Condillac on sense perception but also the broader cultural influence of

Rousseau inspired the founding of the modern disciplines. The book therefore concludes with an overview of some more recent figures, and the threads by which their work can be traced to religious ideas discussed in earlier chapters: in Britain, David Hartley, Joseph Priestley and Francis Galton with his nature-versus-nurture formula; and in France, Hippolyte Taine, Alfred Binet (creator of the 'mental age' test, subsequently IQ) and Jean Piaget himself.

CHAPTER I

Development and the Origin of Psychological Concepts

The history of developmental psychology has two strands: one as a formal scientific discipline dating back a hundred years, the other as what I call the developmental idea – a view of what it is to be human that stretches back two millennia. The first strand is merely a passing phase of the second.

Two millennia is a fairly recent segment of human history. The developmental idea had a starting point well within the period of written record. If, before that, the very existence of a permanent interior development covering the whole lifespan and marking one's personal identity seems to have gone unacknowledged, there are two ways of interpreting this. The first is circular: that people long ago were themselves too undeveloped to recognize as a scientific fact that every human individual has an interior identity which develops over the course of a lifetime – and that aeons had to pass before we humans became clever enough to appreciate the fact. The second is to consider development as such – not just the concept or the theory but even, in important ways, the thing itself – as a creation of human history rather than simply a given fact of nature.

This book takes the second view. Perhaps the very idea of development has altered our natures by interacting with them, and turned them in a developmental direction – if only because we keep on talking about the thing. The fact that the idea (and therefore the interaction) began only at a certain point along the human timeline means that our natures are the product of a series of contingencies, such that under other circumstances something different for humankind might have come about.

Through a long and more or less seamless historical transition past concepts, categories and theories have turned into our present ones. The developmental idea has come to dominate our overall definition of the human being. In fact, its historical character and roots lie not *only* in the monotheistic religions but, more deeply, in human beings' awareness of the bedrock of universal experiences – change, time, mortality – through which we have always encountered ourselves and each other. The developmental idea is this awareness in one of its historically specific forms: that is to say, the most recent one, our own. Monotheism's contribution was to establish as a principle that time is linear, in opposition to the view that it is, for example, cyclical. Two thousand years ago a definition arose of what it is to be human that would eventually become the developmental one: personhood as *permanent interiority structured by linear time*, oriented towards a *goal* (redemption, perfection, maturity – all indicating some sort of completion). Linear time extends into a future which, predictable or not, does not keep bringing you back where you started, and it continues into an eternal afterlife or an equally eternal damnation.

To start with, this linearity was something new. Although centuries were needed for it to become a widespread presupposition, it was theorized almost from the beginning. The early Christian writer Irenaeus (*c*.130–202) proposed that the purpose of the human timeline was 'recapitulation'. We had to take off again from where Adam had fallen and follow a trajectory that would lead to recovery of his original happiness and perfection. (The term 'recapitulation' would turn up again in nineteenth-century psychology as the core principle of modern developmental psychology's academic founder, G. Stanley Hall.)

Another early Christian, Augustine of Hippo (354–430), laid down the idea of a permanent individual identity, which he labelled *homo interior*. Later, following the Reformation and Counter-Reformation, religious debate became concerned with finding where 'saving' grace lay, within this human interior. How did grace arrive in 'the elect' – those few people (God's chosen) who were predestined for salvation? And how did it play out over the linear time of their lives on earth? The elect were a fundamentally distinct type of human being from the 'reprobate' mass, in whom grace was absent and who remained stuck in a static condition with hellfire as their destiny. Then, from the early eighteenth century, the idea of grace began to be reconciled and merged with that of human nature – a thought previously frowned upon. In this context, 'saving' grace began to be reconstituted as cognitive ability and natural maturity, and the elect as normal people (nature's chosen), while the reprobate majority was reconstituted as an intellectually undeveloped minority: idiots, imbeciles and the feebleminded.

Saving grace was thus brought down to earth, and in its new, cognitive form has become a common currency. One illustration of this important episode comes in the work of the devout naturalist, Charles Bonnet. Possibly the very first person to label himself a 'psychologist' in his *Essay on Psychology* (1755), he asked himself here what 'psychology' actually is.

1 Development and the Origin of Psychological Concepts

His answer was that it consists in 'the Economy of Grace'. This esoteric theological term had meant, for previous generations, the inequality of God's allocating 'saving' grace to some humans and not others. In Bonnet's text, however, it means *both* this *and* the unequal distribution of natural human abilities such as cognitive and moral ones.

With the gradual rise of the developmental idea to the surface of early eighteenth-century intellectual thought came also the beginnings of an *explanatory theory* for it. Two particularly important theoretical issues featured in the century leading up to its explicit appearance in Rousseau's *Emile* (1762).

The first of these was an increasing obsession with finding ultimate causes that determine particular human natures and identities. The obsession continues today. But at that point the determinism was of a divine sort. God had irrevocably decided before the beginning of time every individual's interior status and its ultimate end point. Whether you were saved or damned was something you could do nothing about. This idea would eventually transition into the genetic determinism more familiar in today's psychobiology. In the transition, determinism would also acquire its own specifically temporal character, which I call 'stadial determinism'. That is to say, human interiority in itself, over and above the individual's determinate pre-natal status, started to be seen as passing, during its earthly lifespan, through a 'pre-formed', pre-programmed, purely psychological structure that 'unfolds' in a staged series and can be marked off by calendar time.

The second issue immediately prior to Rousseau and relevant to our history is the idea of the General Will. This term is well known to historians of political thought if not of psychology. It was first coined by certain mid-seventeenth-century writers to indicate God's will for human beings, concerning their afterlife destination as just described. The theory was driven by a newly felt need to justify the operations of order and justice in the universe. In medieval thought, order had been largely spatial in conception: a static cosmos with descriptive rather than predictive laws. However, the seventeenth century was witnessing exceptional sociopolitical disorder and injustice. Unpredictable earthly events had highlighted the mutability of human lives, and the search for a *temporal* order on earth and in the cosmos was growing, which helped to reinforce linear conceptions of the human interior. However, there was a problem. All men and women were born in a reprobate state, prior to God's choice of a few for rescue. It was the condition of reprobates to remain static, and of the elect to undergo change. Failure to change, therefore, could be seen as an unjust and disorderly decision by God himself. After all, individuals could do nothing to initiate the change by themselves, and so God seemed to be the creator of their deficiency. Where was the divine perfection here?

The problem was explained away by saying that God's will to save was only a 'general' will, not one that influenced the fate of this human being rather than that one. Rousseau took this idea about divine justice and used it to formulate one about political justice: there was a civic General Will, according to which justice on earth is determined by a social decision-making that somehow prevails over particular individual choices. And in the burgeoning psychological outlook, this idea of a *general* political will was accompanied by the idea of an *abstract* individual. The agency of what Rousseau called 'the abstract man' is not limited by divine decree, but it *is* circumscribed by the stadial norms of the individual interior. This theory had parallels in the contemporary arrival of 'progress' as an equivalent theory of sociopolitical order. Like development, it too had its 'stages'. In fact, the psychological theory may well have influenced the political one as much as vice versa. (Rousseau's equally important contemporary, Turgot, the best-known pioneer of progress as a political theory, had a few years earlier defined and written about social progress as *The Successive Advances of the Human Mind*.)

I have started out, then, with two suggestions. The first is that psychological development as such – its actual content, in addition to its social function – is not something self-evidently natural but a partly or even wholly human creation emerging contingently from the midstream of human history. The second is that modern developmental psychology is a continuing outgrowth of the religious outlook, not the abandonment of one for the other. Christian ways of thinking have become psychological ones that retain a common underlying metaphysic. Later chapters explain these transitions in more detail, and meanwhile some introductory remarks about both these suggestions may be useful.

Psychological Development and Historical Contingency

One major historical overview of developmental psychology from within the discipline opens with the appropriate metaphor: 'A scientific field comes of age when it begins to acknowledge its history. If so, then this volume marks the growth of developmental psychology beyond its adolescence.'[1] The

---

[1] (Eds.) Georg Eckardt and Wolfgang Bringmann, *Contributions to a History of Developmental Psychology: International William T. Preyer Symposium* (Berlin: Mouton, 1985). See also Willem Koops and

implication is that its adolescence began with the onset of the formal discipline at the start of the twentieth century, and that it has now reached its maturity. But it had a childhood too, which had been going on for the previous nineteen centuries. As for its birth, one rarely comes across the acknowledgement that the developmental idea was 'born' at all. Is it not obvious? We seem to see psychological development around us, especially in children, in whom it is conceptualized by analogy with physical development. However, there is a problem in comparing interior development with the development of bodies. Bodily development is a natural kind, a stable aspect of nature. If psychological development were likewise a natural kind, what exactly would be its definition? A definition of intangibles – cognition, emotions, moral thinking, for example – can only be in the head of the observer; unlike the child's body, it depends on who is doing the defining. Of course, it is self-evident that an individual personality *changes* over the lifespan, but less evident why change has to be cast in the role of *development* as distinct from something else.

If a primary task for the historian of psychology must be to try and stand outside its basic terms and concepts in order to observe and understand them properly, the first principle underlying the concept of development is change. Once we have said that, we have reached bedrock. Nothing else lies beneath the absolute principle that 'change' exists. Change just *is*. Analysis can penetrate no further. The idea of development is not itself bedrock; it is only one way of interpreting time and change in human experience. There have been and will be other ways. The developmental idea belongs to a specific era and place. Awareness of change will inevitably feature in the picture any era has of that experience. There are succeeding pictures of change, each of which will consist in a set of 'absolute presuppositions';[2] and each era sees its own conceptual picture as an ahistorical, unmodifiable and absolute truth – even though the succession of eras will always prove it to have been temporary and its theoretical framework redundant. The veracity of the absolute presuppositions is tested not by the ensuing era, since the latter's own new presuppositions will themselves be tested one day, but simply by time.

Frank Kessel, 'Developmental psychology without positivistic pretentions', in (eds.) Koops and Kessel, *Historical Developmental Psychology* (New York: Routledge, 2020); and Sheldon H. White, 'Developmental psychology in a world of designed institutions', in (eds.) Koops and Michael Zuckerman, *Beyond the Century of the Child: Cultural History and Developmental Psychology* (Philadelphia: University of Pennsylvania Press, 2003), p. 63ff.

[2] On this see R. G. Collingwood, *An Essay on Metaphysics* (Oxford: Clarendon, 1998 [1940]); *The Idea of History* (Oxford: Oxford University Press, 1993 [1946]).

Conceptual history provides a firm base from which to do the testing. My claim is not, therefore, that the developmental idea is merely relative, sociologically speaking. It concerns the idea's historical specificity. It is one thing for sociologists to challenge the 'natural' status of what is considered normal development, quite another to work out how the developmental idea was born, and how its sense of the natural and the normal arose. This can be done on the basis of historical texts which are there for all to read and to weigh evidence on that basis, without falling into a futile scepticism.

However, if the developmental idea began only two millennia ago, that leaves plenty of previous historical time unaccounted for, most of it unrecorded. We might therefore look for some deeper-lying common motivation antecedent to Christianity – something that may or may not be inbuilt within human experience. 'Might' because there is a point so far back at which the picture goes blank. Did the original humans in the Great Rift Valley even have the notion of an interior existence, let alone of corresponding group identities? Without such a notion, they could hardly have had the idea of development.

Perhaps the cross-historical question should be: what, as human beings, do we register when we come across unknown fellow humans, and what do they? The philosopher Thomas Hobbes (1588–1679) thought the primary feeling was fear. Less negatively, it might be simple curiosity. But the question remains, how do we deal with the unknown when from the outside it looks like us? The last two thousand years show us a pattern of responses whereby, whatever the feeling which the question provokes, it alternates with reassurance. In the period described in the later chapters of this book, the dominant historically specific feeling was what might be called 'anxiety', the developmental idea being a late historical product of it.

Recent generations have managed the tension between anxiety and reassurance by creating conceptual boxes to put people in. The mind sciences supply a whole rationale of human subcategories, labels and definitions. These may be considered as facts of nature, or they may be considered as a superficial and overdiagnostic imposition upon our humanity – or they may be simply useful approximations. Whichever is the case, 'putting people into boxes' is a cliché of the modern era. Even after human groups started being strictly categorized by internal characteristics, at some point part way along the historical timeline, new boxes have kept appearing – then disappearing. Thus the very *objects* of psychological knowledge, let alone our interpretations of them, do not prove durable. The precise current assembly of categories, their presumed objectivity and associated definitions, concepts and theories, not to mention the ethical value thereby added to or subtracted from this or that group, are on the historical evidence just as fragile and evanescent as past categories proved to be.

The ethical implications of the developmental idea are unavoidable. It is not just that the ideas of the last two millennia have had consequences in the social world; the consequences have fed back into further ideas, with further consequences. For example, in the everyday version of the developmental idea, children's acquisition of characteristics is a good. But losing some of them is *also* a good. And so implicitly, the discarded state in general – infancy – is bad, 'childish', at least if it fails to correspond with the strict laws of calendrical time. This creates a confusion of values. On the one hand, if the developmental acquisition of normal – that is, adult – characteristics is good, so surely is the speed at which developmental stages are reached. After all, the very fact of getting *from* one stage *to* the next is advantageous. On the other hand, this contradicts the scientific certainty of developmentalism's fixed temporal structure, which claims that infants cannot do certain things ('empathize' or 'reason logically') before a certain age. Defining a young human being's personhood by the expectation that their structured developmental stages will proceed in strict tempo, neither before nor after they should, comes with reassurance in the former case and anxiety in the latter.

Today, developmental psychology is a prolific expert discipline, reaching out to the everyday world of parents, teachers and toy manufacturers who put plastic bath ducks for six-month-olds in packaging that says (I have a gift for my granddaughter in front of me): 'Meets Developmental Targets: Logical Thinking, Language Acquisition, Fine Motor Skills.' Its expertise might once have focused only on developmental stages in infants born with some already detectable disability; today, however, normality is etched into place by pathology. All new parents of appropriate socioeconomic status are provided with scientific information about the date when their child should start doing something or leave something else behind. It is as if childhood in general were a clinical condition. Although there are ways in which children's lives have improved, this may not be one of them. It reveals the developmental idea's unspoken premise to be a deficit model of childhood. Indeed, the very first published paper by the world's first self-identifying developmental psychologist was entitled 'Children's lies'.[3]

My hypothesis, just stated, about a behavioural 'pattern' involving anxiety and reassurance could itself be seen as a psychological one. It is in any case purely speculative. But what is not mere speculation is that

---

[3] G. Stanley Hall, *American Journal of Psychology*, 3 (1890), reproduced as 'Children's lies: their psychology and pedagogy', in *Educational Problems* (New York: Appleton, 1911).

when thinkers of the past have had ideas they have often written them down. And the conclusion I draw from my reading of the conceptual record is that whereas today we see development as a given, and any anxiety about development as a product of it, in fact the reverse is true: the very idea of development is a product of that deeper, non-specific anxiety (curiosity, fear etc.). The pattern of anxiety that produces categories of human interiority is more deeply rooted than the categories themselves. The role of the developmental idea is to provide the corresponding reassurance. It does so by offering certainty of knowledge about what it means to be truly human – in *this* way and *no other* – and by assessing the presence or absence of true and full humanity in others.

Anxiety, then, about what exactly? What, in the human being's interior identity, is the thing that ought to be developing, the ultimate marker? This has varied historically and continues to do so. Over the last three centuries a specifically human intelligence or cognitive ability has been first among equals. And my point here is less speculative: *if* anxiety is the issue, then it has *certainly* become attached to this particular item, as modern pre-natal technology shows. It is too easy to assume that when the formal discipline of psychology took shape in the late nineteenth century, it did so in order to investigate fixed aspects of human nature, one of which was intelligence (and particularly its deviations and absences). In fact, the new discipline investigated things it was simultaneously forging: not just a new terminology, nor even new conceptual categories to describe underlying natural things, but the things themselves. There is a huge history to the rise of intelligence, a category whose content and defining characteristics have come and gone and are not agreed upon even in the present. But for the purposes of this book, cognitive ability is developmental or it is nothing; it is key to the present scientific phase of the developmental idea.

The phrase 'cognitive ability' is used in this book very broadly, for ease of reading. It covers what writers of the early modern era, rooted still in directly religious sources, meant when they wrote about 'reason'. Reason in that period – roughly, from the sixteenth century to the end of the eighteenth – signified many aspects of interiority in addition to modern cognitive ability; what united them was rather their absolute distinction from the will. Cognitive ability did not arise as a rival to other qualities – emotional, moral etc. – as if we could choose one or another of them from some cross-historical marketplace. The boundaries among such qualities become fainter the further back we read, until at some point they erode altogether. They swam into focus relatively recently, from a formerly undivided space. If interiority is a historical item, then, so are its subdivisions. In the scientific version of the developmental idea, cognitive ability has the dominant though not exclusive place, and so occupies a similar place in this book. There is plenty of literature arguing the ethical importance of moral or emotional attributes over more narrowly cognitive ones in the modern sense, and it is no good setting different kinds of development at each other's throats. To query our current cognitive obsession simply in order to promote some other, arguably more desirable way of denoting the essentially human trait would leave unexamined the developmental principle that threads through all of them today.

While the modern cognitive tradition requires the individual to develop autonomy in a quasi-juridical sense of 'competence', the psychoanalytic tradition has focused on developing autonomy in human relationships, in the sense of emotional well-being. Jean Piaget and Sigmund Freud are usually presented as opposites in developmental terms, and it is true that the cognitive and psychoanalytic approaches have fought a terminal battle for professional influence – psychoanalysis currently having the higher body count. But in the long historical term they are two sides of the same coin. At the core of developmental psychology lies the idea of mental age, where abnormality consists in 'retardation' or 'delay'. At the core of psychoanalysis lies maturity (albeit of a neurotically fragile kind), where abnormality consists in 'arrest' at the Narcissus stage. Both suggest an inner life defined by the *chronological appropriateness* of predictable, normative *phases*. And both establish thereby a rationale for external observation of something whose source is interior and invisible.

With hindsight it is difficult to see how our current categories of mental existence or the very notion of a mind – and thus the lifespan 'development' of any of them – can be any more valid than the ones our furthest ancestors might have used, if indeed they had anything comparable to say. However, if they have all gone on to acquire an observable reality of their own, it is because they were not *quite* fabricated out of thin air and are thus not *quite* relative. They built on older categories which now seem obsolete but whose impact we cannot escape because their previous and continual accumulation has decided who we would become along the way.

From Religion to Psychology: The Historical Continuity

Those older categories arose in the context of religious beliefs that may puzzle the modern reader. How could anyone have swallowed, for example, the idea they might roast eternally after death, especially as they would be unable to do anything to prevent it? And what on earth might that have to do with modern psychological categories most of us take as read?

Historians of psychology interested in the era before its establishment as an academic discipline have tended to look for their primary sources either in the philosophy of mind or the history of medicine, rather than in the history of religion as such. But from the late Middle Ages onwards, it was writers with a religious purpose who first gave a labelled profile to human interiority, subdividing it into what they called 'faculties' and 'operations'. Their accounts of it were more detailed and definite than any philosophical discussion about the mind claiming to be above the fray. They were also culturally specific. The theory of election (the so-called predestination of souls), for example, was used in civil and international war propaganda.[4] Yet these and similar texts also helped the relevant branches of modern psychology by refurbishing the presupposition of a fundamental intra-human divide between elect and reprobate as a divide between the developmentally normal and abnormal, and between adulthood and childhood as specific and distinct ways of being human. These texts are not the whole history. But they are a much larger part of it than usually supposed.

Both religion and the mind sciences can be subdivided into doctrine, belief and presupposition. Doctrine is a set of formal, enunciated principles; belief is a less fixed form of doctrine and can also involve an internal conversation with oneself; presupposition is belief without awareness even of the possibility of conversation or of alternatives. The three sit alongside and interact with each other; and at various points they also appear in historical sequence. (Rigid) *doctrine* degenerates into (arguable, less structured) *belief*, whose explicit versions eventually disappear but whose (residual) *presuppositions* nevertheless remain, a fact only ever discovered in retrospect. And precisely because presuppositions, being residual, go unrecognized by the person holding them, they help to reconstitute apparently discarded beliefs in quite new versions at whose deeper levels the permanence of the presuppositions continues to operate. Then out of that more or less new belief springs new doctrine. In our case, the new doctrine is developmentalism.

The first principles underlying the doctrines, beliefs and presuppositions of psychology are rarely subjected to philosophical enquiry. Although the philosophy of mind probes the question of what minds are, its focus tends to be on sense perception; it rarely investigates the lifespan as a whole. At least two well-known twentieth-century books seemed to engage with the

---

[4] Remarkably, no overarching treatment of the theory of election so far exists, outside purely theological studies that treat it as a still live issue. Historians of religion nevertheless provide much helpful context; see, for example, Patrick Collinson, *The Reformation: A History* (New York: Modern Library, 2003).

importance of time: Martin Heidegger's *Being and Time* and Paul Ricoeur's *Time and Narrative*. However, they do not provide an external take on 'development', and that is because their deepest roots lie in precisely the kinds of Christian tradition that gave rise to it. They were partly successors to the end phase of that tradition, exemplified in writers such as the theologian Friedrich Schleiermacher and his nineteenth-century successors, thanks to whom salvation became universally accessible and religion finally located more within the human interior than in the letter of doctrine. The possibility was thereby open that election (interiority, as once perceived) might be the status of – almost – every human being and therefore constitute normality (interiority, as now perceived). Moreover, the importance which Heidegger and Ricoeur went on to give to the characteristic of speech within this universal humanity closes off exactly the sort of contribution that might come from the 'undeveloped' and as yet speechless infant, or from the developmentally 'disabled' adult – those whom the developmental idea is most anxious about.

Why does the historical continuity from religion to psychology matter? It matters because religion still, in our own era, furnishes the materials for the layperson's sense of self. Speaking personally, my superego is a rational atheist – but my ego is a two-millennia-long sedimentation laid down by Christianity. Of course, long historical chains like this can be stretched too far. In the physical sciences, for example, there are present-day theologians making the claim – which I suspect is nonsense – that Augustine's theory of time was an anticipation of quantum theory. Nevertheless, what is required of the reader in a modern intellectual milieu still drunk on its liberation from the shackles of Christianity is a willing suspension of unbelief (so to speak). In order to get an outside perspective on the human and mind sciences we must first get inside theology. The fact that this is the crucial path to any history of psychology worth the name may well be closely connected to the fact that it is the one which those of us who are rational atheists are primed to resist.

It could be objected here that psychology has since undergone a refining process, and has now finally discovered category boundaries that are reliable and of optimum sharpness, or are at least getting there. Yet all of the discipline's multiple parentage has so far failed to produce any broad and commonly agreed rule-bound science that might stand its ground even for a couple of centuries: no Newton, no Lavoisier, no Darwin. And so there is nothing to stop it from going round in circles, just as theology once did. A category – 'development', or its goals of 'normal intelligence', 'emotional maturity' etc. – is posited whose validation takes the form of deductions drawn from its already postulated existence. Medieval theologians proved God deductively in just this way. Moreover, for Augustine and Aquinas, the grand architects of Christian theory, God *is* Intelligence. Conceptual history reveals thereafter a more or less seamless transition from Him to It.

The theory of election is a further example of this. I call it the 'theory of election' rather than the 'doctrine' because from a conceptual historian's standpoint it has no less right to be called a theory than development has, and was held across religious denominations. Once the embers of this previously esoteric Augustinian theory were stoked by Reformation and Counter-Reformation, no dispute was more deadly. What is grace? Who has been given it? When and how does it arrive? The last of those questions could only be resolved by staggering its receipt across the earthly lifespan. Failure to acquire grace constituted, by definition, suffering – in the afterlife. By the mid-nineteenth century the small group of God's elect had expanded to include a larger part of the species, as an agglomeration of more or less intelligent and mature individuals (at least among North-West European males). The classification of human interiority in terms of nature merged with human beings' possession of grace – nature and grace having once been mutually exclusive. The language used to describe this merger was dominated by an increasingly active set of human abilities that were seen as impacting on the external environment and as instruments of progress and development of a social kind. It was failure of such abilities to develop over time, that is, developmental disability, that now came to be seen by definition to constitute suffering – in this life, rather than the one to come. Today's developmentalist disciplines are thus one historical manifestation of the deeper-lying and more long-term principle of a fundamental intra-human division that for the last two thousand years has seemed necessary to all ways of perceiving and describing one's fellow humans.

Historically speaking, the two forms of status – elect and cognitively able – are simply passing descriptions of an optimal interiority, the one feeding into the other. The reader may of course find all this talk about interiority suspect. The word sounds vague, liable to act as a holdall. If I can give no pat definition, that is because the practice of delving inside oneself and behind the appearances of others, having arisen at a certain point in the course of human history, has since been in constant fluctuation. I have asked whether our first ancestors even conceived of each other's characteristics as exterior/interior, and whether the very attribution of interiority might not be, in the first place, a product of anxiety. To rephrase this question as a modern autism specialist might, did our earliest ancestors have 'Theory of Mind', that is, did they attribute intentions to others, or was this a product of later psychobiological evolution? The word 'Mind', however, evokes too many of its more recent and infinitely varied applications from the last few centuries, and is therefore too confusing to do the job required of it. (I use it here only when a particular historically specific context demands it.) The word 'interiority' is more broadly applicable, even if it begs just as many questions. It too had its own specific historical onset when Augustine coined that phrase *homo interior*.

In saying that religion and modern developmental psychology belong to a single outlook, I am being dismissive of neither. Psychology does not usually involve or even recognize deep historical analysis of its foundational ideas because to do so would reveal that its causal claims, rooted in nature, are actually moral ones rooted in a specific historical framework. This is not necessarily a critique, but it is a fact of life. In this respect psychology is no different from the other human sciences, such as politics or economics. Its historical slot is the history of ideas rather than alongside the history of, say, physics or medicine. And only by understanding the transitional status of the developmental idea can we understand what its role in our lives might be.

Nor, in connecting a religious definition of what it is to be human to our own supposedly secular, cognitive one, am I merely drawing an analogy. Religion and psychology share common social and anthropological functions which are obvious in practices with individuals (e.g. counselling) and in institutional contexts (e.g. the segregation of impure out-groups). But there is more to it than that. It is the formal conceptual content too that is an organic extension of medieval theology. Nor is the modern discipline a secularization of its medieval counterpart; rather, it has assumed the latter's sacral status. If Christianity can be defined as the 'conduit' through which human experience was 'drained of the secular',[5] the modern developmental idea has a similar role, since outside its terms one is scarcely recognized today as having a human nature at all.

---

[5] R. A. Markus, *The End of Ancient Christianity* (Cambridge: Cambridge University Press, 1998), p. 15.

CHAPTER 2

The History of Christianity and the First Principles of Development: Linear Time, Interiority, Structure

The concept of psychological development, and the developmental psychology that holds it in place, presupposes that the human essence consists in interiority structured by linear time, pointing towards a goal – a future that marks its species identity. This concept and its combination of those several elements had a historically specific onset. In it, timeline, interiority and structure all hold each other up: remove one and the rest fall. The combination is just one historically specific variant – one that has replaced (and will one day be replaced by) others – of the abiding truth that the human being changes. The more specific idea of human time as an irreversible arrow, heading towards a fixed destiny, has led to interiority acquiring a permanence as 'the mind', which with its own detailed framework of categories and subcategories subsequently became seen as structured above all by the succession of temporal stages.

1: Linear Time

In the developmental idea, time is linear. Other ways of describing human time were characteristic of other historical eras and perhaps still lead an underground existence. One example of an entirely different concept of change, once dominating how the human lifespan was perceived, was cyclical, a concept modelled on the return of the same natural events such as planetary phases or the seasons. Another was the arc-shaped line; here, the value is placed neither on a future goal nor on a return to the beginning but on the midlife peak of the arc, which is followed by a descent into a sort of second childishness. Yet another version can be found in the etymology of the word 'develop' itself, which originally meant to unfold (by antithesis with 'to envelop'); in this version if human individuals do have a goal, it is already enshrined in their beginning. Of the three, it was this last that fed the historical transition towards a whole scientific theory of development, as interest gradually shifted from the starting point to the goal or end point. It shows how one set of presuppositions in psychology does not get *replaced* by the next, as if an external force were acting upon an inertia, but flows into it like an underground watercourse.

Today's positioning of linear time and development at the centre of human nature, which in terms of its social history is also an *ideology* or reification, is an inevitable distortion of the deeper-lying principle of change. Distorted because lopsided: it separates growth from decay, goal-orientation from being and living from dying, the second term in each pair being bundled offstage. Onstage, boundaries between human sub-groups are imposed which are ultimately arbitrary but which the developmental idea actualizes as a social practice. The restricted ideological picture of what it is to be human takes a certain creature hostage and presents it to us as the child. In this picture, the difference between 'child' and 'developmentally disabled' is still unclear. If the developmentally disabled person is childlike, 'delayed' on a 'developmental plateau', then it is also the case that children – all children in general – are developmentally disabled. The difference between the two states only becomes clear well into the second or even third decade of existence when that chronologically younger creature comes up with the ransom by 'fulfilling their potential' and achieving a certain cognitive normality and emotional maturity, while in a small number of cases they fail even to begin to do so. The occupant of the dominant ideological niche is then revealed: it is the developmentally non-disabled non-child, who thereby constitutes the normal adult.

The very notion of a cognitive, emotional and moral development circumscribes the childhood identity. Where interior development is assumed to be a natural kind, children must be a separate subspecies of the human; this then justifies their social position and ethical treatment. In other words, the developmental idea, like the modern forms of social organization into which it feeds, involves a conceptual segregation of the child. And if the developmental idea is also characteristically *goal*-oriented, the goal is set by the prior external authority of long-standing norms of scarcely perceived religious origin, mediated by present-day secular social actors including (to begin with) the family. I can truthfully say that my granddaughter is *changing* all the time, but I cannot say that she is *developing* without my having some prior, normative idea of where over time that development is and should be heading. Without a goal, there could be no development. The goal is not hers, autonomously; or even if it is hers in part, this is still only within parameters already ordained for her.

The question for us is not the goals or the power relationships involved but the premise itself, 'development'.

Psychological Development and Absolute Time

What are the historically specific assumptions about human time that inform developmental psychology and the human sciences generally? I have said that we must go back to the beginnings of Christianity, but first we must understand their modern sense, itself a historical phenomenon rooted in the scientific revolution. It arose out of the brief historical window when, following Isaac Newton (1643–1727), time took on what seemed to be an independent existence. In Newtonian physics time and space became absolutes, separate from each other for the purposes of explaining physical events. The notion of time as an absolute then informed the human sciences' conceptualization of interiority. The application of absolute time to psychology was reinforced by contemporary teleological arguments for the existence of God: the very first Christians had believed in the imminent return of Christ, but following their disappointment came a greater interest in how human beings might prepare themselves internally for redemption over a longer timescale, perhaps during an intervening 'kingdom of the saints' on earth. This was very much in the air in Newton's time. It fed into an accompanying science of the human interior, corresponding with his physics in the sense that it too had a teleological basis.

The Newtonian window in physics was brief – a couple of hundred years, after which quantum theory and the space–time continuum would elide his separation of absolute time from absolute space, and since when physics has rejoined the longer-term nexus in which time and space belong together. Meanwhile, however, the developmental idea in its formal psychological sense, originally parasitic on that Newtonian vision, has sunk roots of its own. If 'development' is a presupposition, it is partly because psychologists still think in terms of those eighteenth-century concepts of absolute time – long after the parasite's host science departed.

The extent to which we regard as strange those other, non-linear accounts of change just mentioned correlates with the extent to which we take for granted our own presupposition of it as developmental. The onset of monotheistic religion had been crucial because it engaged in a deep conceptual shift that led to the favouring of time over space, line over cycle and change over stasis, in descriptions of the external cosmos. (Buddhism too, whose mass expansion occurred only in the last century BC, was an attempt to break the cycles of reincarnation.) This shift took centuries to complete. For a long time, in a residually static and spatial picture of the universe, things on the one hand just *were*, and on the other did not seem just to abide by themselves but were dependent for their existence at every moment on the will of the Creator who had the job of continually sustaining them.[1] Thus the early Christian's identity was premised on simple endurance; throughout the first millennium and beyond, redemption and the goal of salvation remained an esoteric doctrine.

Although by the end of the Middle Ages certain temporal explanations of the cosmos were beginning to make an appearance, the early human sciences were still dominated by spatial concepts. To give one example, the *intellectus*, that aspect of divine reason in which the reason of human individuals might hope occasionally to participate, took two coexisting forms: the potential and the actual – a distinction drawn from Aristotle. Today, it is potential intellect that dominates (children fulfil intellectual 'potential' which, one day along the timeline, will become 'actual' performances), whereas for medieval writers the distinction between potential and actual had been not temporal but proximal: the 'actual' intellect – that is, the intellect in its activated state – was adjacent to the divine intellect, and was warehoused in the 'potential'. The picture was a spatial one.

Anthropologists have sometimes described the modern concept of time as replacing a 'primitive' world view in which time and space were a single inseparable entity and which in some cultures even had the same word for both.[2] Spatial fixity still dominated descriptions of the physical universe in Aristotle, for whom proximal criteria were primary: the *perfection* of the cosmos was defined by *distance* from the earth, the most perfect location being the outermost sphere (the 'fixed' stars).[3] Time was of some importance, inasmuch as the extremity of this distance was a function of the speed at which it had to revolve in order to preserve the (static) harmony of the whole, or because it described the motion of planetary orbits which are crudely structured by cyclical 'phases'; but, largely, time was a subsidiary element in the overall picture of the cosmos. Christianity put an end to this.

Alongside the residue of other models (cyclical, arc-shaped, unfolding), certain kinds of non-permanent interior state – some ascribed to

---

[1] Georges Poulet, *Studies in Human Time*, translated by Elliot Coleman (Baltimore: Johns Hopkins University Press, 1956), p. 3.
[2] See, for example, Alan Kolata, *Valley of the Spirits: A Journey into the Lost World of the Aymara* (Chichester: John Wiley, 1996).
[3] Aristotle, *De caelo* 1.12.

momentary visitation, others to changes in bodily temperament and disposition – subsisted well into the early modern era, and contrasted with the unalterable permanence of election and reprobation. Writers of the period did not consider this multiplicity of models a problem. In some sense the models still coexist today. In biology, for example, even though it cohabits with psychology, the assumed course of a living creature is arc-shaped (growth, optimal state, decay) – whereas *homo psychologicus* ascends by structured stages from infancy through adolescence towards its own specific type of perfection (adult maturity), from which point onwards it carries on along a more or less even plateau of normality until it suddenly falls off a cliff (death, elderly dementia).

Within that multiplicity of models, however, a significant break with polytheistic cyclical accounts of time had been taking place almost from the start of Christianity.[4] The establishment of settled agricultural production and accompanying extension of social administration had already led previous Egyptian and Babylonian emperors to flirt with a kind of monotheism, but in their case the god in question was the emperor himself, whose accession was defined by his own status as the sole source of authority. A firmer social basis for the idea of a single godhead was provided by the Romans, whose first 'emperor' overlapped with the young Jesus. Although Muslim and Jewish philosophers heavily influenced Western European thought along the way, including some major elements of a prototypically psychological science, I confine myself to Christianity because it was there that the final passage from religion to the modern mind sciences would occur, some elements of which did not get bolted into place until little more than a century ago.

Redemption and Recapitulation

The New Testament theme of redemption through Christ, which achieved prominence during the second millennium, reinforced the sense of time as movement towards a divine end, represented in human terms as perfection. The subsequent and gradual shift of this goal from heaven to earth, and the subsuming of perfection under terms like 'normality' or 'maturity', would subsequently allow modern concepts of cognitive, affective and moral development to emerge more or less seamlessly out of Christian models of interiority and linear time. A human life of cyclical repetition, whose

---

[4] On this, see Robert C. Knapp, *The Dawn of Christianity: People and Gods in a Time of Magic* (London: Profile Books, 2017).

idea of perfection lay outside it, was replaced by life conceived of as an irreversible trajectory whose perfection or rewards lay at the end of it – a conception influenced (each in its own way) by the advancing armies of empire, ever-encroaching administrative outreach and pilgrimage. This last is particularly important to us because the metaphor of *internal* pilgrimage would feed directly into the developmental idea itself; the hundreds of texts of which Bunyan's *Pilgrim's Progress* is just the tip were not merely naïve precursors of a more sophisticated modern discipline, nor did the modern discipline simply wipe the slate clean.

The importance which the later Middle Ages started to give to time has been seen by social historians as part of the shift from repetitive, seasonal cycles of agriculture to the linear time of capital accumulation.[5] The explanation from social history is strong, but it is intertwined with a conceptual history that has its own separate course. As we have seen, some of the roots of the developmental idea lie in analogies drawn from the physical universe. Just as modern astronomy replaced the medieval *description* of the phases of Jupiter with mathematical formulae involving the *prediction* of its movements, psychologists have adapted this conceit in order to predict the developmental paths of 'typical' or 'normal' human characteristics.

Linear time was not the only theme of early Christianity. Some of its writings admit the unity of (spiritual) growth and decay and the oneness of coming into life and dying. As T. S. Eliot wrote, echoing them:

> Time present and time past
> Are both perhaps present in time future
> And time future contained in time past.

And if time is eternally present, then 'all time is unredeemable' and so, cyclically, we 'arrive where we started'. However, this mystical-sounding stuff had a currency across all monotheistic religions (Kabbalah Judaism and Sufi Islam, for example). What marked Christianity off was the story of redemption. The concepts of linear time and redemption were necessary to each other. Redemption of the individual and of the 'fallen' species as a whole assumed a straight line from past error to future salvation. In cyclical time, eternity and perfection coexisted in some alternative realm that was merely parallel with the earthly one. In linear time, the perfection of life everlasting comes at the *end* of the earthly course and is permanent.

---

[5] See, for example, E. P. Thompson, 'Time, work-discipline and industrial capitalism', *Past & Present*, 38/1 (1967), pp. 56–97.

In this sense the future is a goal that can be foreseen (even if it is not predictable in the case of individuals).

The first shoots of the linear theme were already appearing in the second century AD, when Christianity was still just one among many thriving cults. The decline of the cyclical mode of thinking was intensified for these cults by Jesus's failure to come back to earth as promised. In response to this failure the first major Christian theorist of personal growth, Irenaeus (c.130–202), proposed that the central task of the human species on earth is to plot the line towards its own species goal. To be a follower of Jesus meant to 'recapitulate' the life of Adam, but with a happy ending instead of a fall.[6] Adam before the Fall had been man in his infancy, a state of relative perfection though still requiring spiritual growth. When his progeny reprised that journey, their future state would be even more perfect than the prelapsarian Adam's. This thought of Irenaeus's later became essential to Christianity's historical vision of salvation.[7]

It is worth noting as an aside here that the term *recapitulatio* would resurface in the modern theories of individual psychological development espoused by nineteenth-century race scientists and child psychologists, on the principle that 'ontogeny recapitulates phylogeny'.[8] With interiority honed into cognitive 'intelligence', social 'normality' and emotional 'maturity', such characteristics turned the static medieval vision of a 'ladder of nature' with its vertical hierarchy into something horizontal and temporal.[9] The idea of a future perfection at the end of linear time reinforced that of the human trajectory as being, like a line, either straight ('normal') or deviating ('deviant'), creating the basis for an anxiety that would be displaced to the conceptualization of children.

Early Christian Fathers such as Irenaeus and especially Augustine (354–430) did not start with a blank page but were engaging intellectually with contemporaries. Non-Christian Stoics had written crudely of stages in the development of children, albeit in affective terms and without the linear sense of a goal.[10] But most previous pagan conceptions were cyclical and/or arc-shaped, drawing for their depiction on observations of the natural

---

[6] St Irenaeus of Lyons, *Against Heresies* (Ex Fontibus, 2010), Book 4.
[7] Jan Miel, *Pascal and Theology* (Baltimore: Johns Hopkins University Press, 1969), p. 13.
[8] G. Stanley Hall, *Adolescence: Its Psychology and Its Relations to Physiology, Anthropology, Sociology, Sex, Crime, Religion and Education* (New York: Appleton, 1904).
[9] See Arthur Lovejoy, *The Great Chain of Being: A Study of the History of an Idea* (Cambridge MA: Harvard University Press, 2001 [1936]).
[10] See Lawrence Becker, 'Stoic Children', in (eds.) Susan Turner and Gareth Matthews, *The Philosopher's Child: Critical Perspectives in the Western Tradition* (Rochester: University of Rochester Press, 1998).

world with as much emphasis on decay as on growth. This was what the early Christian writers sought to challenge. If the Church Fathers started to think beyond the spatial and the static, it was precisely because time was specific to *homo interior*. As Paul had commanded, 'Be ye transformed by the renewing of your mind.'[11] The linear trajectory of human time was already seen as a renewal of the interior human life, and important for that reason alone.[12] Augustine got this partly from his reading of more philosophically oriented Christians like Plotinus, whose need to get over their initial dependence on unreliable externalities such as the imminence of Christ's return had led them to a more intellectualist view of the human essence.

Linearity had its downside – time rushes on towards an end – but the upside was that the concept of 'end' had a second, normative sense: that of a goal. The goal was to be with God, and thus to overcome time. Augustine's belief (a) that time's arrow is irreversible, and (b) that psychological time is separable from physical time, profoundly influenced the centrality of time in explaining the external world and would later help to give us Newtonian science. In psychological time, the question of what was *re*formative – relinquishing the old Adam – lay at the heart of what the developmental idea would later represent one-sidedly as simply *formative*, in the modern 'scientific' sense. With Augustine, time had come to be the central feature of what it means to be human. Its linear version implied both a starting point and a qualitatively different point further on: a time over which change, notionally for the better, has occurred. At the end of time, he says, 'imperfection' gives way to 'completeness',[13] a sense of which is inscribed today in the ideal normality of adulthood.

Time as the Explanation for Personhood

It is hard to avoid dividing our discussion into individual, species and society, because that is how recent history has already framed the question for us. In Irenaeus's concept of recapitulation, what stands out is the development of the species as a whole: Adam represents humankind in its entirety. As for progress, in its sociopolitical sense, an embryonic concept of this too lay within religion before becoming explicit and secularized in the mid-eighteenth century. In early Christianity and

---

[11] Paul, Epistle to the Romans 12.2; see also 2 Corinthians 4.16.
[12] Gerhart Ladner, *The Idea of Reform* (New York: Harper, 1967), p. 451.
[13] Augustine, *Confessions*, 10.4.

Empire the three categories (and particularly that of the individual) were less distinct from each other than they are today. Nevertheless, linear time was a presupposition that inherently promoted a kind of individualism.

The concepts of individual interiority and linear time have a special relationship. They depend on each other. The modelling of the human experience by interior rather than external events started out as the mapping of one's personal religious status. During the Protestant schism and Counter-Reformation the condition of the individual interior and methods for its observation would become a central and public issue. Such pre-scientific models of interiority were already like modern ones inasmuch as they were mysteries whose cultural codes had to be obeyed by individuals, via social enforcement if necessary. The difference between the two is that today's developmental idea is a coherent abstraction to whose exclusive and rigid linear dimension all empirical detail is bent. Its forebear, by contrast, was only one among a coexisting range of descriptive and explanatory frameworks.

For example, although the medieval division of the individual lifespan into numbered stages corresponded with early Christianity's 'ages of man', which were indicated by numerological patterns in external nature (the four seasons or the sun's diurnal quadrants, the seven planets or the seven days of the week), these ways of representing time, unlike today's, laid no claim to explanatory status. In modern developmentalism, with its abstract model of the individual, causal explanations for the interior 'nature' of the younger individual come from externally imposed and arbitrarily structured 'stages' reached at strictly fixed points along the lifespan. Generally speaking, the more detailed and extensive a scheme of interior categories, the more complex their causality itself becomes (psychiatric genetics is a modern illustration of this point). The infant supposedly becomes capable of, say, 'empathizing' or 'forming abstractions' only at the precise point in time when the prescriptive theory says they do. These structured stages determine the human creature under consideration, even if empirical observations can be made from beyond the developmental straitjacket that challenge it.[14] The very concept of developmental time is premised upon defining the species by its cognitive (affective, moral etc.) ability. The idea of ability as potential ('ability' being the standard translation of the Latin *potentia*) separates children from the rest of humankind. It shuts

---

[14] For a critique from within developmental psychology itself, see Betty Repacholi and Alison Gopnik, 'Early reasoning about desires: evidence from 14- and 18-month-olds', *Developmental Psychology* 3 (1997); Gopnik, *The Philosophical Baby: What Children's Minds Tell Us about Truth, Love, and the Meaning of Life* (London: The Bodley Head, 2009).

down a whole range of possible explanations as to why a younger human being might do or not do something; where linear time and development are absolute presuppositions, it reduces causality to a date on the calendar. Medieval views on interior stages may have been as arbitrary as our own will one day turn out to have been, but it was arbitrariness of a more relaxed sort.

Linear Time, Historiography and Social History

To the extent that sketchy notions of social progress (though it was not called that) are detectable in the late medieval era, they were already bound up with individual progress, including interior progress. In economic life, well-off peasants knowing the value of money no doubt had a linear sense of what their goals were and to what end their acquisitions of land might be heading. And although ordinary people may not have cared to apply theological principle to their everyday activity, this did not mean that the perception of links between the two kinds of linearity, socioeconomic and conceptual-theological, was impossible. As fifteenth-century economies recovered from the Black Death, people were already dimly aware that the trajectory of their world was open-ended. With this increasing awareness of non-cyclical, unpredictable socioeconomic change, the Reformation would go on to redefine avarice in a way that rendered the progressive acquisition of capital and finance a godly activity, a symbolic way of clearing one's debt to the Almighty. It indicated a will to pay off the wages of sin, and was thereby 'redemptive' in both senses of the word. It aligned economic externals with the journey of the soul in pursuit of an identifiable goal, and in a future that lay beyond the cyclical repetitions of agricultural life.[15]

Recognition of such internal-external interconnections in the linearity of time affected the writing of history. Late medieval historiographers' burgeoning interest in the past, over and above its usefulness merely for homiletic purposes, marked the end of the long shift from an oral to a written culture and the consolidation of memory in writing.[16] If

---

[15] On these matters, see Keith Wrightson, *Earthly Necessities: Economic Lives in Early Modern Britain, 1470–1750* (London: Penguin, 2002).
[16] See R. N. Swanson, *The Twelfth Century Renaissance* (Manchester: Manchester University Press, 1999), p. 64; also Brian Stock, *The Implications of Literacy: Written Language and Models of Interpretation in the 11th and 12th Centuries* (Princeton: Princeton University Press, 1987); and Michael Clanchy, *From Memory to Written Record: England 1066–1307* (London: Edward Arnold, 1987).

ecclesiastical and canon law were increasingly a chronicle of record, so too was the historical enterprise itself. The idea of progress, however embryonic, was partly an outcome of this increased importance of written record and its firmer sense of a past, which in turn provided a firmer and longer-term basis for planning the future, in a context of administrative proliferation. True, late medieval historians mostly used history to back up their own moralizing and to service the present rather than analyze the past on its own terms (how much more so than we do today is another matter). Be that as it may, the trajectory they envisaged was already linear in many respects. The Christian timeline had dissolved the Stoic emphasis on fate. Square one, which fate always brings us back to, was replaced by point zero, the start of a line leading to another point further along the line. The past-future continuum was bookended by known points: the Creation at the start and the Last Judgement at the end, even if the actual length of time between these events was an unknown.[17] Within this timespan, the linear format facilitated notions of a temporally structured progress of the human species.

Such a conception started earlier than one might think. It is detectable at the very start of the twelfth-century Renaissance, to which today's conceptual historian can trace many 'early modern' ideas. It appears, for example, in the widely read religious educator, Hugh of St Victor (c.1096–1141), who inserted within the stretch between the Creation and the Day of Judgement a discrete subsection running from the birth of Christ to the present moment. This reinforced the dating system devised a few centuries earlier;[18] instead of starting from the Creation as Judaism had done, Christians dated from the Incarnation, creating something more like an arithmetical number line (as did the Islamic calendar, which dates from the Prophet's arrival in Medina). It encouraged people to view the future as itself a part of history, and as built into the structure of linear time. The late medieval enthusiasm for prophecy now amounted to a whole futurological science, rather the occasional oracular outburst it had previously been. Meanwhile, the idea began to grow that individual possessors of a finite or corrupt intellect might approach the divine intellect as if the difference between the two were a matter of degree rather than kind. Later on, with Francis Bacon (1561–1626), the idea of history as human advance would come to be conceived as a unitary enterprise, with the prospect of collective species perfection in broadly cognitive terms.

[17] Swanson, *The Twelfth-Century Renaissance*, p. 55.
[18] See Judith Herrin, *The Formation of Christendom* (Oxford: Blackwell, 1987), p. 6.

The incipient idea of progress by its very existence sprouted disputes about the structure of change. For example, within different theories as to how many 'ages of man' there were (seven, six, four), important differences arose as to which age constituted the present moment. Whatever the answer, it signified that late medieval historians had some concrete basis for believing that human beings, both as individuals and as whole societies or as a universal species, change over their lifespan irreversibly. And even if historians have since thrown the idea of progress out of their toolbox, they cannot ignore its presence in the society around them now, particularly in respect of education and psychology. Once the genie of linear time was released, it sparked a cultural tension between progress and its necessary concomitant, degeneration, across a whole range of fields. Today, the line often runs downhill, reflecting the facts of cosmic entropy, climate change or just routine gloom about social decay. But, equally, decay jostles with a psychopolitical vision whose very raison d'être is onwards and upwards: a brighter future for you and your family. The developmental idea as a science, like the pedagogical practices and conceptual apparatuses that flow from it, is an intrinsic component of this necessary social optimism. If today both psychology and the lay population find the notion of decay hard to cope with, it is the consequence of 'development' being something to which time is of the essence.

2: Interiority

In psychology the existence of a permanent interiority seems to be the given upon which everything else, including its development, is predicated. However, the very notion of a permanent interior identity is dependent upon that of linear time as much as vice versa. Moreover, the distinction between an inner self and an external world is just one historically specific way of looking at human lives, one which predominates in the modern world but which may not have been there when our species first emerged and which may at some point disappear.[19] With the idea of a permanent individual interior came also a concern with the interior status of unfamiliar others. Christianity tended to prohibit speculation about this, at least as regards their afterlife status. God alone knew. Nevertheless, the temptation proved irresistible, and in the end Christian beliefs would hugely expand

---

[19] See Charles Taylor, *The Sources of the Self: The Making of Modern Identity* (Cambridge: Cambridge University Press, 1989), p. 3ff; also Larrry Siedentop, *Inventing the Individual: The Origins of Western Liberalism* (London: Penguin, 2014).

our repertoire for probing and classifying the inner lives of our fellow humans. It helped to found the discrete categories – cognitive, emotional, moral etc. – that would inform the developmental idea.

Before Christianity

Before monotheism, systematic descriptions of a *permanent* interior identity were scarce. Pagan religions had posited a quite different kind of relationship between internal and external. Whereas modern psychology describes a movement from inside to outside, starting from 'mind' and resulting in behaviours and performances, pre-Christian accounts tended to start from the outside and go in. Spirit possession, for example, was an external invasion. Moreover, this kind of change was instantaneous, rather than gradual or progressing in structured stages; after possession was over, individuals reverted – usually – back to their original state. Time was a switch, indicating temporary presence/absence.

Let's call this 'shamanism'. The label must be taken with a large pinch of salt; even as a technical term in anthropology it is used very loosely, and is possibly a colonialist imposition. I am using it instead as a simple flag of convenience for any perception of interior change as originating outside the person. (It must also be said that shamanism is not only a feature of so-called primitives; Aristotle too asserted that human rationality enters 'from outside', and that in the last analysis it is not a 'permanent' essential property of human beings.)[20] Some anthropologists have seen shamanism as one of the core components of early societies that seeped into later organized religions.[21] In this sense, modern psychology carries its mitochondrial imprint. Psychologists share with those earlier practitioners the task of mediating between the social or moral order on the one hand and the realm of an invisible interiority on the other. The role of both shamanism and psychology is to frame a 'central morality cult', whose explanatory labels impose a monopoly on the public consideration of behaviour in aspects of life where the usual legal and political mechanisms do not reach.[22]

Today's mind scientist can, it seems, absorb the impact such a crosshistorical criticism might inflict simply by giving it a positive twist. A recent president of the American Psychological Association, for example,

---

[20] Aristotle, *On the Generation of Animals*, 736b25; *Topics*, 129a ff.
[21] See, for example, Ioan M. Lewis, *Ecstatic Religion: A Study of Shamanism and Spirit Possession* (London: Routledge, 1989).
[22] Lewis, *Ecstatic Religion*, p. 4.

claimed that shamans were just indigenous psychologists;[23] the fact that the two occupations are comparable, far from subverting the scientific soundness of today's profession, makes past primitiveness the warranty for its present sophistication, by casting the latter as a truth that transcends history. In shamanic beliefs, the human interior (if it existed) was unreachable and unobservable.[24] In the modern era even behaviourists often assume the positive existence of interiority, if only as a sealed box. In both cases this helps confirm the expert status of the observer, the behaviourist's expertise consisting as it does in an ability to read external signs, just as anthropological 'shamans' confirm their status by a specialist ability to communicate with the spirits doing the possessing.

From ancient spirit possession to the medieval monk's divinely contemplative state, thence to the awareness of being 'in grace' and therefore elect, and finally to the normal interiority of the psychologically developed subject – the continuing thread in all these is the invisibility of the interior content, an invisibility which requires expertise in monitoring and testing of what separates some human beings from their fellows. The shaman, by the definition given in the previous paragraph, mediates between presence and absence. Defining the human species (currently, for example, in terms of the presence of cognitive or developmental ability) calls into question the human status of individuals who fall outside the definition. 'Human' is therefore in both cases 'a fluid term ... Someone who appears human at one point may take on a different shape at another time.'[25] It is just that 'primitive' shamanic markers of change were instantaneous and temporary rather than, as with today's developmental ability, phased and irreversible.

Expansion of the Inner Life in Early Christianity

The difference between pre- and post-monotheistic outlooks on interiority thus lies in their respective representations of time. In ancient cyclical paradigms, spirit possession occurred immediately and tended to vanish just as quickly; in the monotheistic paradigm, to be with God is point B at the end of a timeline which started at a point A (the Creation) or A + 1 (the Incarnation, the Hijrah etc.). And whereas in

---

[23] Stanley Krippner and Patrick Welch, *Spiritual Dimensions of Healing: From Native Shamanism to Contemporary Health Care* (New York: Irvington, 1992); see also Jeanne Achterberg, *Imagery of Healing: Shamanism and Modern Medicine* (Boston: Shambhala, 1985).
[24] Lewis, *Ecstatic Religion*, p. 170.
[25] Graham Harvey and Robert J. Wallis, *Historical Dictionary of Shamanism* (Lanham: Scarecrow Press, 2007), p. 95.

shamanic religions the possessing 'spirits' visiting you here on earth are your ancestors, not a unitary Holy Spirit, in monotheistic religions you get to see deceased family members again, if at all, only at the end of the timeline, in heaven.

The importance of interiority for the early Christians lay in their hostility towards the materialism of the immediately pre-imperial Roman philosophers' account of the soul. They contrasted their own notion of its intangibility as an interior realm. In the final century BC the materialist philosopher Lucretius had distinguished between a specifically human soul (*animus*) and a universal one (*anima*).[26] *Anima*, like the Greeks' *psyche*, was the 'form' that the otherwise inert matter of a living body takes when it moves; *animus* was that body's individual 'disposition'.[27] Although the two were interrelated, neither of them featured a permanent inner identity. Early Christianity provided one, and this idea of an interior existence extending over time gave rise to attempts to demonstrate the reality of its invisible content.

This theoretical shift towards interiority introduced by the early Church Fathers occurred in a specific sociopolitical context. Irenaeus's recapitulation theory was part of a broader project to systematize doctrine and thereby amend the chaos of apocalyptic and often incompatible beliefs among the disputatious Judaeo-Christian sects of the first century. He is noted for having been among the first to provide Christianity with an ideological structure, by systemizing the construction of heresy. His linear vision – expecting to see God in the future rather than here and now – predicted the regularization of a bureaucratic ecclesiastical (and imperial) order. In this practical hegemonic form, 'Christendom' – Christianity as a temporal enterprise on earth – emerged from the First Council of Nicaea in AD 325, convened by the Emperor Constantine. Within a few years Christianity had become the Empire's official religion. Its Nicene belief system aided the promotion of a civic mentality. It also laid down rules for ecclesiastical order, in which the organizational grid upon which Constantine based his regional system of bishoprics was coextensive with that of the Empire's administrative bureaucracy.

---

[26] Translation of such terms is always an issue. It is important to take account where necessary of the contextual distinctions between the two, as later between soul and mind or *l'âme* and *l'esprit*. Nevertheless, for our purposes these all constitute historical aspects of interiority. Taken together, they form a Procrustes' bed. Sometimes the meanings are interchangeable; sometimes the difference between them is big; sometimes it is small and sometimes (as here) it is small but also highly significant.

[27] Lucretius, *On the Nature of Things*, 3.99.

Social organization and the very principle of a permanent inner status thus began to reinforce each other. The categorizing of interior identities can be traced back to events like this; it belongs with the history of administrative decision-making about membership rules. These rules were effectively set by the Council. The second of its twenty canons established a minimum number of years for the examination of 'catechumens' – that is, aspiring converts. Probationary requirements were systematized, even if the number of probationers remained tiny. Whereas Christianity's first-century street cult had continued the loose initiation rituals of existing Jewish sects, the induction formalities were now centralized. The assessment of interior status as a universal vetting mechanism (the modern version of which is the cognitive ability test)[28] was born from this. Its first form was the catechism. The fact that Constantine himself remained an unconfirmed catechumen may have been due to modesty, or it may rather have been that he was adding his personal stamp to the linear trajectory – ignorance, preparation, maturity – by modelling it. Either way, the point is that the existence of an internal cognitive realm was posited in part by Christendom's very own organizational structure, its controlling functions and their political importance.

As a catechumen you did not just need to recognize personal sin through confession, you also had to prove yourself through your cognitive understanding of basic principles. Understanding of this kind was hard to distinguish from doctrinal loyalty.

At the doctrinal core of the controlling functions stood recognition of Jesus's combined human and divine status. The Arians, Nicaea's rivals for dominance among the disparate Christian sects, had ranked Jesus below God because he was created only at a certain point along the historical timeline; hence Nicaea responded by insisting that Jesus and God were of the same divine substance. This tells us how doctrine came to involve the *correct display* of interiority. The goal at the end of the interior timeline, salvation, was only achievable by a divine Jesus's intervention to atone for human sins; the timeline was determined both by the goal itself and by the necessity of there being only one single path towards it – and this path was a monopoly of the Nicaean Council. Arian resistance thus had to be quashed because it was a concrete obstacle to the very future of the human species. But Arianism's so-called creeds had in fact been loose and varied, making it something of a straw man. It was Nicaea's insistence

---

[28] See Theodore Porter, *Trust in Numbers: The Pursuit of Objectivity in Science and Public Life* (Princeton: Princeton University Press, 1995).

on uniformity *as such*, even more than the actual doctrinal content of that uniformity (the divinity of Jesus), that was important. With uniformity came the church's excommunicatory powers, which again were coextensive with the Empire's uniform legal system; people excommunicated on religious grounds were often denied a role in the Empire's secular institutions.

Augustine and Homo Interior

In pre-Christian cultures people tended to think about fulfilling their social roles in terms of the continual acquisition, loss and reacquisition of honour through external action: a reflection of the cyclical movements of the stars. Fictional heroes like Odysseus or Gilgamesh had their moments of introspection, but these did not amount to a lifetime's personhood. Systematic reflection, along with the self-monitoring function of conscience, came about as people took upon themselves the social role and values of Rome's citizens rather than its warriors. If the warrior judged himself and others by external criteria, the citizen did so by self-reflection and self-restraint. Augustine's era signalled this shift of balance within the structures of an Empire where notions of citizenship were required to reinforce a fatally stretched imperial bureaucracy. His baptizer and mentor Ambrose (*c*.340–397), the man who delivered Nicaea for the Roman state, actually started his career as Governor of Emilia-Liguria; the Emperor then reassigned him a few steps across the office floor to become Bishop of Milan, for which he was later canonized. Equally, Augustine's teachings arose not in a social void but in the concrete setting of an imperial outpost where his mother had been a local devout Christian and his father a sinful pagan Roman administrator.

Augustine was interested in time precisely as a way of explaining what goes on inside the individual, rather than (as many later philosophers have been) in what time means to that individual as an observer of the external world, or in whether time has an objective existence.[29] I have said that the concept of linear time is formative of the concept of interiority as much as the other way round. In Augustine's much-discussed account of time, written not long after Nicaea, he criticized the pagan philosophers' measuring of time by the stars, external objects that followed a cyclical pattern.

---

[29] On this, see Matthew Drever, *Image, Identity and the Forming of the Augustinian Soul* (Oxford: Oxford University Press, 2013), p. 92; Gerald O'Daly, *Augustine's Philosophy of Mind* (Berkeley: University of California Press, 1987), p. 153.

Instead, he claimed, the very reality of time is constituted out of the internal realm of the human subject. He was not saying that time is relative. Rather, time on earth was simply a 'distention' of the human mind: an unhealthy expansion of it.[30] Time only began with the Fall. The Fall was the beginning of history; the arrival of the elect in the City of God will be the end of it. And what was true of the species was true for the individual too: time *constitutes* the human being's interiority as such, in the form of a personal history. Outside history there was no 'mind' to speak of; Adam before the Fall was too full of timeless bliss to be doing anything we might call 'knowing' or 'thinking'.

So the mind is developmental or it is nothing – at least that is the presupposition we have absorbed over the last two thousand years. Although for Augustine the mind's regrettably dilated condition blocks the way to being with God – a situation unavoidable because of original sin – the path of time is nevertheless the only path there is. It has to be travelled if the human interior is to be cleansed. This is achieved by discovering the spiritual within it. You cannot hope to find God – a God at the end of time whose understanding is deeper than the deepest possible human understanding – unless you first find yourself. Augustine inserted a substantial role for cognitive ability, inasmuch as one achieved 'participation in the divine' through Bible study and interpretation[31] (though it must also be said that for him the overriding factor in human psychology was the will).

Augustine is important for the further reason that his thought was *the* primary influence on the late seventeenth-century debates about grace and election, out of which the concept of interior development arose in its modern form. Most Church Fathers before Augustine had believed that human beings have free will or at least some agency in their own salvation, partly in order to counter pagan belief in fate:[32] there had to be some point to doing good. Augustine himself supported this view in his first treatments of the topic. Later, though, he changed his mind.[33] His theory of God's elect – the choice of a few for heaven from before the beginning of time and the absolute necessity of hell for the rest – would for later generations

---

[30] Augustine, *Confessions*, 11.27.
[31] Andrew King, 'St Augustine's doctrine of participation as a metaphysic of persuasion', *Rhetoric Society Quarterly*, 3/4 (1985).
[32] See Giulio Maspero, 'Anthropology', in (eds.) Lucas Mateo-Seco and Giulio Maspero, *Dictionary of Gregory of Nyssa* (Leiden: Brill, 2010), p. 41.
[33] Augustine, *De libero arbitrio*, about which see Eleonore Stump 'Augustine on free will', in (eds.) Stump and Norman Kretzmann, *The Cambridge Companion to Augustine* (Cambridge: Cambridge University Press, 2001).

involve the notion that God's choice also involved the insertion of a certain quasi-mechanistic operation *within* the individual's psychology that played a part in determining their afterlife destination. This seemed on the one hand to concede something to pagan accounts of fate; on the other hand it created the idea of a 'little man inside', as a mental parallel to his bodily form.[34] The result was an interiority that was both *determinate* and *separable* from the body.

Augustine's thought illustrates how the human interior – a place, as it were – was also *interiorization*, an event. Or rather it was a continuing series of events. The conception arose both of a *permanent* interiority conceived as just explained, and, inextricably, of consistent interior *change*: a picture that would increasingly dominate early modern concepts of human reason and thence the emerging mind sciences. It also gave rise to the notion of self-monitoring, in which internal self-exploration taught people to regulate their own behaviour. This is illustrated by Augustine's view of the relationship between the strictly human *animus* and the part-divine *anima*. The meanings of these terms overlap to some extent in his writings.[35] But equally *anima*, in the sense of 'form' to the body's 'matter', also became form to the *animus*, the individual's everyday interior disposition; it thus constituted an apparently objective psychological mechanism, a means by which the mind monitors itself as it undergoes change.

Lay Sainthood and Election

So much for theory. But whose interiors are we talking about? What actual individuals? Interiority in Augustine's sense existed only as an aspiration; the expansion of a whole culture of interiority and its temporal structure applied to a still very narrow set of people. It spread slowly at first, in fits and starts (Augustine's writings did not reach much of a public even among elites until the late Middle Ages). Saintly interiors were ascribed mainly to people isolated from popular life: the hermit, the monk and the nun. There was also a medieval 'cult of saints', which led to the canonization of several European kings and the principle of hereditary sanctity of rulers. This kind of saintly CV was an elite hobby horse, requiring nobility of birth and/or a bishopric;[36] it afforded exceptional closeness to God and (as with

---

[34] Gareth Matthews, 'The inner man', *American Philosophy Quarterly*, 4/2 (1967).
[35] Augustine, *Confessions*, 10.6. See O'Daly, *Augustine's Philosophy of Mind*, p. 7ff.
[36] André Vauchez, 'Lay people's sanctity in Western Europe: evolution of a pattern', in (eds.) Renate Blumenfeld-Kosinski and Timea Szell, *Images of Sainthood in Medieval Europe* (Ithaca: Cornell University Press, 1991).

shamans) the additional social privilege of acting as 'intercessors . . . orchestrating the communication between God and the ordinary citizen'.[37] There were lay saints too – but only occasionally, where the criterion was posthumous honour paid to the performance of miracles rather than to a holy interior.

Slowly the hagiography of visible externals such as social status or miracles was joined by the inner holiness of whole lifetimes.[38] The description of these was still vague at first (the indwelling 'light', for example, that early Christian thinkers had got from Neoplatonist philosophers like Plotinus). This began to change in the late Middle Ages. In 1215 the Fourth Lateran Council initiated 'a crucial recognition of the personal conscience, of interiority against exteriority' by stipulating annual confession. This led to an 'acceptance of particularity and personality' of individuals.[39] But we still have to ask: *whose* confession, exactly? What social and intellectual class of individual? Even with the arrival two centuries later of the printing press and with it a vast social extension of biblical literacy, Jean Gerson, one of Europe's foremost religious authorities, was still issuing widely read instructions to the priesthood that described sin entirely in external, behavioural terms.[40] Interior states were not on the list. His volume was bound together with an *ABC des simples gens*, but this too was merely a reduced, accessible version of the main text. Only with the Reformation and Counter-Reformation would sainthood, and interior status in general, become fully available to the laity, in the form of election. This coincided with the expansion of humanist education rather than being challenged by it. A more cognitive-type understanding of the catechism was starting to be seen as a necessary component of putative election. The religious culture was becoming textual in a sense that went beyond Bible reading. It defined more sharply the status of non-readers: children and 'simple people' (still meaning, at this point, the majority of the population).

The interior *absence* personified by these groups helped to firm up the concept of interiority itself. Internal self-monitoring, on the part of the still small saintly minority, was centred increasingly on the theory of election.

---

[37] Brigitte Cazelles, Introduction, in (eds.) Blumenfeld-Kosinski and Szell, *Images of Sainthood in Medieval Europe*, p. 2.
[38] Michael Goodich, *Vita Perfecta: The Ideal of Sainthood in the Thirteenth Century* (Stuttgart: Anton Hiersemann, 1982), p. 3.
[39] Swanson, *The Twelfth-Century Renaissance*, p. 150.
[40] Jean Charlier de Gerson, *Le traicte des dix comandemens de la loy* (Paris: Jehan Treperel, 1495), D.iiii. recto.

You examined yourself for signs of your own elect status. The prospect of salvation was blind, and fear of unavoidable damnation persisted for a very long time. Even as the mind sciences were becoming formalized, hell would still be a real place that terrorized the mature Charles Dickens and Abraham Lincoln, not to mention the adolescent Max Weber (Calvinist mother) and James Joyce (Jesuit-inspired aunt). If good behaviour was not the solution, nor was internal self-examination on its own. To be saved, you also had to be already chosen, and you could not choose to be chosen. Since human beings do not control their own ultimate destiny, it must be caused by some determinant that is external in origin but has also been inserted within them (a sense in which seventeenth-century Christian theology resembles the shamanism of pagan practice).[41]

Interiority and the Idea of the Individual

Without the theory of election, 'the individual' could not have come to be conceived in human science terms as being allowed (or alternatively, denied) 'rights' and 'competence'. That is because election discriminated. It discriminated between these people over here, whose interior condition will change, and those people over there, who will not change. Not only will they not change, they do not have interiority in the first place. Reprobation – absence of election – is by definition *not* an inner condition; just as John Locke said of his cognitively disabled 'changelings', reprobates are entirely 'determined' by exterior forces.[42] Reprobation is not a temporal condition at all, precisely because it rules out interior change. All men are born damned because of original sin, and while a few are got out of it, those who remain unrescued are, again by definition, not individuals. They are simply a stolid unchangeable 'mass': as Augustine called it, the *massa damnata*. There is a strong bond between the concept of the elect and the emerging one (much discussed by historians and sociologists) of the individual, and it lies in the capability of both for change.

We cannot just assume the strength of religious belief among laypeople of the past among whom waves of scepticism can be detected,[43] but if the self-reflective person did have a nagging preoccupation it would, prior to the rise of the mind sciences, have been 'Am I saved?', not 'Am I normal?' Had the concept of normality actually existed then, it would have been in

---

[41] See Bernard Saladin d'Anglure, 'Rethinking Inuit shamanism through the concept of "third gender"', in (ed.) Graham Harvey, *Shamanism: A Reader* (London: Routledge, 2003), p. 239.
[42] John Locke, *An Essay Concerning Human Understanding* (Oxford: Clarendon, 1975), p. 265.
[43] See John H. Arnold, *Belief and Unbelief in Medieval Europe* (London: Bloomsbury, 2005).

some medical context organic to the body: for example, there was the broadly accepted theory of an optimal balance between sanguine, choleric, melancholic and phlegmatic temperaments, any imbalance being detectable by external behavioural observation. These were in any case merely dispositional; unlike most of today's typologies, they came and went, did not have blame attached and were not deterministic markers of a fixed personal identity. Nevertheless, labelling of some sort was required. The turbulence which late medieval administrators and elites encountered in the social activity around them led them to start seeing it as a turbulence of individual subjectivities, and therefore to try and set up an internal control function. They began seeking 'right order' in the individual's thought processes as much as in their actions.[44] And the more they looked for order, the more disorder they found. It fed an increasingly systemized obsessiveness about categorizing human interiors that would one day give birth to the mind sciences.

The need to categorize internal descriptions was a directly political issue. The probing of dubious subjectivities went side by side with the idea that there was something *socially* destructive about wrong doctrine: hence the increasing importance attached to heresy (executions for heresy began only once Christianity had entered its second millennium). Moreover, some historians have suggested that what was offered as evidence of heresy was often, in fact, 'the product of those persecuting it': there were no heretics, only 'people given the label heretic by someone else'.[45] Heresy might often be just an ill-timed interpretation of religion that would shortly after become acceptable doctrine. ('Theology' was another late medieval coining, its very appearance the admission that intellectual proliferation was spilling beyond the restricted, mainly monastic setting of biblical exegesis.)

Encouraged by the ubiquitous example of Augustine's *Confessions*, the individual – that is, the individual cleric and not yet many other people – was supposed to spend some of his time looking inside his own heart, the heart being in this period the bodily organ of thinking. Introspection had the potential to let a hundred flowers bloom, and therefore had political consequences. The late medieval religious philosophers replaced earlier Christianity's Neoplatonist idea of a unitary and motionless World Soul with the idea of the soul as a plurality, such that the increasing amount of social mobility in the everyday world was matched by a theory of *individual*

---

[44] Gerd Tellenbach, *Church, State and Christian Society at the Time of the Investiture Contest* (Oxford: Blackwell, 1940), p. 126ff.
[45] Arnold, *Belief and Unbelief*, p. 192; see also R. I. Moore, *The War on Heresy: Faith and Power in Medieval Europe* (London: Profile, 2012).

souls. Aristotle's newly translated *De Anima* ('On the Soul') taught them (a) that the soul was not a unity but an attachment to the individual, and (b) that it consisted in motion – an idea by which the soul became attached to the Christian sense of time, to its linear direction and its goal of perfection through salvation. In the same period the recounting of profound spiritual meditations within and about the self, inspired by Augustine's *Confessions*, turned into a whole genre.[46] The rarefied air of scholastic philosophy was permeated by the classical instruction, 'Know thyself.' At first this still just meant, loosely, 'Remember what species you belong to.' Your species is above the animals. It is quite possible that outside of religion, ordinary people in everyday life always felt themselves to be their own person; but it was only when the instruction was deployed across early modern forms of social organization that this everyday *homo socialis* would start to become also an individual *homo psychologicus*.

The late Middle Ages also saw a shift of focus from God the Father, a punitive patriarch, to God the Son, a suffering individual. In the very first Christian narratives, God was out in the external cosmos doing battle with the Devil, to whom we humans had succumbed. Jesus, however, was 'God in us', and being partly human might resemble one of us, as well as holding out the promise of salvation. Interiorization, for this human individual, uncoiled the cyclical time of fate and the seasons to become an extending thread. One's known point of departure was followed by an uncertain journey but a known destination: redemption or abandonment, salvation or damnation, perfection or degeneration. The intervening uncertainty would later be smoothed out and made safe by the developmental idea.

Individuals who accommodated their sense of self to this prospect of non-cyclical change now had more than just an instinct for survival. There was the prospect of 'enhanced' survival: improved socioeconomic status in this life, and – not unconnected – a possible salvation in the next. Historians have tended to discuss the rise of individualism and the individual reasoner either in the context of high philosophy (consciousness, the self), or of political and social thought (rights, competence) involving the freeing up of labour, the expansion of markets and capital accumulation and the extension of bureaucratic authority. Religious belief forms an intermediate level between the philosophical and the social, affording a more precise discussion of the role of interiority in this.

---

[46] John Frederick Benton, *Consciousness of Self and Perceptions of Individuality* (Cambridge MA: Harvard University Press, 1982), p. 263.

2: Interiority 45

Historians of political thought tend to be interested in the idea of the individual as it surfaced later, in the eighteenth century or at the earliest in the civic humanism of the Renaissance. This is understandable. What could have been gained by representing yourself as an individual in previous, bonded forms of social organization where your legal capacity was unclear and any conceivably 'natural' individual rights in practice non-existent?[47] Nevertheless, the individual was alive and kicking outside philosophical texts even in antiquity and certainly in the Middle Ages.[48] Although there was no such word as individualism, it seems to have always been enough of a threat to require the control by labelling of population groups, albeit without (at first) purely psychological descriptors.

We owe to the scholastic theologians of the late Middle Ages not only the basics of our modern psychological vocabulary ('faculties' such as 'memory', 'imagination', 'reason' etc.) but also the word 'individual' itself, which they employed in their theory of universals. A 'universal' is a category that appears to unite particulars by their common characteristics; the Latin *individua* was used for particulars in contexts where their function was purely quantitative. This theory of universals was no ivory tower exercise, since the paradigm case of a universal was nearly always 'man' – a category united by the fact that all particular humans share the common characteristic of reason. The convention was adopted in humanist discourses because it provided a (circular) rationale for placing 'man' at the centre of everything. This universal human may not yet have been an aggregate of individuals, as the modern human sciences construe it. Nevertheless, the latter, more modern sense of the individual has roots in the late medieval 'manufacture of norms'.[49] What was manufactured was not merely the *interpretation* but the actual *substance* of an interiority which, together with its various 'faculties' and their specific 'operations', was now seen as a permanent fixture, formative of assessable individual identities.

---

[47] On the background to this, see Richard Tuck, *Natural Rights Theories: Their Origin and Development* (Cambridge: Cambridge University Press, 1979).

[48] Timothy J. Reiss, *Mirages of the Selfe: Patterns of Personhood in Ancient and Early Modern Europe* (Palo Alto: Stanford University Press, 2003), p. 242.

[49] On this, see Julie Brumberg-Chaumont, 'Logical skills as a new social, intellectual and anthropological norm in medieval elites: the origin of "logical man"', in (eds.) Claude Rosental and Brumberg-Chaumont, *Logical Skills: Socio-Historical Perspectives* (Leiden: Brill, 2021); and (eds.) Véronique Beaulande-Barraud, Julie Claustre and Elsa Marmursztejn, *La fabrique de la norme: Lieux et modes de production des normes au moyen âge et à l'époque moderne* (Rennes: Presses Universitaires de Rennes, 2012).

The Systemization of Psychological Faculties

Positive categories of the individual human mind emerged among monastic and university-educated elites. Crudely put (there are many variations), the mind was identifiable by the three broad faculties of memory, imagination and finally judgement, which was sometimes 'reason' or some other term; its activity came in the form of specific 'operations' such as logical reasoning, abstraction, attention, consciousness and (under other names) information-processing. This kind of individual defined himself also by his possession of what were known as 'the common ideas' (*communes notiones*), meaning common to individuals of a certain social caste who had the ability to self-monitor their own operations. The operations described the set of individual capabilities that would later go on to act as a model for the whole species. What endured throughout that later transition was the question: which individuals? After all, even today the answer is still: only some.

The history of psychology conventionally sees medieval faculty psychology as the main precursor of the modern discipline, and this is correct inasmuch as it introduced a terminology still recognizable today.[50] However, its 'faculties' and 'operations' must be set alongside those other, religious rather than cognitive, categories driving the developmental idea that I have already mentioned. Lay sainthood and election were more fundamental features of interiority than simply having all your faculties, though the more secular-sounding (to us) cognitive-type categories were important too. Of course, the two were interwoven. Augustine had divided the soul (*anima*) into a 'trinity' of memory, understanding and will, which seems partly to prefigure later faculty psychology by virtue of its tripartite structure.[51] But it was an obscure contemporary of his who first stabilized the three main faculties as memory, imagination and reason, and who linked them anatomically to separate cavities of the brain.[52] Bishop Nemesius wrote in Greek, which few read, and his work was not translated into Latin until the eleventh century. Aside from the sketchiest of earlier hints by the Roman Empire's master physician Galen, his is the first example of a compartmentalized psychology confirmed by its association

---

[50] For a thorough account of the period, see Simon Kemp, *Medieval Psychology* (New York: Greenwood Press, 1990).
[51] *De Trinitate*,14.15.12, in *Augustine: Later Works* (Philadelphia: Westminster Press, 1955), p. 115.
[52] Nemesius, *On the Nature of Man*, translated by R. W. Sharples and P. J. van der Eijk (Liverpool: Liverpool University Press, 2008).

(unquestioned today) with corresponding material components of the brain.[53]

This also made possible a more fixed intellectual identity. Although the word 'psychology' would not itself be coined until the end of the sixteenth century – initially as a defence against materialist theories of the mind – the theoretical framework already existed for a detailed organization and compartmentalization of mental life. The main faculties structured interiority in those people who motivated themselves by inwardly directed reflection. The monastic life, beyond supplying legendary examples of asceticism, gave its inmates space to cultivate and distinguish the 'operations' just described. Then, with intellectual renewal in the later Middle Ages, came its secular parallel among the *literati*, the lawyers, bureaucrats and administrators whose literacy (defined largely as knowledge of Latin) entitled them to look down on a majority population of lay 'idiots' largely lacking such operations. The job of these professionals was contradictory. On the one hand, they codified and applied formal authority in the functions of state and church; and bureaucracy likes fixed, static categories, to which any notion of change spells danger. On the other hand, their skills were required precisely in order to deal with change, in the form of the extended and intensified administrative outreach over gradually dissolving social and economic bonds and the consequent recognition of new, proliferating population categories.[54]

As these categories acquired a more detailed and sharply defined content, their ideal types could first be spotted within the *literati* themselves. To put it another way, modern psychological norms and their presentation as natural kinds started out as the self-attributions of a certain social caste that were related to its day job. The old paradigm of the learned man who expressed his moral superiority to social chaos and sclerotic imperial bureaucracy by retreating to the monastery gave way to that of the learned man who, employed by that very same bureaucracy, engaged with the chaos and tried to master it. And as their starting point, members of this social caste began to reassemble an absent social order within themselves. Cognitive activities treated today as natural psychological kinds have their roots in medieval elites' internalizations of their own external activity, as we shall see in more detail shortly.

---

[53] See Goodey, 'Blockheads, roundheads, pointy-heads: intellectual disability and the brain before modern medicine', *Journal for the History of the Behavioral Sciences*, 41/2 (2005).
[54] On this, see Leonard E. Boyle, *Pastoral Care, Clerical Education and Canon Law, 1200–1400* (London: Variorum Reprints, 1981), p. 112.

The manufacture of faculties and operations of interiority, together with appropriate forms of monitoring, was a function of the more general extension of norms accompanying the spread of written laws about behaviour. The historical identity of interior categories and that of socially sanctioned behaviour were interdependent: understandably so, inasmuch as the optimal performance of each category was represented in the self-description of the people establishing the sanctions. The early universities and especially their academic theologians were at the forefront in this. It was their alumni who dominated the writing and application of legal systems in both church and state. As the new literacy took further hold of ruling institutions, law and administration, with the new universities as their training ground, were creating expertises of their own. The tasks of written intellectual labour offered ways of denominating not just the *products* of the mind – that is, its ideas – but also the *workings* of the mind, prefiguring modern psychological categories that would be involved in the creation of exclusions and pathologies.

At the start of the second millennium, with literacy and documentation finally dominant, the constituent operations of modern cognitive development, far from being pre-existing 'natural' entities in the process of being discovered, were being invented more or less from scratch out of the external bureaucratic forms imposed by written record-keeping. True, this structuring of interiority by faculties and operations still presented a largely static picture. The arrival of temporal and developmental elements came not from within the faculty psychology model itself but with the aid of the quite different notions of interiority in the theory of election and predestination; as we shall see in the final section of this chapter, these were focused on how divine grace arrives over the lifespan. However, since the modern disciplines draw their surface discourses directly from faculty psychology, we should summarize its operations here in order to understand how they were later adapted to the temporal perspective and its developmental norms. In short, how did those 'operations' arise which the later, formal psychological disciplines would describe as developmental?

Logical Reasoning

Literacy encouraged reflection about an inner reality in the human subject whose logical capabilities might coincide with the logical properties of texts.[55] The medieval logicians, in their intellectualization of religious

---

[55] See Stock, *The Implications of Literacy*, p. 241.

culture, came up with the division between an external, 'artificial' logic and an internal, 'natural' logic. Large areas of modern human science rest on this supposition that there is on the one hand logic as a set of formal, objective procedures which somehow exists 'out there', untouched by human hand (so to speak), and on the other a logic or logical reasoning which is the most refined capability of the human subject. Over the centuries various ways were found to express this, until today the human sciences – economics, education, law, social policy, bioethics – presuppose that they are two sides of the same coin: that they *correspond with* each other. This correspondence, in its optimum form, is then used to justify scientific notions of order in humankind: the classification of the human species within nature as a whole, the subclassification of human groups vis-à-vis each other; and the internal order of the individual seen as a broadly cognitive entity, a thinking being.

Pre-Christian writers had said nothing about the human subject *possessing* logical reason. Aristotle allocated to human beings a special place in the world, in an ethical sense. But his syllogistic logic, though it uses 'man' as one of its illustrations, treats him no differently from any of its other illustrative objects – 'chairs', for example. Medieval thinkers departed from Aristotle in establishing a positive feedback loop between logic as system and the place of logical reasoning in man's interior nature: men do logic, chairs do not. This created the circularity that holds together the modern human sciences' fixed frameworks for observing one's fellow humans.

Logic was the basis for all scholastic knowledge (*Scientia*). Albertus Magnus (*c.*1200–1280), doyen of the late medieval intellect, instigated the Dominican Order's decision in 1259 to teach logical skills to all mendicants and friars, which helped to establish logical reasoning as a social norm.[56] In academic logic, chairs and the rest had now largely vanished from the discussion. 'Man' became the paradigm case for elaborating the relationship between universals and particulars. This convention, reinforced later by humanism, coincided with the medieval picture of the cosmos as a 'ladder of nature', its central rung occupied by human beings because they straddle both its top half (immaterial reason) and its bottom half (material nature). This picture could then be represented as itself a logical proposition, in which the human being's place in the universe is, as the Arab philosopher Ibn Sina (Avicenna) put it around the year AD 1000, the

---

[56] Julie Brumberg-Chaumont, 'Les débuts de l'enseignement de la logique dans les *studia* dominicains et franciscains en Italie: une organisation précoce et innovante', in (eds.) J. Chandelier and A. Robert, *Les savoirs dans les ordres mendiants: XIIIe-XVe siècles* (Rome: Ecole française de Rome, 2021).

'necessary consequence' of his essence: 'If this thing is a rational animal, then it is a man.'[57]

Abstraction and Information-Processing

In medieval thought, the sorting of particulars under general terms or universals – 'abstraction' – began to be promoted as a central operation of cognitive activity. Again, Aristotle was claimed as the source, and again the link is weaker than one might suppose. It was his medieval Latin translators who invented the verb 'to abstract' (*abstrahere*), inserting it in passages where he himself had simply used various everyday verbs (to lift, to remove, to take away etc.). The Greeks had neither a verb nor a reifying noun, 'abstraction'. Aristotle did say something apparently along these lines, but he did not give it a strictly psychological significance. Allocating particulars to general headings was something Athenian philosophers just happened to do when they got together and talked. The idea of abstraction as a crucial internal operation of the modern subject is a legacy of the late Middle Ages which themselves initiated the 'early modern'.

This coincided with the expansion of bureaucratic expertise. The professional rationales of the *literati* and their written record-keeping provided the model for the 'operations' of their own elevated interior status. Filing, itself the sorting of single recorded items under general headings, consequently turns up in the human psychology as the sorting of particular conceptual items under universal ones. It has been noted that psychological terms originate ultimately from metaphors involving analogues from the material realm.[58] However, it should be added this process takes place in a specific historical context. Here we catch in flight something of a different order from mere metaphor: namely, the translation of a concrete social activity into a psychological concept, at the moment of that concept's inception. The trick by which the externally observable reality of the one is smuggled into the invisible realm of the other, as the basis for validating categories of interiority, is transparent.

As for 'information-processing', though the phrase itself is modern, here the Greek connection is stronger. The professional intellectual caste known as the Sophists stated that certainty of knowledge was possible: it was after all *their* knowledge, from which they derived their own social

---

[57] Avicenna, *The Propositional Logic*, translated by Nabil Shehaby (Dordrecht: Reidel, 1973).
[58] David E. Leary, *Metaphors in the History of Psychology* (Cambridge: Cambridge University Press, 1990), p. 49.

position. They were forerunners of the medieval *literati* in that they were hand in glove with political authority in Athens and early Rome, and responsible for devising written law. We know about their information-processing model of knowledge only from Plato's satirical account of it in his *Theaetetus* (though writers impervious to the joke have often attributed it to Plato himself). The mind, said the Sophists, is like a wax tablet. We perceive objects in the external world through our senses, and the 'signs' of these objects are recorded on the mind as if it were a wax tablet on which text is engraved. They drew this metaphor from the communications technology of the time, since their own students would have been taking notes by this method. We can see here a recurring historical pattern – from the wax tablet or *tabula* (as in *tabula rasa*) to the e-tablet – whereby the knowledge achieved by the internal activity of information-processing owes its sense of certainty to being modelled on the external object recording that knowledge.

Attention and Consciousness

The modern concept of attention, and attention deficit, is a legacy of what the theologian had once aspired to in his study. For Augustine, attention was an aspect of the will, a sign of the will's positive relationship to the understanding. Is your inner being with God? Have you succeeded in overcoming its distention into time, with all the 'multiple distractions' and preoccupation with the senses which time induces?[59] Attention was an active state. The Latin word was usually not *attentio* but *intentio*, carrying a sense of effort.[60] You could not just wait for God to arrive, since the Devil would leap into any hiatus.

Increasingly in the late Middle Ages and especially with the Reformation, attention was likewise demanded of the lay congregation during sermons and the liturgy; if they were not listening, the Eucharist could not have its transformative effect on the elect soul. One's state of mind at the precise moment of receiving communion demanded a conscious certainty of one's standing in the eyes of God – a principle that reflected the wider cultural shift from shame (temporary failure to live up to an external role in the eyes of others) to guilt (a sinful and intractable inward state with permanent

---

[59] Augustine, *Confessions*, 11.29. For a detailed account, see O'Daly, *Augustine's Philosophy of Mind*, pp. 43–5.
[60] Hilary Powell, 'The quest for *quies mentis*', in (eds.) Felicity Callard, Kimberley Staines and James Wilkes, *The Restless Compendium: Interdisciplinary Investigations of Rest and Its Opposites* (Berlin: Springer, 2016).

consequences).[61] The late medieval take-up of Augustine's confessional mode led to introspection being considered a duty for each individual congregant, while the significance of Holy Communion and its effect on the recipient became the core of ecclesiastical dispute. The idea of transubstantiation, established as orthodoxy only in the thirteenth century, contributed much to the birth of the distinct discipline that would come to be known as 'theology'. Protestantism, in particular, by rejecting the miraculous aspects of transubstantiation, intellectualized the inward aspects of the Eucharist, introducing an epistemological emphasis. Do I understand what the bread and wine is doing to me, in view of its symbolic rather than material character? And, almost the same thing, am I certain of my elect status at this moment or, if not, am I receiving it hypocritically? Attention was turning into a kind of constant monitoring of self, and thus of the 'consciousness' that would later become an object of study for psychology. (The etymology of French usage makes this clear, where 'consciousness' is *la conscience*.)

Interiority and Exclusion

Joined to the cognitive operations and categories described in the previous sections, forms of exclusion familiar in modern psychology were also arising. It will become clear in later chapters how absolutely necessary some presupposition of conceptual and, consequently, social exclusion has been to the linear model, continuing from the presence/absence framework of shamanism and spirit possession. Just as the linear temporal outlook in some sense *created* cognitive ability as we understand it, so the late medieval proliferation of psychological categories brought a sharper definition of its deficiencies and disabilities.

At a deeper level of meaning, disability, prior to being absence of ability, is absence of *change*. In modern psychology, the 'operations' originally devised by a minority to describe their own activities and mark their own elite or elect status have come to describe the normal, 'able' majority of the population. Although medieval psychology's 'operations' were initially conceived of as having a static character, religious perceptions of the human being were simultaneously interpreting deficit along temporal lines, thus creating sharper categories of the child and the 'developmentally disabled' person (under varying historical labels) in particular.

---

[61] On this, see John Frederick Benton, *Consciousness of Self and Perceptions of Individuality* (Cambridge MA: Harvard University Press, 1982), pp. 263, 271.

The developmental idea, in its early religious forms, helped to forge such boundary lines, rather than merely reinforcing ones assumed to have always existed in nature. I have pointed to the circularity inherent in the human sciences' principle of a subjective logical reasoning that corresponds with logic as objective system. This created exceptions to the rule, which demanded an explanation: what or who lay beyond the circle? On the threshold of the early modern era, and only then, did the preoccupation with cognitive ability and formal logic provoke the question: what if the premise 'man is a rational animal' is false? What if something looks *homo* physically, but is not *rationalis*? Here I do not mean rational in the diffuse, discursive sense shared today both by psychiatry and by its sociological critics. I mean the deeper hypothesis that there are some human-looking creatures whose existence we have to prevent, because (as modern bioethicists such as Peter Singer have argued) they are *lower* than beasts.

In the late Middle Ages we already come across such hints at species exclusion in descriptions of the masses as *subhomines*, lacking the faculty of reason. On the one hand, such labels at the time stayed rhetorical. The rule of thumb for membership of the human species, indicating a shared human 'substance' if nothing else, remained (as it had done for Aristotle) physical resemblance to one's progenitors. On the other hand, there was an increasing sharpness of intra-human distinctions that came about partly because the specific intellectual labour of the *literati* was becoming the normative model of human reason – norms being required because the lives of more and more individuals were no longer socially and economically bonded.

Take, for example, the invention of the jurisprudential category *idiota a nativitate* or 'idiot from birth', first mentioned in the fourteenth century (though it only entered legal procedure in the sixteenth). 'Idiot' at the time meant layman – in which case idiots were a majority of the population. The phrase translates literally, then, as 'layman by birth', since in law *idiota a nativitate* was restricted to the class of estate holders; this person is singled out because he has turned up in a place where he ought to belong but does not. He does not belong because he does not have the ability to manage his estate despite being the legal heir. Legally, if not necessarily in the everyday perceptions of ordinary life, it was only by being in full possession of an earthly estate that one could be in full possession of cognitive faculties, and vice versa.

In religious terms, by contrast, lacking cognitive faculties could sometimes be seen as a positive. The idea that one might possess a specifically human reason, detached from its divine source, was an invitation to pridefulness. Augustine cites the benefit of having people around who are stupid (*stulti*) on the grounds that their moral behaviour may be exemplary. However, on each of the occasions he does so it serves an entirely different ethical argument, and so his 'fools' turn out to be a mere rhetorical device.[62] Similarly, the later medieval 'holy fool' had the rhetorical role of mitigating the church's reputation for venality. Invoked when needed as a safety valve, the holy fool was a moral critique presented as embodying the values of 'community', including the subordinate masses, against the elite. The holy fool's intellectual vacuity was a positive contrast to the worldly cunning of established institutions, including religious ones. It reflected Jesus's disciples, '*idiotae*' in the Vulgate Bible, who started off in an undeveloped state but were then changed by their apostlehood. The odd lowly person here and there could be picked out by God and given, say, an instantaneous grasp of Latin (it would have to be Latin), as proof of Providence. These were sudden transformations rather than outcomes of development.

In the history of intellectual and developmental disability the holy fool is therefore a red herring. The more important religious link to modern concepts of disability is reprobation. What religion and the law increasingly had in common was an overlap between the category of childhood in general and that of the cognitive developmental disability relevant to the period. The legal category of the *idiota a navitate* provoked the idea of the person thus disabled as permanently childlike. The importance of an individual's status *at birth* – right at the start of the lifespan – began to sideline the importance and likelihood of providential cure. One could not sit out the whole lifespan just waiting for the sudden moment when one's inborn status as a rational being might be confirmed.

The conglomerate conception of fool and child – fools *as* children, and children *as* fools – is late medieval in origin. Alongside this there was also the positive deployment of childhood as a moral critique; child prophets were promoted, and even the idea of a children's crusade to the Holy Land. But these would have had no point without the contrast of an intellectual authority in church and state that was literate and thereby specifically adult. Just as the central economic preoccupation of the period, land distribution and management, created for the law courts a new form of temporally defined incompetence that was innate and permanent and therefore (as 'idiocy') a separate category from madness, which came and

---

[62] For a more detailed analysis of the passages in question, see Goodey, *A History of Intelligence*, p. 187ff.

went,[63] so children in general were being redefined as having incipient but by the same token deficient intellectual and emotional interiors – in short, as developers. (Male children, that is; in jurisprudential terms all females were non-developers.) The Middle Ages initiated the process by which children would become, as they are today, *candidate* human beings. A teleological element arrived later, as the burgeoning educational disciplines sought to guarantee the functioning of a whole society and whole nations. Since the start of the nineteenth century the goals and the very content of social progress have been allocated a place within the childhood interior and somehow constitute it. Children make progress, but equally, 'progress' makes 'children'.

3: Temporal Structure

So far we have established that the concepts of interiority and linear time did not arise independently of each other. The third interactive element in the developmental idea, which is the *structuring* of the first two, illustrates again how the developmental idea is just one, historically specific way of representing the deeper-lying problem of change. The question of structure arises because there are certain problems intrinsic to conceiving time as linear. For example, as the philosopher Henri Bergson pointed out, a line immobilizes that which was conceived as mobile, and assumes fixity or regularity in what may in fact speed up or slow down; moreover, because time is experienced as an interpenetration between past and present, human experience cannot be registered by points on the calendar.[64] The monotheistic religions dealt with the problem by seeing change over the lifespan both as a line and as consisting of discrete 'stages'. These allowed for ceremonies, observation, assessment and controls, denoting a fixed and regular temporal structure that would later become central to the scientific procedures of the developmental idea.

Change as such can either be law-governed and gradual, or it can be providential and instantaneous so as to cancel any previously stable identity. This theoretical distinction between gradualist and instantaneous accounts of major change in human life in general and mental life in particular can be detected from the start of Christianity,[65] and would

---

[63] See Eliza Buhrer, '"But what is to be said of a fool?": Intellectual disability in medieval thought and culture', in (ed.) Albrecht Classen, *Mental Health, Spirituality and Religion in the Middle Ages and Early Modern Age* (Berlin: De Gruyter, 2014).
[64] Henri Bergson, *Time and Free Will: An Essay on the Immediate Data of Consciousness* (London: Routledge, 2002 [1889]).
[65] On this, see Robert H. Mounce, *The Book of Revelation* (Grand Rapids: Eerdmans, 1998), p. 24ff.

become especially sharp following the Reformation and Counter-Reformation. You could only expect salvation if, in this life, you had already received 'saving' grace, which set you up for afterlife. It tended at first to be seen as a one-off event; yet this raised doctrinal disputes which in the end could only be resolved by staggering the reception across your earthly existence. Grace became incremental. The modern developmental disciplines are a direct historical outgrowth of these gradualist theories of grace in the individual.

A variety of early Christian attempts at structuring the human timeline borrowed mystical numerologies, associated with the natural world, from pre-Christian thought: four (the seasons) and seven (the planets) were popular.[66] The most influential model was Augustine's. Since his purpose was 'the complete "Christianization" of philosophy',[67] he had to engage with the accounts of his immediate philosophical predecessors, for whom time had been a mere measure of change in the external universe (the Aristotelians), or a side effect of motion (the Stoics), or a secondary aspect of The One, which was actually timeless (the Neoplatonists). Augustine's more linear scheme fleshed out the trajectory of Irenaeus's 'recapitulation'. He subdivided it into the 'Six Ages of Man', though it was actually six plus one because it implied a seventh age, the afterlife. The microcosm of the individual encompassed the macrocosm of the species, and vice versa: the six ages each human being passes through are those which the world as a whole is passing through.

Augustine's first stage, infancy, corresponds to the period from Adam to Noah, the next four (childhood, adolescence, youth, maturity) to ensuing periods of Old Testament history; the sixth and last earthly stage, old age, is the one we are now living in. Old age may indicate decay, but it corrupts only the 'exterior' man; the interior man, by contrast, is daily being renewed, 'whence comes that sempiternal rest which is signified by the Sabbath', the seventh day.[68] Bodily decay is precisely an anticipation of the final stage of everlasting rest, where time has been abolished and a blissful stasis reigns. On the one hand there is this discontinuity between ages one to six and age seven; on the other hand age six represents an ideal interior maturity, and in this sense the route from six to seven – from life on earth to the afterlife and from human to divine intellect – looks less like a hiatus

---

[66] See J. A. Burrow, *The Ages of Man: A Study in Medieval Writing and Thought* (Oxford: Clarendon, 1998), especially pp. 55–94.
[67] Stephen Gaukroger, introduction to *Antoine Arnauld: On True and False Ideas* (Manchester: Manchester University Press, 1990).
[68] Augustine, *De diversis questionibus*, 1.58, cited in Burrow, *The Ages of Man*, p. 80.

and more like a flow. The soul simply tips from one into the other. Augustine's picture thereby – potentially, at least – elides the ontological gulf between time and eternity, a gulf which his depiction of time as the 'distention' of the soul none the less insisted on. (We shall see in Chapter 6 how this paradox became important for the rise of early modern theories of the mind.)

Isidore of Seville (c.560–636) took up Augustine's account of the six ages of man and introduced it into the mainstream of medieval thought. In so doing, he turned Augustine's vague formulaic structuring of human change into a pattern that could be plotted against calendar time. His interest in nature, deeper than Augustine's, prompted him to detail the functions of each stage and their relationship to the body. He left several different versions, but in his most influential one the human ages occupy regular spans of calendar time which he calls, metaphorically, 'weeks'. The first two ages, infancy and childhood, are crammed into the first 'week', whereas adolescence has a span of two 'weeks' due to the intensity of its activity, including that of the intellect (this one specific reference to interiority is not analyzed further). Three 'weeks' are then allocated to young adulthood because of its need to accumulate physical strength. Maturity (*gravitas*) – which in the modern developmental idea is the only thing that counts – lasts just one 'week', and old age lasts four.[69]

One problem with the structuring of change in both Augustine and Isidore was that of what constitutes a 'point' in time. Not only is there a primary distinction to be drawn between the instantaneous and the gradual, there is also a distinction to be drawn *within* the gradual – between change as a series and change as continuous flow. Both men had seen the earthly lifespan as consisting of unproblematical leaps from one separate stage to the next. However, there was no conceivable explanation for what happened other than Providence, each leap being a simple one-off event.

From the late Middle Ages onwards we can trace a felt need to explain temporal 'leaps' in naturalistic terms. A major theological text from the late fourteenth century, Walter Hilton's *The Ladder of Perfection* (c.1390), describes the metaphorical journey of the soul, reflecting the increased freedom of social movement in Western Europe. It expresses both a confrontation and a confluence between the spatial and the temporal world views. Hilton, like Augustine, wrestled with the problem of how the divine realm can be reached by merely human creatures whose intellects, inevitably corrupted by the flesh, are always at a seemingly infinite distance

---

[69] Isidore of Seville, *Differentiae*, 2.19, cited in Burrow, *The Ages of Man*, p. 74, n. 46.

from that goal. Contemporary mystics, such as the anonymous author of *The Cloud of Unknowing*, thought the distance could be covered (on the rare occasions that it was covered successfully) in zero time. Hilton, whose criteria were more cerebral, denied this. He conceded to mysticism the static 'contemplation' of the divine as the goal, but it was only the final goal. One could reach that point only over time. An extended and steady advance was required, albeit with interim goals: what he calls, in a phrase striking for the period, a 'process of time'.[70]

Herein lay the problem. How does Hilton's 'process' (noun) actually process (verb), so to speak? How might one describe its temporal operation? Hilton's English noun was then possibly a neologism, and this suggests that the underlying concept had a special significance for him. It went beyond Augustine's and Isidore's demarcation of human interior change by single dateable events marking one stage from the next, which had ignored the functional problem of how the changeover happens at all. Stages on a journey cannot be discrete: you do not just beam down from one location to the next.

The answer according to Hilton was that each stage must incorporate all the lower or previous ones. Since God is 'the highest' point, he says, 'process' involves 'climbing' a ladder 'step by step' towards 'contemplation', this latter being one's 'highest' and quasi-divine intellectual state. So far so good, but for Hilton the metaphor of rungs remained inadequate. It simply reproduced the problem of continuity between points. What exactly *was* the process that got you from one to the next? His answer was that the goal is a 'union', in which 'contemplation by cognition ... and contemplation by affection ... ' are both superseded dialectically, over time, by the next and 'third part of contemplation' which 'lieth *both* in cognition *and* in affection'.[71] Moreover, the metaphor of rungs might lead to the mistaken belief that a divine, infinite realm can be reached by your own efforts, which are in fact corrupt, mortal and finite – when in fact the last act of 'process' will be your sanctification by a God who inexplicably bestows saving grace on you or, equally inexplicably, refuses it regardless of your climbing skills. If there is a subjective element in interior change, it is simply 'the process of time *through feeling of grace*'. Hilton does mention the 'hard work' involved, but this means putting up with knockbacks, not

---

[70] Walter Hilton, *The Scale of Perfection* (Grand Rapids: Christian Classics Library, 1995), p. 180.
[71] My italics. On all this, see Ad Putter, 'Moving towards God: the possibilities and limitations of metaphorical journeys in Hilton's *Scale of Perfection*', in (ed.) Peregrine Horden, *Freedom of Movement in the Middle Ages: Proceedings of the 2003 Harlaxton Symposium* (Donington: Shaun Tyas, 2007), p. 333.

some autonomous and positive will or agency which you might credit yourself with, let alone any purely cognitive understanding.

The Theory of Election

The problem inherent in thinking of linear time as having 'points', which Hilton had discussed in terms of man as a species, carried over into the burgeoning concept of the individual interior. Initially the life of the Christian had only one significant 'point', the one where the timeline crosses from earthly existence to the afterlife. Other such points, and a more extended and complex temporal structure, came about as Christian doctrine ramified. An important late medieval novelty was Purgatory, the upshot of some obscure hints in Augustine.[72] Purgatory was bounded by two points, death and the soul's admission to Paradise; it thus formed a discrete passage of time between them, during which the required purification of the heavenbound soul took place. This stage represented a bridging of the ontological gulf between time and eternity, between process and completion; it assumed the existence of a mixed community between living and dead, in which the living help the dead onwards to the next stage in the temporal trajectory.

Reformation theologians rejected Purgatory, but only by maintaining that concept of bridging and attempting their own version of it. They too proposed a community transcending the living and the dead, but it was also a more limited one, a 'kingdom of saints' that consisted exclusively of the living and dead elect, and offered the prospect of a future that unfolds towards a somewhere different from the present. In the realm of socioeconomic change, that 'somewhere' was coming to be acknowledged as unpredictable; in religion it took the form of a conscious project to render the end of the temporal journey predictable. The millennium, the kingdom of God on earth where the elect 'saints' would rule, was one example. It replaced the merely passive expectations of earlier Christians, whose take on earthly life had been grim in the extreme, with the goal of a shared earthly glory prior to paradise. This hope was bolstered by the calendrical mapping of human existence; earth was now, for the individual, 'a self-reflexively temporal and thus epochal space, in which not knowing where you are might be disorienting but not knowing *when* you are [was]

---

[72] Augustine, *Enchiridion*, chapter 69. See Jacques le Goff, *The Birth of Purgatory*, translated by Arthur Goldhammer (Chicago: University of Chicago Press, 1984).

terrifying'.⁷³ The number of fixed 'points' along the earthly timeline proliferated, together with an inevitable multiplicity of explanatory links among them. There had always been baptism, but now there were more points, spread out over the staggered arrival of faith through regeneration, then justification, and finally sanctification. Anxiety about the structuring of linear time thereby increased, and was central to the theory of election.

The obvious divide between Protestantism and Catholicism goes without saying, but for our purposes the institutional schism was less important than the theoretical dispute that arose over election – a dispute which existed between opposing wings *within* Protestantism, as well as *within* Catholicism, and which transcended the better-known ecclesiastical divide. The dispute in all its variety marked an underlying shift in the West European world view and its understanding of time. By the early seventeenth century, the institutional schism was set: on the one hand a loose range of Protestant doctrines (Lutheran, Calvinist, Arminian etc.), and on the other hand the Catholic Counter-Reformation that emerged from the Council of Trent (1545–1563). What theologians of each of the two alike quarrelled about among themselves, within their own denomination, was the question of who was damned and who saved, and why. For the history of the human sciences, the fight between Catholic and Protestant ways of thought is less important than this subdivision cutting across them over predestination; and that is because in both the structural framework denoting how the individual changes over time was of paramount importance. The linear concept of interior time had a cultural presence deeper than any institutional schism.

Election, having once been a recondite abstraction, was generating major public disputes towards the end of the sixteenth century, and brought with it ever more minute and precise considerations of religious status, based on the observation of others as well as of oneself. Predestination had certainly been discussed in medieval scholasticism, but remained esoteric. Now it began to spill in all directions. At issue was your destiny in the afterlife. God had already decided where you were headed. Possibly even before you were born, you had been chosen ('elect') and were on the way to heaven, or you remained reprobate and hellbound. Could you do anything to alter this decision – say, by giving all your possessions to the poor, or by abstaining from adultery, or even by

---

[73] Samuel Loncar, 'The Protestant Reformation as a metaphysical revolution', https://marginalia.lareviewofbooks.org/protestant-reformation-metaphysical-revolution (accessed 9 September 2018).

acquiring cognitive ability in the form of 'the understanding'? Were you saved by sheer faith, a product of the grace planted within you externally by God, or did your own earthly merits and abilities play at least some role? Having lain in theological obscurity for the thousand years since Augustine (similar issues had also arisen in Judaism and Islam), they burst into life following the Reformation.

Answers were multiple and contentious. However, their subtle variations are less important for our purposes here than the way in which, out of them as a whole, would come a conception of the human being that prefigured the modern developmental idea. Debate reached a climax in the early seventeenth century. The historian has to be wary, because the labels denoting the various schools of thought were applied after debate had already begun, often abusively by opponents, and were often stretched to breaking point. Nevertheless, we shall only get by here by using them, perhaps with imaginary scare quotes. Within Protestantism the main doctrinal battle was between Calvinists and Arminians, and within the Catholic church between Jansenists and Molinists – though for this last label I will be substituting the term 'Jesuit' as the more relevant one for our context.

The Predestination Disputes

Calvinism and Jansenism had something in common, as did Arminianism and Jesuitism. (Protestant) Calvinists and (Catholic) Jansenists both emphasized that, since your interior status as elect or reprobate – and therefore saved or damned – had been decided at birth or before, it was prideful to think you could do anything to alter it. To be 'good' in this life was one thing; to be 'righteous' – that is, excused from the inborn original sin of your species – was quite another, and it was righteousness that was the decisive factor. (Protestant) Arminians and (Catholic) Jesuits objected to this way of putting it because it suggested a harsh, even a malign God. Surely he does not command people to obey him when, even if they do, it cannot alter their destiny? Decreeing someone's damnation before they have had a chance to prove themselves makes God the author of sin. Besides, what would be the point of your doing good or understanding your catechism if you have been denied any moral agency of your own?

However, Arminians and Jesuits believed just as much as their opponents in the ultimate determining role of divine grace. They did not actually think you could get to heaven just by trying, though that was the charge made against them by Calvinists and Jansenists. (And even the latter did not accuse them of believing that everyone could be saved; when Jesuits and Arminians spoke about atonement being 'universal', they meant merely that Christ's self-sacrifice was an offering to everyone, not that everyone was in a position to take it up.) Modern commentators sometimes represent the Jesuits and Arminians as anti-predestinarian. But there are limits to what this could have meant at the time. Absolute anti-predestinarians did exist here and there, but they were oddities; theologians across the board more or less enthusiastically believed in election, that few were chosen, and that they were divinely determined. As the Jesuit Cardinal Bellarmine put it, 'The number of the reprobate will be as the multitude of olives that fall to the earth, when the olive tree is shaken; and the tiny number of the chosen will be as the few olives that, having escaped the hands of the gatherers, remain in the highest branches and are picked separately.'[74] Dispute was rather about the significance of earthly behaviour *in view of* one's predeterminate interior status. If human individuals did seem to have at least some margin for manoeuvre, or thought they had it, how did it work and how big was it?

At the very least, suggesting to congregants that human agency might have some effect was an inducement to their good behaviour and attempts at understanding. The actual Jesuit and Arminian belief, however, was that human effort counted for little. For a long time they would justify leading their flocks up the garden path like this. Ordinary people were not to be trusted with a doctrine whose apparent harshness might lead them to reject God altogether. Theologians could handle the esoteric truth of predestination, but the vulgar masses needed a vulgar truth – that is, not really a truth at all. A less cynical way of putting this is that Jesuits and Arminians accepted a divine determinism but reacted to the objections about its harshness by trying to negotiate a path through the middle. Some individuals commendably went in for good works and understanding; others did not. God had endowed these others with 'sufficient' grace but foresaw from the start that they would not make use of it. Conversely, in those who did try hard, their 'perseverance' had to be accompanied by God's 'saving' grace or these efforts would not have any effect. Either way, God already knew who was going where. Despite the opposition's charge that Jesuits and Arminians were allowing individual human effort to trump divine determination, theirs was just another version of predestination. At best, goodness and understanding might be a *sign* of election; but they could certainly not be its *cause*.

---

[74] Cited in P. J. Thuesen, *Predestination: The American Career of a Contentious Doctrine* (Oxford: Oxford University Press, 2009), p. 60, referring to Isaiah 17.6.

Between Jansenists and Jesuits in particular the dispute belonged mainly in France, and is important both because of its political consequences and because of the route it tracks (examined in later chapters) towards Rousseau's *Emile*. The Jansenists' hallmark from the start was not so much their view of election but their reputation for piety, which contrasted with what they saw as the Jesuits' 'libertinism' (a term originally denoting freedom of thought but given a sexual connotation subsequently by its opponents). Jansenists had a particularly chronic anxiety, more so than most Calvinists did, about the risk of lapsing from their elect status and becoming recontaminated. By 1653 when Pope Innocent X (under pressure from the French state) condemned Jansenism as heresy, it had started to become a rallying point for anti-Jesuit forces in the political sphere too, so that the ascendant Jesuits tended to bracket anyone who disagreed with them as 'Jansenist' fellow-travellers. Visible (with hindsight) at this point is the kernel of Jansenism's later role as a general pre-revolutionary 'mentality of opposition' to the absolutist state, which sparked a second papal pronouncement of heresy in 1713.[75]

Whereas the Jansenists' emphasis was on God the all-powerful, the Jesuits' was on God the all-knowing. Since he knows beforehand what efforts individuals will make in accordance with their predestined elect status, free will and necessity (agency and predestination) may be 'congruent' with each other. For this the Jesuits referred back to Paul, in Romans 8.29–30: 'For those God foreknew he also predestined to be conformed to the likeness of his Son, ... And those he predestined he also called; those he called he also justified; those he justified he also glorified.'[76] The idea of congruence was the most they could offer as consolation. After all, what would happen if everyone, including the last conceivable human being in all of human time, were hypothetically salvable? There would be no need for hell, no need for redemption; the Creation would have been in vain, and so there would be no religion either. And if there is hell, there must be people to send there. This presupposition, shared by all sides, ran deeper than any argument about the criteria for sending them.

At issue centrally was the unconcealed bluntness of Jansenist and Calvinist determinism: the individual is powerless. But that was their weak spot: how could an all-loving God be so cruel? Their bluntness was

---

[75] Richard M. Golden, *The Godly Rebellion: Parisian Curés and the Religious Fronde 1652–1662* (Chapel Hill: University of North Carolina Press, 1981).

[76] For context, see Robert Sleigh Jr, Vere Chappell and Michael della Rocca, 'Determinism and human freedom', in (eds.) Daniel Garber and Michael Ayers, *The Cambridge History of Seventeenth-Century Philosophy*, vol. 2 (Cambridge: Cambridge University Press, 1998).

due, said the Jesuits, to an over-dogmatic and quasi-Calvinist interpretation of Augustine (Augustine was cited in support by both sides, though it depended which bit of him was being cited). The (Catholic) Jansenists themselves saw no reason to abandon Augustine's hard line on election just because some (Protestant) Calvinists also held it. They accused the Jesuits of being 'Semi-Pelagians'. This very common insult referred to the early Christian ascetic Pelagius, on whose reported doctrine of free will Augustine had honed his own hard-line doctrine of necessity.[77] In fact the idea of effective human agency for salvation was held by perhaps no one in its entirety, and 'Pelgianism' was thus always in this sense a straw man.

Jansenism, Jesuitism and the Elect

There were other groups within Catholicism aside from the Jansenists, notably the Dominican Order, that took the harder line.[78] But to help trace the later trajectory of the developmental idea we must focus on the Jansenists in particular. A seminal figure for them had been Michel de Baye (1513–1589), the teacher of Augustinianism to a new generation of Catholics under whose influence the young Cornelius Jansen (1585–1638) came. For Baye, original sin expresses itself not just in habitual vice; it is natural and transmitted by heredity: that is, not only by divine determinism but also quasi-biologically, by the very sexual act through which the human being comes into existence in the first place – an obsession whose roots lay in Augustine's account of the Fall.[79] But even for a gloom-monger like Baye there had to be a chink of light. He found it in the elect individual's aspiration to prelapsarian innocence – not through agency and effort as such, but by a self-abnegation before God that would remove the bodily taint of original sin.[80] Love of God in this sense was enshrined in the concept of 'charity', which would become central to Jansenism and to Pascal in particular, and which also embraced love for one's fellow humans.

In France, where Jansenism took root, the suspicion arose that it was a betrayal of Counter-Reformation principles. There was indeed

---

[77] See James Wetzel, 'Predestination, Pelagianism, and foreknowledge', in (eds.) Eleonore Stump and Norman Kretzmann, *The Cambridge Companion to Augustine*.

[78] (Eds.) Jordan Ballor, Matthew Gaetano and David Sytsma, *Beyond Dordt and De Auxiliis: The Dynamics of Protestant and Catholic Soteriology in the Sixteenth and Seventeenth Centuries* (Leiden: Brill, 2019).

[79] See Augustine, *The City of God*, Books 13–14.

[80] On Baye, see M. W. F. Stone, 'Michael Baius (1513–89) and the debate on "pure nature": grace and moral agency in sixteenth-century scholasticism', in (eds.) Jill Kraye and Risto Saarinen, *Moral Philosophy and the Threshold of Modernity* (Dordrecht: Springer, 2005).

circumstantial evidence. Jansen was inspired to write his magnum opus on predestination only after realizing how much he agreed with the Calvinist line on election at Protestantism's decisive Synod of Dort in 1618–19, where it had prevailed over the opposing Arminian one.[81] There was nevertheless one important difference from Calvinism, namely Jansen's belief in the possibility of lapse. The elect, once endowed with grace, could also lose it, and be sucked back into Augustine's 'mass of the damned'. Many Calvinists, by contrast, believed that once grace arrives it stays, and that the sign of your own election was precisely your sense of certainty about it. Although this provoked a certain epistemological anxiety (you might be certain, but how could you be certain you were certain etc.), it did not run as deep as the Jansenists', for whom lapse was an ever-imminent abyss. Calvinist election had a built-in sustainability, known as 'sanctification' (the upkeep of grace that follows 'justification' or excusal from original sin); the Jansenists had only penitence, which carries no guarantee and therefore must be unceasing.

Jansen himself was constantly cited by the effective founder of the Jansenist sect Jean du Vergier de Hauranne, better known as the Abbé de Saint-Cyran (1581–1643). As a result, Jansen's work achieved notoriety when Saint-Cyran was imprisoned by Cardinal Richelieu, to whom the Jesuits had allied themselves. Champions of hard-line predestination accepted the 'Jansenist' epithet pinned on them, among them several operating at a higher theoretical level – notably Antoine Arnauld, Pierre Nicole and above all Pascal. These are well-known figures in the history of philosophy, and it is they, rather than Jansen himself, who represent what history has come to know as 'Jansenism' in its initial phase. Jansen's *Augustinus* was partly a response to Luis de Molina's seminal account of Jesuit doctrine.[82] What started as esoteric and nuanced differences over the Augustinian revival then became a frame of reference for disputes about ecclesiastical power. The predestination disputes grew partly from the Jesuits' influence on state authority during the minority of Louis XIV. As a pressure group within and around the French state (which the Jansenists did not try to be) they felt, and for a long time were, politically secure, and this, plus the puritanical exclusiveness of the Jansenists, allowed them to occupy swathes of the wider Catholic territory beyond their own order.

---

[81] Cornelius Jansen, *Augustinus* (Louvain: Jacob Zegers, 1640). See Antoine Adam, *Du mysticisme à la révolte: les jansénistes du XVIIe siècle* (Paris: Fayard, 1968), p. 73.
[82] See Luis de Molina, 'On Divine Foreknowledge', in *De Concordia*, translated by Alfred J. Freddoso (Ithaca: Cornell University Press, 1988).

The Jesuits' idea of 'congruence' between predestination and human agency enabled them to gloss over the contrast between man's divinely created being and his fallen nature. In this vein, some of them went out on a limb to elevate human nature rather than (as their opponents did) condemn it. They placed human nature itself on the timeline and gave it a corresponding goal; it might 'become ever wiser and more perfect, without limit or end, and resemble an infinite goodness and wisdom'.[83] Nevertheless, this could only happen 'with the grace of God': in other words, the human nature this author is thinking of is still that of the elect alone. The majority were not even in a position to start the journey, since God had pre-selected them for the everlasting bonfire. Moreover, any optimism was matched by the equally extreme pessimism of other Jesuits: for example, the notorious preacher Jacques Bridaine who some decades later would famously if momentarily panic most of Paris into believing that only a handful of people from throughout history would ever be saved.

Grace: Instantaneous or Gradual?

Once the theory of election became key, the temporal aspect of human interiority started to dominate debate, in two ways. The first involved the question as to when the external decision about one's afterlife status had been made. Supralapsarians believed God had determined it before the beginning of time. Sublapsarians believed that determination came only with the Fall. The Jansenist view was a variant of the latter: the decision came only with the Fall, but it was not even made directly by God, since it had been freely willed by the sinful actions of Adam. And Adam had transmitted it by heredity to his descendants. This signified that election and reprobation were rooted within human history. After all, for Christians in general Adam and Eve were not mythical in the sense that (say) Zeus and Hera had been for the Greeks – they were real historical people who existed on the timeline of the species.

Secondly, if elect status were (or ought to be) central to every person's self-awareness, then manifest signs of it had to arrive within one's earthly lifetime, which one could monitor. The arrival of grace was the crucial moment. 'Grace' was the ubiquitous concept to which modern thought

---

[83] Louis Richéome, *Adieu de l'âme dévote laissant le corps*, cited in Dale van Kley, *The Religious Origins of the French Revolution: From Calvin to the Civil Constitution 1560–1791* (New Haven: Yale University Press, 1996), p. 52.

later reacted, even more so than 'faith'. In a strictly religious context, grace meant a special dispensation or formal pardon from inherited original sin. But even then there were almost as many definitions and qualifying adjectives for grace as there were individual theologians. In order to make any headway, we must ignore this complexity and keep in mind one common denominator: namely, that God's grace has two forms – one belonging to all of us by virtue of our being human, and one given only to those of us who are destined for heaven. In both cases grace is given (and in the second case also largely withheld) regardless of our own merit. The determinism that had once been enshrined in the pagan and Stoic ideas of fate, rejected by Augustine, re-entered as the theory of election. Before Christianity came along, fate had been located in the wrong place – in the external world of nature and of non-linear, cyclical time. With the idea of predestination, Augustine and his legacy had given fate and determinism one foot *inside* the workings of the human interior.

Anxiety about people who looked like members of the human species but might not be had achieved its first full expression in the late medieval idea of heresy; but in the Augustinian revival of the sixteenth century, heresy got overtaken in importance by reprobation. Heresy was external (wrong doctrine) and behavioural (sodomy etc.); reprobation was internal. All humans without exception are born reprobate because of original sin. Despite possessing the 'sufficient' or 'general' grace that comes automatically with membership of the species, we are all guilty and therefore all deserve hell. But because God is also infinitely good, he must surely have chosen to rescue at least some individuals. Having made his choice before any of us existed, he endowed this elect few during their lifetimes with an additional 'saving' or 'effective' grace that ensured their rescue.

Moreover, if there were two types of grace – that which belongs to everyone by virtue of their human birth, and that which provides salvation for a few – the question of how the elect arrive at the second kind of grace from the first had to have an explanation that could be presented in terms of linear time. In the special grace of the elect, the dominant explanation was at first its singularity. It was a lightning strike: unavoidable, and consequent upon God's having implanted a 'seed' at baptism; the endowment of elect status was thus the act of a moment, an interiorization belatedly triggered by a prior ritual. But out of the constant argument and counter-argument described above came a more complex and gradual explanation. In this version, 'saving' grace came about as the insertion (from outside) of faith, occurring in stages over the lifetime of the elect. This was the case even for supralapsarians who believed that salvation was allocated before time began, since in this case too the actual stages of election did not begin until after the individual had arrived on this earth. And so the axis of discussion about human interiority *had to be* the structure of change.

As far back as the twelfth century, even before the theory of election became the centrepiece of discussion, writers were coming up with 'an extraordinary range of images indicating the process of renewal and reform' within the individual.[84] But how such changes actually occurred was another matter. For the time being, the principle of instantaneousness still applied. Sixteenth-century Protestant theologians then went beyond this to highlight the three-stage process of regeneration, justification and sanctification. These three components had already been mentioned by Aquinas, for whom they were purely metaphysical and did not form a temporal sequence within the individual. Now they did. Regeneration was the initial cleansing; justification was the excusal of original sin and insertion of faith; and finally sanctification gave the whole a permanent, preservative solidity. Of the three, it was sanctification that would feature largest in the transition from the elect into the normal, since its particular function of *sustaining* the elect condition on earth approximated most closely to the idea of a *permanent* interior identity, in which role it eventually made regeneration and justification redundant.

A certain kind of gradualism, then, ran out the winner. In so doing it also demonstrated that the instantaneous and the gradual are not necessarily incompatible. It is a false antithesis, since (as Hilton's example shows) gradualism poses insoluble questions of its own. It turns out to be discontinuous. Because it necessitates a sectioning of time into stages, this begs the question as to how one temporarily steady state yields to the next without the 'yielding' itself being instantaneous. The problem of discontinuity was still being recognized at a philosophical level by Rousseau in the eighteenth century, and would remain a major puzzle for Piaget in the twentieth. What we can say, at least, is that the theory of election bequeathed to the modern developmental idea, as a normative principle, the notion that there is a point in time before which something cannot happen, and a point immediately afterwards by which it really ought to have happened, otherwise no further change will take place.

---

[84] Caroline Walker Bynum, *Metamorphosis and Identity* (New York: Zone Books, 2001), pp. 19ff, 78; see also Giles Constable, 'Renewal and reform in religious life: concepts and realities', in (eds.) Robert L. Benson and Constable, *Renaissance and Renewal in the Twelfth Century* (Oxford: Clarendon, 1982), p. 39.

CHAPTER 3

The History of Education: Rearing the Elect Child

I have already noted how important the mid-seventeenth-century Jansenist movement was to the history of the modern developmental idea. This and the next chapter will expand on the point. The structuring of linear time helped to isolate the concept of childhood as a *special case* of development, and so the present chapter is about the Jansenists' approach to children's education while the next will look at embryonic notions of development in Pascal, who was closely associated with them.

The history of education is intertwined with the history of childhood in general, and a few preliminary remarks on the latter will be useful. Some pre-Christian writers saw children as a distinct category, but in a restricted sense. The Greeks, for example, had plenty to say about their education and their acquisition of characteristics, but crucial elements of the developmental idea were missing. It is difficult to identify from classical Greek culture the place where a sense of permanent interiority might lodge. Greek *paideia* ('upbringing'), the education of the elite, saw ability and goals in terms of behavioural performance; the soul (*psyche*) was the animating principle of the body, not a separable internal realm. True, Plato thought all human beings are born with innate knowledge; in his dialogue *Meno*, he famously has Socrates tease out innate but previously undisclosed arithmetical knowledge in a young slave. But this is an 'unfolding' model rather than a developmental one; moreover, what is innate here is the actual knowledge itself, its content, not a temporally structured interiority.

Early Christianity may well have encouraged a view of children as moral beings,[1] but in the process they started to be also a *separate category* of moral beings. Childhood subsequently became a discrete form of interior status: a conceptual segregation that roughly coincided with the notion of childhood interiority as 'promise'. This meant God's promise of election which

---

[1] Odd Magne Bakke, *When Children Became People: The Birth of Childhood in Early Christianity* (Minneapolis: Augsburg Fortress, 2005).

demanded change and an accompanying temporal structure, of which childhood was the crucial first phase. Some such notion can equally be inferred in the movement for a humanist education that was associated with names like Erasmus and claimed to place more emphasis on children's freedom. The modern child and its sharper definition are the upshot of both.

'He seems to make infants a separate species,' complained one reader of the English Calvinist writer, Richard Baxter.[2] There was and is no logical reason why such a conceptual separation should guarantee benign outcomes (in fact some of Baxter's congregants thought the opposite – they suspected the Calvinists of wanting to beat their children). Historians of childhood, however, have tended to see the separation as a positive historical shift. One claim has been that before the modern era children were seen as small adults, or that the adult–child relationship shared overlapping features with that between master and servant.[3] Only once early modern educators grasped the importance of an age-appropriate curriculum, it is said, could the child cease to be dismissed as an 'idiot' whose family was simply waiting for his majority, and become 'a particular human being with behavioural modes valuable in themselves'.[4] The opposing claim has been that childhood has always had a separate classificatory significance, at least in affective terms.[5] This second school of thought simply imputes a distinct conception of childhood to the whole of history: they never were conceived as miniature adults. However, this disagreement is only about chronology. Both sides approve the notion of children's difference. Either way, difference is a good thing. The point for us is that both represent a retrospective view from the modern standpoint which cannot see children in the same way as other human beings because they are developers and not developed.

The Elect Child

The rise of a more precise, age-related schema and the Jansenists' practical monitoring of the childhood interior was a secondary outcome of their deeper anxiety about intra-human distinctions, and specifically about how to distinguish the elect from the contaminating surroundings of reprobation. The

---

[2] John Tombes, *Anti-Paedobaptism* (London: Henry Hills, 1654), vol. 2, p. 199.
[3] Philippe Ariès, *Centuries of Childhood: A Social History of Family Life* (New York: Vintage, 1962); Patrick Ryan, *Master-Servant Childhood* (New York: Palgrave, 2013).
[4] Richard Trexler, 'Ritual in Florence: adolescence and salvation in the Renaissance', in (eds.) Charles Trinkaus and Heiko Oberman, *The Pursuit of Holiness in Late Medieval and Renaissance Religion* (Leiden: Brill, 1974).
[5] See, for example, (eds.) Katariina Mustakallio and Jussi Hanska, *Agents and Objects: Children in Pre-Modern Europe* (Rome: Acta Instituti Romani Finlandiae, 2015).

previous century's Anabaptist sects had already preached that people should not be baptized until they were adult and capable of exercising their own will; infant baptism merely 'sowed a seed' or 'gave a sign', which was not enough. At the height of the seventeenth century's predestination debates, disputes over the structure of the human timeline were crucial. Subsequent arguing about temporal structure focused on the detail of (dis)continuity from one stage to the next over the life course, and on the divinely determined series of transformative events that constituted the leap from elect child into elect adult.

The Jansenist belief that one could lapse from one's preordained elect status created an extra layer of anxiety about childhood, thus demanding that elect status be reinforced from the very start. They imputed to childhood interiority a special vulnerability, insisting as much on this as on the tripartite phased structure of irreversible change (regeneration–justification–sanctification) espoused by Calvinists and other Reformers. Although calendar dates did not yet dominate totally, the importance of objective temporal mechanisms of change within the elect rivalled those of external ritual. Fear of lapse helped the developmental idea itself to develop, to become a historically matured theory separated from the more obvious facts of bodily development. It marks a forward connection to the secular cognitive perfections and pursuit of normality that arose in the subsequent history of psychology, as well as echoing the human soul's aspiration to mystical perfection in Augustine's *City of God*.

Reformation and Counter-Reformation alike provoked quarrels over the exact chronological age at which grace and therefore faith might be implanted within the elect child. It is true that the more relaxed view still stood whereby election sprang to light early, in the shape of 'gifted' children (today's jargon phrase has direct roots in 'the gift of grace') – those whose interior status is already as if adult. Nevertheless, the more the very essence of grace was that it required Jansenist 'purity' or Calvinist 'preparedness', the more childhood became a state of compulsory deficiency. In an assertion that informs modern concepts of childhood generally, Saint-Cyran remarked: 'Virtues in everyone, but particularly in children, are only acquired with much time ... It is not the same with vice.' Vice is immediately present in infants in its most concentrated form, owing to the concupiscence of the reproductive act, which was why 'the devil has possession of the infant soul in its mother's womb'.[6]

---

[6] 'Entretien de M. de Saint-Cyran avec M. le Maistre', in Nicolas Fontaine, *Mémoires ou histoire des solitaires de Port-Royal, Edition critique*, ed. Pascale Thouvenin (Paris: Honoré Champion, 2001 [1748]), p. 408.

Baptism, though still an absolutely vital sacrament activating the child's notional election, was not as Pelagius had seen it a total cure for original sin; it was merely, as Augustine saw it, a seed, the onset of a precarious 'convalescence'.[7]

For the Jansenists, the further back in infancy you are, the more you are in thrall to the Devil: a dynamic concept, as developmentalism itself would also turn out to be. The platitude had always been that all human beings, regardless of age, are children in the sight of God; therefore, as the biblical Paul had said in his own account of predestination and his dismissal of human agency, we are 'by nature the children of wrath'. But whatever Paul may have meant by 'nature' (*phusis*) at that point in history, predestinarians now took it to mean congenital. As Paul himself had seemed to imply (theologians are still disputing the point) humans are *born* 'the children of wrath'.[8] The projection of predestinarian anxiety on to those human creatures closest to zero on the number line of linear time would help to create the modern child. Jansen's mentor, Baye, had at least tried to ward off the obvious accusation of harshness here by saying that in infants the lusts of the flesh are not actual; they are merely 'dispositions', 'imputed' to them.[9] In other words, the demonization of children made necessary a concomitant discourse about conserving the purity attributable their elect state.[10] Notions of certain children's innocence, already well entrenched in the Middle Ages, now acquired a new, more modern contradictoriness that would enable childhood in general to be othered by being also sentimentalized.

As for cognitive ability, the medieval archetype of the creature young in years but miraculously old in wisdom (*puer senex*) had been no mere exoticism. It had lain at the core of Christian belief, alongside the more linear theory of 'spiritual ages' described in the previous chapter.[11] Wisdom did not have to correspond with chronological age, and was providentially available at any time of life. In short, it was still possible to transcend the natural stages (which are also limitations) of linear time. The Jansenists' model of the child, however, ruled this out.

The original Jansenist groupuscule of politically marginalized nobility was anxious partly because of its own precarious position. In the case of their own children – that is, those of their extended families – precariousness led to

---

[7] Markus, *The End of Christianity*, p. 57.   [8] Ephesians 2.3; 1 Timothy 2.4.
[9] De Baye, *Opera* (Ridgewood: The Gregg Press, 1964), p. 7.
[10] See Frédéric Delforge, *Les petites écoles de Port-Royal, 1637–1660* (Paris: Cerf, 1985), p. 20.
[11] On this, see Christian Gnilka, *Aetas Spiritualis: Die Überwindung der natürlichen Altersstufen als Ideal frühchristlichen Lebens* (Bonn: Hanstein, 1972).

preciousness. The ultimate anxiety was a backsliding child (who in the later secularization process would become the 'backward' child). We have seen how childhood interiority as a concept, like that of developmental disability, is as much the product of the linear model as an already existing natural category. The profile of the modern 'developmentally disabled' person comes in part from that of the reprobate; and the fact that the linear model creates the profile of the modern child too means that these categories, reprobation and childhood, interconnect. Both are universal experiences from which one wishes for people to escape. Just as everyone is born a child, so everyone is born reprobate: what is universal about man is not, positively, his reason, as the medieval scholastics despite their reservations would have said, but his innate deficiency. Human creatures taken hostage by the idea of linear time – children – are born, like the reprobates that we all are, as candidates for rescue.

However, rescue may turn out to be impossible. Who gets saved is arbitrary. The most you can do at any point in life is stand at the roadside, adopt what might just possibly be the right stance, even stay pure and undergo preparation – but ultimately you can only hope you will get picked up. In this situation the Jansenist educator's task was partly to *protect* younger human beings. He had to shape their interiority as it inevitably changed over linear time from determinate cause to predestined end. He was a potter as much as a sculptor. This foreshadowed the ambiguous role of the tutor in Rousseau's *Emile* and, through him, some of the liberal education theories and practices of today.

Schools for Jansenist Children: The Context

The Jansenists put childhood at the heart of their vision because they saw education as the way to give practical effect to doctrine. Their first spiritual and ideological headquarters was the Abbey of Port Royal near Versailles. Saint-Cyran had begun there with a couple of pupils in 1638, but his imprisonment by Cardinal Richelieu almost immediately thereafter meant that nothing of any size started up until the mid-1640s, when the Jansenist educational project was able to break cover for a few years. These primary age schools (the word *écoles* could equally mean 'classes') were then shut down in 1660 by Louis XIV, as their Jesuit opponents were achieving ascendancy at court. (This was also the point at which Louis reached his majority; for the previous years of his reign he had been the Jansenists' very model of a lapsed child, spoilt by false Jesuit doctrine.) However, in closing them Louis unwittingly gave them a cachet that eventually passed on to the many eighteenth-century French schools which were modelled on them and which would acquire a reputation for breeding opposition to absolutism.

The first Jansenist generation of speculative theologians was seeking a practical level at which to mitigate the threat of damnation, by sealing off its own families' children from the reprobate mass in an isolation tank which they called 'school'. Their interest in education reveals a central conundrum. The Bible says that in the eyes of God all human beings regardless of chronological age *are* children. But if linear time has a selection process at the end, how do these few saved individuals emerge from the reprobate infant state into which they were born like everyone else? There must be no Pelagian-style suggestion that mere humans can achieve salvation by their own efforts. If there is potential for some to not only 'grow' but also 'grow out of' their childlike religious status and therefore out of their initially damned state, what has happened to the original biblical premise that all adults are children in the eyes of God? Surely it has to be rephrased. For religious purposes it has begun to imply, not that adults *are* children, but that they are *like* children. This is a very different matter. In order to be comparable, child and adult categories must be fixed and separable. Consequently, the problems of how exactly one crosses from the first state to the second, and the corresponding anxiety, become more acute.

True, the distinction between the child and the adult was still not clear-cut. Not only are adults still children in the sight of God, the human soul's tendency to lapse is regardless of age. As Pascal put it, 'Everything that can grow progressively better can also decline. Nothing that was once weak can ever be absolutely strong. It is no good saying, "He has grown, he has changed, [because] he is still the same."'[12] It is also worth mentioning here Pascal's pious younger sister Jacqueline, whose decision to enter Port Royal as a nun, initially disapproved of by her brother, fuelled the personal crisis that drove him to 'convert' from mathematical and engineering puzzles and devote the rest of his life to theological ones instead. According to the trenchant Jacqueline, Port Royal's adults should not consider themselves above or more able than the precariously poised children they taught. For the Pascals, faith – personal possession of which guaranteed salvation, and without which you could not be sure you were elect – was the great leveller

---

[12] Blaise Pascal (ed. Louis Lafuma), *Pensées* (Paris: Editions du Seuil, 1962), 780. References correspond to this edition's numbering of the 'Thoughts'. The standard English translation uses the same numbering system: see Blaise Pascal, *Pensées*, translated by A. J. Krailsheimer (London: Penguin, 1966), though translations here are my own.

between chronological ages. However, the price for this levelling doctrine was, paradoxically, that the Abbey's pedagogues did indeed, in practice, begin to 'treat children as distinct beings with their own psychological dimensions, clearly differentiated from other human beings'.[13] And that was because if one eye was on adults being like children, the other, sharper eye had to be on what kind of creature the human child would turn out to be once it crossed the threshold of adulthood.

Curricular Organization

To the most fundamental distinction of all, between elect and reprobate, Jansenism added that between adult and child. And to faith, God's gift to the elect, it added an objective *potential* for growth, if not the kind of growth that involves agency and free will. This new emphasis on time constituted a 'rupture with universalism',[14] inasmuch as it invited separate consideration for children based on their chronological rather than their spiritual age.

The curriculum and pedagogy of the Port Royal schools seem at first sight to belong in the long trend of educational humanism already advocated by Erasmus, Montaigne and others.[15] Like them, the Jansenists claimed that their approach contrasted with the usual force-feeding and rote learning that went on elsewhere. By 'usual' the Jansenists meant Jesuit. In short, the claim had ideological roots, which historians of education have tended to take at face value. True, getting children to parrot answers to a standard list of questions on the catechism was possibly a general feature of Jesuit schools.[16] The Jansenists prided themselves on requiring their own pupils to confine memorizing 'only to that which is excellent', to have their 'honest curiosity' encouraged and to learn in the vernacular rather than in Latin.[17] Yet this was in itself hardly revolutionary, since

---

[13] René Taveneaux, *La vie quotidienne des Jansénistes aux XVIIe et XVIIIe siècles* (Paris: Hachette, 1973), p. 65.
[14] Ibid.
[15] See Allison P. Coudert, 'Educating girls in early modern Europe and America', in (ed.) Albrecht Classen, *Childhood in the Middle Ages and the Renaissance: The Results of a Paradigm Shift in the History of Mentality* (Berlin: De Gruyter, 2005).
[16] Karen Carter, *Creating Catholics: Catechism and Primary Education in Early Modern France* (Indiana: University of Notre Dame Press, 2011), p. 5.
[17] Arnauld, letter to Prince Ernest of Hesse-Rhinfels, 19 April 1683, in *Oeuvres* 2: 189, 193, cited in Brian E. Strayer, *Suffering Saints: Jansenists and Convulsionnaires in France, 1640–1799* (Eastbourne: Sussex Academic Press, 2008), p. 101.

educators even before Erasmus would sometimes favour the interiority of understanding over its 'performative' elements.[18]

As for the curriculum, apart from a weekly catechism class and a modicum of Bible study on the two days a week they attended mass, the core curriculum was Latin grammar and syntax, Virgil, Livy and ancient history, with a combination of reciting by heart and expounding.[19] Since this was already a familiar feature of a humanist education, it is debatable whether it amounted to a 'spectacularly advanced pedagogy'.[20] What was specifically Jansenist and therefore novel about it was not the curriculum as such but its view that study of texts by pagan authors might be the means to avoid lapse from an imputed Christian state of grace.

In addition, the Port Royal educators made reference to age appropriateness, to the tailoring of the curriculum to the individual, allowing for the pupil's own disposition and interests. Nevertheless, the reason for such liberalism was precisely the fragility of their charges' religious status. Unlike the sculptor, the potter had to preserve all of the existing 'clay' of their imputed election; his job was to avoid its inherent tendency to collapse. A first-hand account of the experience of two of the original pupils (who were brothers) ends with a description of how, because their tutor and both parents had recently died, the Devil was surely lying in wait for them and might 'ruin their education'.[21] The aspiration to grow in grace on this earth came with the corollary of anxiety about the risk of lapse. The anxiety was displaced on to the youngest members of the community, reinforcing their categorization as temporarily imbecilic. In this early form of developmentalism, one runs merely to stand still – though at least one is running.

Age appropriateness was in any case already an obvious strategy in strictly schoolroom terms. Famous names of pre-modern educational theory such as Quintilian (AD 35–100) as well as Hugh of St Victor had advised that the pupil should simply move on when he is ready; calendar age was relatively unimportant. But age appropriateness at Port Royal was not of this common sense kind, as their view of the ritual of Confirmation shows. For the church in general Confirmation was an external verification of internal status and even perhaps of a cognitive ability to understand religious texts, but it was not a developmental stage in the sense of having

---

[18] Katherine Zieman, *Singing the New Song: Literacy and Liturgy in Late Medieval England* (Philadelphia: University of Pennsylvania Press, 2008), p. 76.
[19] 'Education des Princes de Conti par M. Lancelot', in Fontaine, *Mémoires*, p. 912.
[20] Philippe Sellier, Preface to Delforge, *Les petites écoles*.
[21] 'Education des Princes', in Fontaine, *Mémoires*, p. 921.

a precise chronological moment. Its administrative details were hazy. The reforming Council of Trent subsequently suggested a precise age, twelve, though even then it added, 'Or, by default, the age of reason,' which might be as low as seven (in today's secular context it is calendar age itself that is ritualized). For the Jansenists, however, because of the possibility of lapse, there was a special anxiety about being *too early*. To confirm small children was an abuse, because 'they might lose the grace they received, all the more so because this sacrament, unlike the Eucharist, is never repeated'.[22] And so they went as far as to insist that religious doctrine (as distinct from Bible reading or catechism) *not* be taught in school. A similar warning with a similar rationale would turn up in Rousseau's *Emile*. Because religion was too hard to grasp at an early age, it would actually increase the possibility of lapse or, in proto-modern terms, hinder their development.

As for the individually tailored curriculum, this emphasis on the particularity of the individual child led to a new universal. On the one hand, as just noted, 'you would do well not to force Confirmation on [the recipient]'; each particular elect individual, 'like the Church itself, has his Pentecost'.[23] On the other hand, this liberal-looking notion, closely resembling the grounds for John Locke's theory of toleration, created its own set of general norms. It led to a new universal in which chronological age was the dominant abstraction and would in turn suppress that very individuality, since each individual child would be judged and assessed in relation to it – as eventually in Binet's 'mental age' score, the prototype of the IQ test. The Reformation and even (in part) the Counter-Reformation had renewed the idea of the One God, as against the medieval worship of particular saints which they saw as harking back to the many gods of paganism; but it only succeeded in reconstructing the 'elect' individual as each responsible to God in his own way, and in leading to a sense of disaggregation that reinforced the necessity for greater strictness of control.

The result was a schema framed by discrete stages. The abstract character of developmental age, as a series of points on a temporal number line by contrast with a 'spiritual age' transcending all chronology, gave observable form to the change of the human personality over time. The very insistence of the Jansenists that every child is an individual and should be educated 'each according to the measure of their received graces',[24] as well as being a practical pedagogy, was also something abstract and symbolic (as it would be in *Emile*). Port Royal's primary sources often revolve around the

---

[22] 'Entretien de M. de Saint-Cyran', in Fontaine, *Mémoires*, p. 414.   [23] Ibid.
[24] Taveneaux, *La vie quotidienne*, p. 67.

experience of just those two children, who belonged moreover to the extended family of Arnauld, its foremost theoretician. As much as a practical pedagogical study, then, they reveal a preconceived paradigm, in which the abstract and generic character of medieval philosophy's 'man' is unwittingly reborn as equally abstract but individual (elect) 'men'.

Preserving the Elect Child's Purity

In medieval religion the appearance of remarkably precocious infants was iconic: a sign of providence and miracles. The icon was now replaced with a temporal goal, involving the preservation of purity. Purity was not the same thing as innocence. Although the Jansenists continued to use this latter term, they meant something different. Children in the Augustinian formula are born guilty; therefore they cannot be innocent in the sense of freedom from original sin. Purity, however, was a possibility, and it consisted in the prospective but precarious election imputed to them as the children of elect adults (i.e. of the Jansenist families themselves). This shift of emphasis came about in a specific social setting. If the abstract 'individual child' were to survive in his elect state, the external environment too had to be pure. In the case of Port Royal, this environment was physical, a monastery. In the utopian case of *Emile*, purity would be guaranteed by the moral and fictional monastery of nature, whose protective constraints resembled that of a physical building. In both cases, the abstract individual's potential for perfection was preserved by a sterile location, away from the everyday world contaminated by reprobation.

State persecution forced several changes of location on the Port Royalists in the late 1640s, when they even faced calls for the children to be removed from their families. In this situation they had to take 'particular care to preserve the children … with shelter, as much internally as externally, from any objects that might corrupt them':[25] externally from the everyday world's temptations, internally from the Devil's assaults on their elect status. In the humanist educational tradition, the physical space for delivering religious instruction was a secular one; teaching was typically done by a visiting priest, but the space itself was untouched by ritual or church services. At Port Royal it was the other way round. The timetabling of religion was minimal (for the reasons just given), but it belonged in the geographical space of a religious foundation and it was the prevailing

---

[25] Pierre Thomas du Fossé, *Mémoires*, vol. 2, p. 259, cited in Delforge, *Les petites écoles*, p. 127.

secular curriculum that had the visiting tutors.[26] Moreover, humanist educators like Hugh of St Victor and Erasmus had indeed advocated mixing the secular with the religious, but discretely, side by side; at Port Royal, by contrast, the secular curriculum and its associated cognitive 'abilities' were seen as a direct prolongation of the spirit of baptism, which had fired up the soul for the battle between grace and nature.[27]

It is in this light that we should view Jansenism's contribution to the developmental idea. The importance of early baptism, said Saint-Cyran, is due to childhood being a town under siege (*une ville de guerre*). It is the 'appropriate moment' for the Devil to attack: 'He espies the space immediately: if the Holy Spirit does not fill it, he will.'[28] Arnauld (1612–1694), Saint-Cyran's successor as the Jansenist community's leader, attacked Calvinists who blithely thought that if 'the children of the faithful' (i.e. their own) died before the age of discretion, it would be all right because they were hereditarily elect.[29] Arnauld was prompted by Calvinist failure to insist on the possibility of lapse. The function of Port Royal's (secular) curriculum was to protect children against the lusts of the flesh, and against any consequent deprivation of the grace that was imputed to these elect young souls. 'He attacks children and they do not fight: one must fight on their behalf.'[30]

So, by contrast both with the rejected 'Jesuit' rote-learning practices and with humanist educational reformers, the Port Royal schools had an extracurricular aim, namely, to ward off the Devil's ever-imminent raids on the children's elect status as he kept 'doing his rounds ... ever seeking an entry into these little minds'.[31] Their prophylactic aim was also in a sense eugenic: to preserve and reinforce the benefit of baptism so that one day they might rear children who do not lapse or degenerate.[32] And the way to do it was to ensure that knowledge of the world (*les sciences*) and piety (*la piété*) kept each other in a close embrace. As children grew in years, mundane cognitive ability was one way in which they might guess at their predestined status, because it was a secondary sign of spiritual growth.

As intellectuals the Port Royal theologians were modernizers. They looked favourably on the new mathematics and scientific exploration, especially (if also critically) of the new Cartesian kind. And in what

---

[26] Delforge, *Les petites écoles*, p. 38.   [27] See Taveneaux, *La vie quotidienne*, p. 67.
[28] 'Entretien', in Fontaine, *Mémoires*, p. 414.
[29] Antoine Arnauld, *Renversement de la morale de Jésus-Christ par les erreurs des Calvinistes* (Paris: Guillaume Desprez, 1672), p. 579ff. See also Pascal, *Pensées*, 571.
[30] 'Entretien', in Fontaine, *Mémoires*, p. 412.   [31] Ibid.
[32] Robert Arnauld d'Andilly, *Mémoires* (Paris: Petitot, 1824), vol. 33, p. 187, cited in Delforge, *Les petites écoles*, p. 138.

Descartes called 'the beast machine', the mass of unthinking animals, they could see a parallel with what Augustine had called the *massa damnata*, the ignorant and reprobate majority.[33] Saint-Cyran linked curriculum to the aim of earthly social progress: as the Abbott, 'I had the plan of building a house which would be like a seminary for the church, as a place in which to preserve the innocence of infants without which, as I constantly perceive, it is hard for them to become good clerics,' that is to say, a competent and responsible elite.[34] True, someone thus insulated might hardly turn out to be the well-rounded civic type that the humanist educators claimed to produce; nevertheless, a certain mundane intelligence was important to the moral perfection of children and vice versa, and the element of cognitive interiority specific to each particular child would coalesce with the imputed elect status that already united them as a saintly community. The precise character of this combination between the religious and the secular marks a distinct difference from the humanism of Erasmus, who thought quite conventionally that children are born 'wild animals' and have to be tamed into their reasoning (i.e. essentially human) nature.

A further indicator of the emphasis on purity was the Jansenist insistence on small numbers in the classroom. Jesuit schools, in addition to their supposed over-reliance on rote learning, had gained a reputation for being too big and undisciplined. The Jansenist educator Pierre Coustel, claiming Erasmus's *The Institution of Christian Marriage* as his inspiration, praised the efficacy of his colleagues' small-group, family-oriented model.[35] The entire school at Port Royal in its heyday never grew beyond fifty, mostly members of a small interrelated group of embattled noble families. An excess of pupils would have made them more susceptible to what Coustel, pre-echoing the motive for modern private and selective schooling, bemoaned as 'contagion'. Fear of being polluted by the mass of the damned and reprobate was as great as the fear of being polluted by a Jesuit religious curriculum.

Moreover, the Jesuits were more inclusive, with an explicit welcome – at least in theory – for those who found it difficult to learn.[36] The Jansenists

---

[33] On the place of early psychology in the history of science and medicine, see Gary Hatfield, 'Remaking the science of mind: psychology as a natural science', in Christopher Fox, Roy Porter and Robert Wokler (eds.), *Inventing Human Science* (Berkeley: University of California Press, 1995).
[34] Saint-Cyran, *Lettres chrétiennes et spirituelles de messier Jean Duvergier de Hauranne abbé de Saint-Cyran*, n.l. 1744, vol. 2, p. 167, cited in Delforge, *Les petites écoles*, p. 20.
[35] Pierre Coustel, *Les règles de l'éducation des enfants* (Paris: Estienne Michallet, 1687), vol. 1, p. 115, cited in Delforge, *Les petites écoles*, p. 163.
[36] See Adrian Velicu, *Civic Catechisms and Reason in the French Revolution* (Farnham: Ashgate, 2010), p. 30.

were hardly inclusive in this respect. True, Pascal warned against valuing intelligence over love of God. But that did not mean cognitive ability was a bad thing. Yes, the intelligence of sinful man could be corrupting. But the issue was not qualitative, it was merely quantitative: what human beings know will never be enough by comparison with what God already knows. Hence Port Royal saw no problem in encouraging pupils to compete intellectually against each other.[37] The famous nineteenth-century historian Charles-Augustin Sainte-Beuve, in his history of the Abbey, noted drily that however much the Jansenists disputed the 'Pelagian' idea that salvation could be achieved by personal effort, most of them suddenly turned into Pelagians when it came to the intellectual progress of their own children.[38] They perceived no contradiction, however. God's will to save was a *general* will that did not take account of personal qualities, and so the redundancy of human effort did not come into it. Coming top of the class was not necessarily a bad sign. Because childhood was the crucial period of combat with the Devil, the chief purpose of school was rather (as it still is today for many in Western societies) isolation from the *massa damnata*, and this overrode any possible risk from taking pride in one's own child's intellect.

Punishment and Supervision

Because the young were more susceptible than adults to the flesh, punishment was a central issue. Pascal reprimanded his older sister Gilberte for caressing her own offspring. Jacqueline, meanwhile, suggested correcting the wilful behaviour of pupils by making them stand with placards round their necks that described their faults in big letters: 'lazy', 'negligent', 'liar'.[39] It is possible that the formal moral punishment of children by deliberate shaming is a relatively modern phenomenon. Quintilian, for example, had been against even physical punishment precisely on the grounds that it inflicted shame.[40] The Jansenists too banned physical punishment, on the grounds that it was counterproductive and would hinder the weaning of children away from their natural fleshly inclinations

---

[37] Jean Racine, *Abrégé de l'histoire de Port Royal*, cited in Delforge, *Les petites écoles*, p. 168. Racine had been a pupil there.
[38] Charles Augustin Sainte-Beuve, *Port-Royal* (Paris: 1840–59), vol. 2, p. 428.
[39] Cited in E. Marvick, 'Nature vs nurture: patterns and trends in seventeenth century French childrearing', in (ed.) Lloyd de Mause, *The History of Childhood: Untold History of Child Abuse* (New York: Aronson, 1995), p. 277.
[40] Quintilian, *Institutes of Oratory*, I, III.

(Locke would join in the argument against physical punishment a few years later). The sense of shame once attached to externals such as loss of 'face' had become attached instead to internal, moral and cognitive phenomena, and became even stronger in later centuries when 'idiots' and 'moral imbeciles' began to be institutionally segregated from their families, with locational boundaries now reinforcing conceptual ones.

Clearly, then, criticizing physical punishment was only the surface token of a deeper attitudinal change towards children that was not so humane: the emergent idea of a necessary connection between (a) more strictly temporal definitions of childhood and (b) the need to justify punishment of some sort, as a principle. Physical assault can often be informal and spontaneous, and it may be that punishment started to become systematic only once it started to take moral, internal forms with labels attached. In other words, moral punishment through shaming allowed a stricter codification of the guilt of original sin. With textbook labels replacing placards, 'lazy' might one day reappear as 'retarded', and 'liar' as 'behaviourally disordered'. The child is blamed for these things because they are obstacles on the linear trajectory towards the goal of salvation or, later, normality. It is the *systemization* of punishment of younger humans that seems new, as much as its precise form physical or moral. There is a rising sense, unfamiliar in previous generations, that childhood *as a general category* (and not only this or that egregious child) might fill the space which society reserves for the possibility of blame.

There was another link from such views on punishment to the modern developmental idea – namely, that the notion of an interior state necessitates external verification in each child. A lapse might be triggered at any moment and so, according to Saint-Cyran, the child had to be under constant supervision. This led to a peculiarly Jansenist version of the humanist principle of small-group teaching. If there were 'lack of surveillance', inevitable with large numbers, children would 'almost immediately lose that innocence, simplicity and modesty which previously rendered them so worthy of God's and men's love, as a result of an unfortunate contagion'.[41] Even at night, the beds were arranged so that all the children could be observed at once:[42] a panopticon, anticipating Jeremy Bentham by a century and a half. And all because 'one of the greatest forms of ignorance in children, and in almost all Christians, is not to know how

---

[41] Coustel, *Les règles*, vol. 1, p. 115, cited in Delforge, *Les petites écoles*, p. 158.
[42] Delforge, *Les petites écoles*, p. 277.

hard it is to return to God and to truly convert having once lost the innocence of baptism'.[43]

The possibility of lapse entailed a law of diminishing returns. When Pascal experienced his famous 'night of fire' it was already a 'second', emergency conversion. The constant note of existential anxiety in his *Pensées* points to his dread of the need for a third. Tolerance to sin was like tolerance to Valium, and the moral of this was: get in early. Assume that children are equal in vice to adults ('a great deceiver is as much a deceiver at ten years old as at forty').[44] The conceptual separation of childhood then lies fundamentally in children being the kind of creature for whom it is especially important not to make allowances. This was what marked the 'rupture' with universalism and with the previous fuzziness about the adult–child distinction: if adults were not children but merely *like* children, then in fact they precisely were *not* children. And if the Devil has his claws on human beings at the outset of life, educational objectives must consist in forcing him to let go as soon as possible. The period from infancy to adulthood, which for Augustine had been indistinct aspects of a single unitary span – that is, the regrettable distention of an ideally timeless soul or mind – now consisted in a temporally graded acquisition of fully human essence that contrasted with the *instantaneous* danger of the Devil's encroachments. The developmental idea, on the threshold of its modern dominance, is a function of the child's resistance to them.

Consequences for the History of Education

Port Royal's families of believers clearly just assumed that it was 'their' children (drawn as they were from the small group around Arnauld's own extended family) who were the chosen. Arnauld says so himself, more or less explicitly, his only qualifier being that this did not preclude their being prone to lapse.[45] This illustrates a more general pattern in the history of education. Humanist educators like Erasmus were clearly key figures but in fact Saint-Cyran, Arnauld and Pascal were just as important – if rather more obliquely. Their model of schooling was part of a view of human interiority across the age range that would later feed into eighteenth-century sociopolitical movements where the elect became 'the people' (*le peuple*): a shift eventually felt in Jacobinism, and still echoing in nineteenth-century French republicanism and its fight against the church's dominance of social institutions.[46]

---

[43] 'Entretien', in Fontaine, *Mémoires*, p. 408.   [44] Fontaine, *Mémoires*, p. 412. My italics.
[45] Arnauld, *Renversement*, p. 584.   [46] See Van Kley, *The Religious Origins*.

The history of education, as a formal academic discipline, tends to be undifferentiated, in the sense that ultimately everyone says the same thing. Historical opponents of its great names – Quintilian, Hugh of St Victor, Erasmus, Comenius, Saint-Cyran, Locke, Rousseau – are non-existent. No grand educational theory was ever set out that explained why one should teach children in a language they don't understand, use the same curriculum for children of six as those of sixteen, teach in groups of a hundred and flog them as the method to help them think for themselves. These are straw principles, against which all the great names in the history of education bat for the same side. The history of education is thus a history with no dialectic. And that is because the antithesis has been suppressed. There is an unspoken presupposition that the children under consideration have to be deemed relevant to educational theory in the first place. The history of education is undifferentiated because the core subject of study is only ever *a certain kind* of child, unified by their potential for being saved or, later, for being normal.

This claim – that the history of education is actually the history of elect children – will seem less odd if we can stand outside our own, present-day absolute presuppositions and see how it still applies in practice. The locational segregation of children with 'developmental' and 'intellectual disabilities' or affective, moral and 'behavioural disorders' more or less compulsorily from the rest is accepted practice today both within and despite the principle of 'universal' schooling. Its roots lie in the preservation of purity. Children and their teachers are sheltered from the contamination of unfamiliar others, just as for the Port Royal educators and their humanist contemporaries the purpose of school was to pull elect sheep out from among reprobate goats. The circumstances may be different, but the substratum of this presupposition does not change. The nineteenth-century rhetoric of universal schooling came to justify this segregation on the grounds of certain children's 'natural' inability to contribute to national competitiveness; in the twenty-first century, the rhetoric is about giving them specialist help. All three examples presuppose deficit in a generic cognitive and moral ability that is itself a historically manufactured representation of interiority. And so, in order to understand the embryonic modernity of Port Royal we must substitute, for the tiny minority of children at the Abbey itself as they sheltered from the polluting ocean of reprobation around them, today's great majority of the normal who are under threat from those who do not 'develop'.

CHAPTER 4

Pascal on the Ordering of Human Time

From the mid-seventeenth century onwards, inklings of the developmental idea in its modern form emerged through major figures from Pascal (1623–1662), through the writers discussed in the following two chapters, to Rousseau a century later. In Pascal such elements did not yet amount to a theory. Dying fairly young, he left in his collected aphorisms known as the *Pensées* no rounded theological system, only what may or may not have been the draft of one. It is therefore easy to pick and choose elements that suit one's own thesis, and the reader needs to bear this in mind in what follows, as they do when reading other commentators. The temptation is to try and unearth a consistency of some sort, any sort, from the mounds of paradox; but it is questionable whether Pascal himself could have made a thoroughgoing theory out of his 'thoughts' even if he had lived to do so. We shall look here at what he has to say in the *Pensées* about a temporal internal order in human beings and its goal of 'happiness' which 'all men seek', and about the relationship between election and the human cognitive abilities and their deterministic causes.

Pascal was much concerned with Order: order in the universe, order (or lack of it) in contemporary politics and society and in a different but relatable sense order within the individual, whose behaviour he divides into three ideal types or callings: the order of the flesh, the order of minds and the order of 'charity' or love of God. Even if in this respect he did not think of the individual as following a developmental trajectory from one such 'order' to the next, his work introduced a significant note of temporality. The *Pensées* were a launching pad for the following generation. Within a few decades, the problem of divine justice (what was orderly or just about God preordaining the majority of us for eternal damnation?) would be refocused on earthly events (what was orderly or just about absolutism?). This shift is well-known to historians of political thought, who have shown how Rousseau helped transform the Jansenist theological concept of a divine General Will into a civic and political one that would account for change and time in mundane social terms. Less well-known is the fact, as we shall see in later chapters, that woven into this transformation was a theory of temporal order within the individual. After Pascal, if not exactly with Pascal, order in the individual human interior gradually came to be seen predominantly in terms of the lifespan.

Pascal had a direct influence on the experimental primary schools described in the previous chapter – for example, he devised a new way of teaching literacy – but his contribution to the developmental idea went well beyond the Jansenists' view of childhood. His religious writings would become the chief reference point for the politically oppositional 'Jansenist' movement that began to emerge a generation after his death; and some of the roots of Enlightenment notions of progress lie in his reconsideration of time in the human interior, in which the concepts of election and of linear development further coalesce.

Temporal Order, Politics and Society

An *enfant sage* if ever there was one (Pascal's world-changing contribution to probability theory came at the age of sixteen), in his *Pensées* he finally abandons the residues of cyclical thinking. God, previously present among the recurring miracles of birth and death and the seasons, is now positioned only in eternity. Man is born at point zero and has infinity awaiting him after death; and in that section of the line running between these two points God remains 'hidden', meaning that one can never be sure of one's election.[1]

Pascal's religion was a call to personal action in time and history. True, 'inclining towards oneself is the beginning of all disorder'; one must instead tend 'towards the general'.[2] But the very acknowledgement of the former possibility reveals Pascal's awareness of the individual's expanding role. True also, not only the species (the natural community) but the society too (the civil community) 'tends towards the good of the body'. But this body politic was at the historical point of ceasing to be a simple property of the monarch, and was beginning to have to grapple with individual wills on a mass scale – what Locke would call 'an army of ten thousand wills'. In this contradictory social context individual interiority expanded to become an object of detailed theorizing.

Pascal's earlier and widely read *Lettres provinciales* (1657) had driven a wedge between the Crown and certain elite families, even beyond the

---

[1] See Miel, *Pascal and Theology*, p. 114ff.   [2] Pascal, *Pensées*, 420.

Jansenist redoubt. The Jansenists adhered none the less to the principle of absolutism. Monarchy, in an idealized form, was for them the earthly instrument of godly power. It was just that with the Jesuits supreme at court, the actual monarch – a young Louis XIV – was in the hands of doctrinal deviants. This gave time a sociopolitical significance for Pascal. Absolutism, at that historical point something of a novel ideology, was sparked by an equally novel sense that state authority is constrained by time. The majestic, static representations of ancient authority and the honour society had given way to a recognition, on the evidence of contemporary civil turmoil, that one thing can lead to another and usually does. Under these new circumstances the function of absolute order, said Pascal, is like managing a 'hospital of lunatics'.[3] In other words, an absolutist state is one that has to constantly react and intervene. That is what it was born to do. And if the politics of change thus lay in acknowledging a temporal dimension, the psychology of change did too.

Just as the violence of the English Revolution forced Hobbes to account for the vice of personal wills it had exposed, so Pascal and the Jansenists were reacting to the injustices of the Fronde, the contemporary French civil wars, which had suggested equally to them a war of all against all. Injustice, as Pascal saw it, arose from a feeling that 'each self is the enemy of all the others and would like to tyrannize them'.[4] Like Hobbes, the Jansenists saw absolutism as the cure. This was not a reactionary retreat to the old honour-based monarchism indulged by the Jesuits. Precisely the opposite: it was goal-rational, in the sense that it pointed (as it did for Hobbes) along a linear trajectory towards a discernible 'collective redemption', both civic and religious.[5]

For Pascal, solutions to the earthly chaos of interpersonal strife and ambition lay in a civic and personally ordered existence. Order would come from something that at first sight seems quite humdrum, a quasi-bourgeois 'honesty' (*honnêteté*): a man's 'virtue' should be measured not by standing out from the crowd but 'by his everyday condition (*son ordinaire*)',[6] which could be monitored internally, by conscience (the *forum internum* or internal arena, as Hobbes termed it).[7] Honesty was quite distinct from an aristocratic type of honour of the sort that was monitored by public shame and duelling. Status criteria in the seventeenth century were

---

[3] Pascal, *Pensées*, 533. On this, see Nannerl O. Keohane, *Philosophy and the State in France: The Renaissance to the Enlightenment* (Princeton: Princeton University Press, 1980).
[4] Pascal, *Pensées*, 597.
[5] J. G. A. Pocock, 'Time, history and eschatology in the thought of Thomas Hobbes', in *Politics, Language and Time* (London: Methuen, 1972), p. 177.
[6] Pascal, *Pensées*, 724.   [7] Thomas Hobbes, *Leviathan*, I.15.

distributed between honour, reason (wit or *ingenium*) and grace. These seem to correspond roughly with Pascal's three kinds of earthly calling. However, he has an agenda. Often he seems to be trying to pass from the first of these (the order of flesh) to the third (the order of charity or love of God) while not getting bogged down in the second (the order of minds). The notional 'honest man' whom his writings are aimed at is someone who espouses civic values and has a conscience, but who tries to get round personal difficulties in religion by an over-reliance on thinking them through, intellectually.[8]

What were these difficulties? Pascal's own anxiety, which he sought both to alleviate in himself and to provoke in his readers (they had to take their religion seriously), focused on one's own membership of the elect. It seems possible to write whole books on Pascal's thought without mentioning election, or by treating it as just one among many equally obscure doctrines at an archaic distance from our own era. Yet it is not something that can be brushed aside and left to theologians. The theory of the elect dictated the whole substructure of Pascal's and the Jansenists' writings. In terms of motivation, what could be more anxiety-inducing than the absolutely real prospect of spending infinity in a furnace with demons pecking at your bowels? Pascal was not writing for an abstract 'general reader', if indeed such a creature had existed at the time, but precisely for the person who might reasonably hope that he – or she (grace was gender-neutral) – might be saved from such a fate but was going about it the wrong way. This stimulated a new type of self-examination, as it had done among Calvinists. What signs of ultimately saving grace could one find in oneself?

Order and Interiority in Pascal

The question here is not whether Pascal's account of election was one of the precursors of a psychological science. Rather, Cartesian science and the Jansenist theology of interiority emerged over a common historical terrain. Descartes's new unifying mechanical system of the universe, while it included a 'machine psychology' of the sense impressions that occur in the 'sensitive soul', still had room for a disembodied, quasi-divine 'rational soul' and for the blind determinism of God's will regarding election.[9]

---

[8] David Wetsel, *Pascal and Disbelief: Catechesis and Conversion in the Pensées* (Washington DC: Catholic University of America Press, 1994), p. 18.
[9] Gary Hatfield, 'The passions of the soul and Descartes's machine psychology', *Studies in History and Philosophy of Science*, 38/1, 2007, and 'Mechanizing the sensitive soul', in (ed.) Gideon Manning, *Matter and Form in Early Modern Science and Philosophy* (Leiden: Brill, 2012).

Arnauld, a great influence on Pascal, is well-known to historians for his critical correspondence with Descartes on such matters. Jansenism also produced the standard textbook on logic which would dominate that discipline until the mid-nineteenth century: *La logique ou l'art de penser*, authored by Arnauld and Nicole with Pascal himself also contributing. The fact that 'logic' and 'thinking skills' are in apposition indicates once again the increasing circularity between logic as objective system and logic as a subjective faculty of the individual mind. This text gave 'psychology' itself – a term which at that time stood for opposition to materialist explanations of the mind – its own equivalently 'mechanical' resonances, which fed into the nascent human sciences.

Such was the immediate intellectual context of the *Pensées*. It must also be said, however, that the main motive for Pascal's account of interiority and introspection came not from 'science' but from his admiration and criticism of the philosophical essayist Michel de Montaigne (1533–1592). Montaigne himself was not over-concerned with election and the afterlife, but what he did do was start a fashion for getting at the truth about human lives and destinies by sitting in one's study (a secularization of the medieval hermit's cell) and examining one's 'self'. What was new here was not just that this was one way of aiming at self-improvement, but that in doing so one improved the public sphere rather than turning one's back on it. Montaigne's most widely read disciple, Pierre Charron (1541–1603), took this notion of privacy and turned it into a normative interiority, subclassifying and labelling human cognitive characteristics as if they were natural kinds.[10] Pascal objected to this rigid picture of the human being as 'gloomy and tiresome'.[11] He rejected any view that might encourage readers to claim for human reason a godlike power of allocating such capacities to fixed slots.

He complained moreover, like Luther, that 'Reason's final action is to recognize the infinity of things that lie beyond it.'[12] However, reasoning was necessary. 'Would to God ... we never needed it ... but nature has withheld this blessing.'[13] Faith was more important, 'a gift from God. Do not think we should call it a gift of reason.'[14] Yet this very need to insist on the point was a sign that by now the horse had bolted – a result not only of people like Charron but also of certain tendencies in Pascal's own work. After all 'Man is clearly made in order to think', and this 'constitutes his greatness'.[15] It is just that he keeps thinking about the wrong things.

---

[10] Pierre Charron, *Of Wisdom* (London: R. Bonwick, 1707), i, pp. 130–1. [11] Pascal, *Pensées*, 780.
[12] Pascal, *Pensées*, 188; see also 45. [13] Pascal, *Pensées*, 110. [14] Pascal, *Pensées*, 588.
[15] Pascal, *Pensées*, 620; 759.

Salvation requires man's will rather than his reason to be the crucial faculty – and even his will is inadequate. Reason is to be desired, but it is also a trap.

Pascal's answer to this conundrum comes partly in his outline notion of a temporal order. When he began assembling and arranging his 'Thoughts', it is clear that Order was intended as the very first subheading.[16] Order is first and foremost God's will, as it unfolds over historical time.[17] Applying this principle to human individuals, Pascal reshapes personhood by attributing to it a temporal structure. (It is not entirely trivial to note here that he also devised the world's first timetabled bus service.) This bears some relation to 'order' in the somewhat separate sense of the way a life is lived. Each of the 'three orders' – flesh, minds and charity – is a vocation. As we shall see later, there is the perhaps unwitting hint here of those orders forming a sequence over the duration of linear time in earthly life. For the moment let us look at the spatial relationship between these orders. Each existed within its own separate sphere and each had its rank within an overall hierarchy. All three orders existed within the ruling layer and, by inference, solely there (the Parisian omnibuses were actually not for everyone, only for nobles and clergymen). In Pascal's view 'the everyday world' of the higher estates in general and of 'our people' – that is, the Jansenists – was favoured in having 'the ability not to concern themselves with things they do not want to concern themselves with'.[18]

Each of the three was an 'order' in the sense of being a specific *method* for seeing one's way through the obvious mutability and chaos of one's surroundings. One sense in which the picture is not purely static is that although election was associated with the highest order, that of charity, it could always lapse and go into reverse. Whereas for Montaigne interiority had been a 'point of rest in an unstable world', for Pascal it thus establishes his own métier as a 'master of anxiety'.[19] Interior stability is an illusion. Interiority is an unceasing journey, in which method may be a hand to hold on to if you keep fumbling for it in the dark or indeed may not be there at all. 'There is enough light to enlighten the elect and enough obscurity to humiliate them,' while there is also 'enough obscurity to blind the reprobate and enough light to condemn them and prevent them from being excused'.[20] His anxiety was not a late Renaissance quintessence-of-dust complaint about external vicissitudes; it concerned

---

[16] Pascal, *Pensées*, 1–12.   [17] Pascal, *Pensées*, 594–598.   [18] Pascal, *Pensées*, 815.
[19] Pierre Force, 'Pascal and philosophical method', in (ed.) Nicholas Hammond, *Cambridge Companion to Pascal* (Cambridge: Cambridge University Press, 2003), p. 21ff.
[20] Pascal, *Pensées*, 236.

the destination of one's inner journey, and could be assuaged precisely and only by focusing on this latter's temporal sequence. Accordingly he divided human beings not rigidly into two, elect and reprobate, but three: those who serve God, having found him; those who live neither having found him nor even searched for him; and those who have not found him but continue to search and hope.[21] As we have seen, this third category appears among his Calvinist contemporaries too (Baxter, e.g.). Blind hope was a way of excusing God's apparent harshness over reprobation.

Pascal is often seen as the defender of a different kind of interiority – faith – against the excesses of reason. The question remains one of emphasis, though. Despite the order of 'minds' being ranked lower than that of charity, 'our intelligence holds in the order of intelligible things the same rank as our body in the extent of nature'.[22] Locke, who in the 1670s would be exchanging ideas with leading Jansenists, is usually seen as Pascal's opposite: a defender of reason against the excesses of faith. But the common denominator and overriding concern for both men was 'excess'. They are both examples of how modern notions of a specifically human reason or cognitive ability emerged historically *through* discussions about faith, which remained a given, rather than through any supposed opposition between them.

In any case, faith itself had become the crux of dispute only relatively recently, with the Reformation and Counter-Reformation. It had grown into part of a multistage series of events over time in one's personal relationship with God, events that consisted of staged internal transitions tracking the timeline of the elect individual's progress towards salvation. Grace added its own sense of objectivity, as the external transmitter of faith, to the timed arrival process. The classic series for the arrival of faith was regeneration, justification and sanctification; as we saw in Chapter 3, for the medieval scholastics this had not been a temporal sequence but rather a fixed, abstract schema floating vaguely above the ups and downs of earthly existence. Now, however, faith itself, being the point around which much of seventeenth-century doctrine had to dance, was reborn for the early modern era as a temporal sequence within each human individual.

The temporalization of divine Order would become characteristic and cross-denominational in the later seventeenth century. Pascal himself, his eye on contemporary civil violence, had started out from Augustine's

---

[21] Pascal, *Pensées*, 160. See also Hélène Bouchilloux, *Pascal: La force de la raison* (Paris: Vrin, 2004), p. 113.
[22] Pascal, *Pensées*, 199.

insistence in *The City of God* on the 'tranquillity of order'. For Pascal personal order was a prerequisite for this, and his three orders or callings were a quasi-sociological way of framing it. The order of the flesh denotes the realm of earthly authority, to which one rightly defers; it produces heroes and statesmen. The order of minds denotes human reason, whose achievements too must be respected; it produces wise men. The order of charity alone denotes saving grace, faith and redemption; it is the realm imputed to the elect, and consists in a self-denying love of God, entailing also love of one's fellow humans. If these three reflected the seventeenth century's grand trio of competing status representations (honour, reason, grace), philosophically they can be linked to orders of reality (third, second, first).

The fact that Pascal was writing in the wake of the Fronde rebellions may explain some of his concern with disorder; however, for him the epitome of disorder was the Jesuits, and the fact that they muddled the three orders when the aim should be to make a dash for charity. Hence Pascal's starting premise that the orders are mutually exclusive: charity consists in a clean break from the other two. In his *Lettres provinciales* he had associated Jesuitism with the first two orders – not because flesh and minds were intrinsically bad, but because the Jesuits substituted arguments proper to these subordinate orders for the argument of charity, which was the only true place for the religious vocation.

When Pascal thought about his own personal internal order, he drew on his study of the external world and its workings. His 'second conversion' of 1654 and consequent turn to studying the human interior and its relationship to God sprang not only from his readings of Augustine and Arnauld but also from his preceding mathematical researches. Mathematics, and especially geometry, was the model for a stable order. The Euclidean principle of discontinuity between spatial orders of magnitude (i.e. from points to lines to plane surfaces), he says, must surely conceal an ultimate unity. There must be a 'connection ... which nature, ever mindful of unity, establishes between things which in appearance are far removed from each other'.[23] This was a characteristic claim of early modern science, intended like Newton's physics to demonstrate the unifying rationale of the divine creation. Pascal acknowledged that it was this theory of his concerning the orders of spatial magnitude in mathematics that inspired his theory of three orders in the moral status of the human being: 'Those

---

[23] Pascal, 'Traité du triangle arithmétique et traités connexes', in (ed.) Jacques Chevalier, *Oeuvres complètes* (Paris: Gallimard, 1957), p. 171.

who clearly see these truths will be able to admire the grandeur and power of nature in this double [geometrical] infinity that surrounds us on all sides, and to learn by this marvellous consideration to know themselves, ... to estimate themselves at their true value, and to form thoughts that are worth more than all the rest of geometry itself.'[24]

If the three orders, despite being discontinuous and at an 'infinite' distance from each other in the spatial dimension,[25] seem nevertheless to also form a unity, that is because they have a temporal dimension which implies connections from one to the other. The discontinuity between points, lines and planes in geometry is replicated in the activity of the human interior by the gaps between one order and another and by the fact that the passage from one to the other requires a leap. Nevertheless, leaps are possible. Leaps are made by 'the heart' (*le coeur*). According to Pascal, the heart is always looking towards the first-order reality of charity as its goal. The mutual exclusivity (as between geometric phenomena) among the three orders is trumped in the last resort by the fact that there is an ultimate goal and a personal, introspective route towards it.[26] Precisely inasmuch as the three orders were also points in time and had a temporal goal, the relationship among them might be rationalized and modernized.

Reason and Human Goals

The need to know what was going on inside each elect person, and their changes of internal status over time, was connected to the collective pursuit of goals. Pascal's approach to the goal of 'happiness' illustrates this. For Augustine happiness existed only in heaven. But what then was the point of our prior earthly existence? Aquinas would go on to distinguish between the 'beatitude' of the next life and a lower-status 'felicity' in this one. Pascal elided this locational distinction. He thought that although happiness is *not possible* on this earth, it is also *the whole point* of our existence here. The second half of this paradox was not lost on his successors such as Leibniz and Rousseau, through to the secular Utilitarians who liked this bit of Pascal if not the rest: 'All men seek to be happy ... It is the motive of all the actions of all human beings ...,' though Pascal the existentialist had typically added here 'even of those who are about to hang themselves'.[27]

---

[24] Pascal, 'De l'esprit géometrique et de l'art de persuader', in (ed.) Chevalier, *Oeuvres*.
[25] Pascal, *Pensées*, 308.
[26] On this, see Buford Norman, *Portraits of Thought: Knowledge, Method and Styles in Pascal* (Columbus: Ohio State University Press, 1988).
[27] Pascal, *Pensées*, 148.

What role and character did Pascal ascribe to the broadly cognitive profile of 'happiness'? Certainly he had more trouble dealing with 'minds' than with 'flesh'. The human intellect is constantly threatening to muscle aside the charitable heart. One example is his famous 'wager' on the existence of God. Clearly such a wager entailed a rational decision. What if the clever atheist, upon dying, is confronted with proof that he had been wrong all along? Consigned to the flames, would he not now think it cleverer to have bet the other way? Whereas, if his atheism had turned out to be justified, no harm would follow from having been a believer. The wager is based, said Pascal, on rational evidence not only from scripture but also from 'nature': placing your bet assumes a positive interaction between the two and therefore some shadow role for individual agency. Pascal appeals both to the potentially charitable, God-loving person and to their natural intellectual disposition, while admitting that this latter has its limitations. 'Philosophy' and 'intelligence', for the potentially elect, are like vitamin pills for a marathon runner. Swallow some before a race, but don't imagine they guarantee victory.

The 'heart' thus described is not contrary to reason: it grasps 'first principles ... such as space, time, motion, numbers', and can lead thereby to the knowledge of God.[28] This is what lay behind his famous aphorism, 'The heart has its reasons of which reason knows nothing.'[29] However, like reason, the heart is also ambivalent. Its goal lies in the order of charitable love rather than of minds and intelligence, but the very fact that the heart involves feelings brings the corresponding risk of an 'animal-like' concupiscence.[30] It is thus also the organ by which the elect can lapse.

As for reason as such, knowledge of God that comes by reason alone is, as we saw, inadequate. 'It is only human, and useless for salvation.'[31] A reasoning human 'nature', however, is not positively incompatible with the goal of salvation. Pascal believed that the stronger one's natural intellectual disposition, 'the more efficient the work of charity will be'.[32] In other words, although his formal arrangement allocates to human reasoning a secondary role, possession of a quasi-cognitive property is functional to his definition of what human nature is. Secular, specifically human reason is no longer, as it had been for almost everyone from Augustine and Aquinas to Luther and Calvin, a potential suspect needing to be thoroughly frisked on entry. It is already inside the joint, and the whole Pascalian world view would collapse without it. Ask who this reason

---

[28] Pascal, *Pensées*, 110.   [29] Pascal, *Pensées*, 423.   [30] Pascal, *Pensées*, 149.
[31] Pascal, *Pensées*, 110.   [32] Broome, *Pascal*, p. 136ff.

belongs to, who is its exemplar, and clearly it belongs to Pascal himself, plus all the people he is trying to convince who are currently stuck in the order of minds. They are real human individuals (this order takes a plural, unlike the other two), the adult equivalents of the children in the Port Royal school with its project for the preservation of elect purity through development and self-development of young minds via a secular curriculum.

Nevertheless, while this reasoning mind constitutes one aspect of interiority, it is to the will that Pascal attributes the sense of forward movement in the order of charity, and to reason only in a subordinate sense. The task of the individual will was to approximate its moment-to-moment movements as closely as possible to those of God. Whereas in much of Protestantism 'perseverance' meant willing the good in the mere hope that one was mysteriously chosen, in Pascal perseverance meant being in grace at each moment as a direct result of constant divine intervention. Secondary support came not so much from reason as from what Pascal calls the 'machine' of ritual, penance and prayer. These created a direct connection to the order of charity. The measurable pulse of the timetabled repetition of ritual helped to mark a true duration for the human individual's interior status, and might be the basis for renewed attempts at its future happiness. Nevertheless, if today it is cognitive ability rather than the will that instantiates and sacralizes the goals of the inner life, that is only by its having acquired its halo from historical notions like Pascal's.

Developmental Nature and Causation

Pascal was starting, still ambiguously, to see nature as a whole as developmental. During the period from birth to death – that is, when God is absent – nature fills the space. With the thread of cyclical time now fully unwound, the schema of the three orders was as much horizontal as vertical.[33] True, horizontal did not yet mean linear in the modern developmentalist's sense. All three orders were still equally necessary elements of human society; the first two were not simply left behind. Just as important, forward movement could be interrupted or even reversed: man's 'double capacity for receiving and losing grace' defines his interiority, and 'there is no point of doctrine *more appropriate to man*' than this.[34] There is something that comes and goes, and even if the ultimate determining force behind man's trajectory is God rather than nature, in respect of interiority,

---

[33] See Pierre Magnard, 'Les "trois ordres" selon Pascal', *Revue de métaphysique et de morale*, 1 (1997).
[34] Pascal, *Pensées*, 354. My italics.

'Nature [too] acts by progress. *Itus et reditus*, it goes forth and returns, then goes further, then two steps back, then more than ever, etc.'[35]

Talk of coming and going raises again the central seventeenth-century conundrum about causation in human lives – about agency and predetermination, freedom and necessity. It must be remembered here that the Jansenists were sublapsarians: God determined your soul's afterlife destination, but his decision came *with* the Fall, that is to say within historical time. You yourself therefore bore the direct responsibility for your posthumous future, even if there was nothing you could do to change its destination. And one upshot of this paradox about responsibility, and of theologians' attempts to wriggle out of it, was that an explanatory space arose for determinism in a more modern sense. The idea arose that the roots of that causality might lie *both* out there in the cosmos *and* within the individual, the difference between the two types being relative. There is a 'master cause' and a subordinate 'following cause', says Pascal:

> If we ask why men are saved or damned, we can in one sense say that it is because God wills it, and in another that it is because men will it. But it is a question of knowing which of these two wills ... is the dominant one, the source, the principle and cause of the other ... And [the will] that is dominant and master of the other is considered as in some sense unique ... because it involves a concurrence with the following will ... It is not that an activity cannot also in one sense be attributed to the following will: but that activity is properly attributed only to the master will, as to its principle. For a following will is such that one can say in one sense that an activity proceeds from it, inasmuch as the following will concurs with the activity, and in another sense that the activity does not proceed from it, inasmuch as the following will is not that activity's origin. The primordial will, on the other hand, is such that one can well say that an activity proceeds from it, but one cannot in any sense say that the activity does not proceed from it.[36]

To sum up this knotty passage on causation: the divine, determinate will no longer simply *encompasses* the human will (as it had done for medieval thinkers); it creates from its superior position a *concrete connection to* the role of the human will, and to this latter's quasi-independent but still subordinate operations.

Medieval psychology had not identified any mechanism that might concretely link the divine will to the human in this way, and Pascal saw this as a weakness. He began instead to lay the foundations, if unwittingly,

---

[35] Pascal, *Pensées*, 771.   [36] Pascal, *Ecrits sur la grâce* I, in (ed.) Chevalier, *Oeuvres*, p. 949.

for some separate and properly human mechanism. Pascal's text is a watershed between pre-modern and modern. Substitute in the above passage 'nature' for God and 'nurture' for the human will, and it is clear that the two formats share the same underlying metaphysic. Their common denominator is the very *need* for a causal account of human interiority and its status – a need that was and so far remains historically specific. The seventeenth century's new and special interest in the deterministic aspects of human interiority was acquiring a sharpened sophistication – and an increasing obsessiveness – prior to its transitioning into modern psychiatric science.

Causality was important for the Jansenists because it raised the question, who first abandoned whom: Adam, or God? Just who had caused the human disaster? The correct answer is of course Adam, and therefore the whole of his posterity. God's abandonment of the majority of human beings was a consequence of Adam's original misdeed, the abandonment of his creator. The Calvinists were wrong because they 'entirely submit the will of man to the will of God' while the Jesuits, at least in the Jansenists' caricature of them, were wrong because they 'entirely submit the will of God to the will of man'.[37] Faced with the conundrum of finding a middle way between necessity and free will, the Jansenists solved it by removing the idea of causality from its scholastic abstractions and postulating instead an objective causal mechanism located within human nature and specific to it.

The Growth and the Lapse of Grace: Two Sides of One Coin

According to Jansenism, God had an overriding will to save humanity only in principle, in general terms; he did not will changes in the predetermined destiny of particular species members by responding to their individual merits. Thus he was 'no respecter of persons' (the phrase is of biblical origin). By the early eighteenth century, the emphasis in the phrase 'the general will', coined by Arnauld to describe divine determinism, had shifted to discussions about whether this situation was just or not – justice now being a higher principle which requires even God to act according to it. The meaning of the phrase shifted accordingly. His being 'no respecter of persons' came to indicate that he judges qualities of personal moral effort as being more worthy than those of social rank; that was how it was interpreted, for example, by Samuel Richardson, the pioneering novelist

---

[37] Bouchilloux, *Pascal*, p. 120.

of the human interior who would impress Rousseau so much.[38] Rousseau's General Will would solve the conundrum of freedom and necessity at a political level, by postulating a common interest that prevails over individual choices.[39]

Pascal stands at the beginning of its parallel and interconnecting path in the history of psychology. We have seen how he and the Jansenists differed from most Calvinists in believing that whatever had been sanctified in the elect could be lost again. Irrevocable excusal from original sin, which is how most Calvinists defined 'sanctification', was not actually possible: anyone who 'offends against God ... no longer has the grace which the sanctification of baptism had given him', even if they belong to the elect.[40] But sustainability of grace must surely lie *somewhere*. If election did not carry with it a guarantee of some sort, the place of humanity in the universe would not make sense. What would have been the point of creating us? And if the Jansenist emphasis on lapse meant that election per se could not absolutely confirm salvation, then the guarantee must lie elsewhere. And for Pascal it seems to have lain in whatever constituted the opposite of, and opposition to, lapse itself. One might have to call such a thing, *avant la lettre*, development. Degeneration of the lapsed soul will continue inevitably unless it is acted upon by an equal and opposite force, a 'counterweight', as Pascal terms it.[41] And the counterweighing force is grace: grace seen in this instance as the operation of the interior, an act or 'duty' of the individual will at some quasi-autonomous distance from its external source in the divine will.

This helps us understand Pascal's existential paradox, that 'duty' is inseparable from 'incapacity'.[42] If the Jansenists, with such a strong intimation of being themselves the elect, were to avoid the horror of lapsing from their own state of grace, there was only one solution: at least keep moving. 'Our nature consists in movement; all rest is death.'[43] Pascal defines internal grace as 'movement' over time, by contrast with the static 'hardness' of heart that defined the reprobate.[44] Standing still was not an option. It invited attack, with the Devil always ready to pounce. One needed to

---

[38] Samuel Richardson, *Pamela; or, Virtue Rewarded* (London: Penguin, 1980), p. 443.
[39] See Patrick Riley, *The General Will before Rousseau: The Transformation of the Divine into the Civic* (Princeton: Princeton University Press, 1986).
[40] Antoine Arnauld, *De la fréquente communion* (Paris: Antoine Vitré, 1664), p. 391; *Le calvinisme convaincu de nouveau de dogmes impiés* (Cologne: Pierre Binsfelt, 1682), p. 125.
[41] Pascal, *Pensées*, 351. [42] Pascal, *Pensées*, 381. [43] Pascal, *Pensées*, 641.
[44] Pascal, *Pensées*, 702.

submit to the 'machinery' of penance following any unfortunate deviation, but that was not enough. The opposite of 'corruption' was not mere purity, itself a static notion, but a superadded, active and very personal 'redemption' for which one had to *grow* in grace – from within, here on earth.[45]

Pascal, like Locke, was a modernizer in the sense that he saw the central problem in epistemological terms. Human spiritual growth consisted in a fight against despairing doubts about the 'hidden' God who might turn out to be an absent God (absent, at least, from the aspirant's life). In this sense, then, the idea of interior development started its positive conceptual life as a kind of *pushback* against the Devil. Pascal's term 'counterweight' (*contrepoids*) was perhaps too feeble for what he himself was seeking to express. Aquinas's grace, both the universal ('habitual') and the special ('saving') types, had been ultimately static entities; their arrival came at different points – the first in the embryo, the second at some non-specific point after birth – but they were not self-moving. For the Jansenists, however, interiority implied forward movement. Pascal nails the importance of this for his existential gambler in three words: *vous êtes embarqués*.[46] You are on your way – you, the person reading this. In Pascal's order of charity, the interiority of grace is neither static nor stable. Restoration of it becomes ever more difficult with each lapse. A whole principle of countermovement is therefore required. When he says, for example, that 'Man is full of natural error which is ineradicable without grace,'[47] he is saying that the *process of eradicating error* actually *constitutes* the positive ability to overcome it. Countermovement cannot come in the external form of agency or even of obedience to ritual, but instead in the form of an objectively existing causal, quasi-cognitive mechanism *within* oneself – even if one does not ultimately have the power to direct it.

From Jansenist as well as some Calvinist doctrine is born the idea that such an internal causal mechanism is a natural kind of its own. However, this does not make Pascal a founding father of modern psychology. For him, divine will needs to be co-present with the individual will at every instant,[48] as was the case with Descartes's view of existence as depending from moment to moment on God's creative force. Its infusion has to be continuous. Grace had no element of self-generation, and in that sense Pascal was still at one with the scholastics.

---

[45] Pascal, *Pensées*, 442.   [46] Pascal, *Pensées*, 418.   [47] Pascal, *Pensées*, 45.
[48] See Michael Moriarty, 'Grace and religious belief in Pascal', in (ed.) Hammond, *Cambridge Companion*, p. 144ff.

The Temporal Structure of Internal Order in Pascal

The notion of an interior movement that pushes back still begs the question we encountered in Chapter 2 as to how one fixed stage of that movement can possibly transition into the next. As we saw, the preferred solution whether medieval or modern has always been dialectical: that the forward movement of stages happens by incorporating the previous ones. In Pascal's three moral orders the ultimate order, that of charity, somehow transcends the other two; and it is there that the connection occurs between the divine will and the subaltern individual will. For Augustine such a connection could only occur beyond death, in the mystical 'City of God'. Pascal's talk instead of a 'Christian Republic', as a 'body entirely made up of thinking members (*un corps plein de membres pensants*)', seems to position the timeline's goal closer to life on earth.[49]

The goal was still a supernatural one, and in his 'republic' he probably includes the dead elect as well as the living elect. Nevertheless, rather than leaving the orders of flesh and minds behind, reaching the order of charity and ultimately the love of God requires and incorporates equivalent 'satisfaction' in the other two orders; taken together, they all constitute a temporal projection in which man can foresee his goal of future happiness. Happiness no longer has to be a now-or-never state. Hence the first two orders have their own positive aspects. The order of the flesh involves sense impression, obtainable from the 'machinery' of church ritual, and this connects the flesh to the divine; if you have lapsed, you will do better to clutch at the immediate feelings derived from ritual than from your intellect, because they are better than the intellect at keeping you going over time. The order of minds involves 'enjoyment' which, though distracting and in its way a sort of attention deficit, can be seen as positive because it 'keep[s] intellectuals busy at their own level'.[50] The inadequacy of the human intellect means that it cannot operate without also getting constant support from those positive elements of the order of the flesh. The third order alone, that of charity, can reveal to the individual the reality of his election, but it can only do so by encompassing the previous two. Thus the three orders may be mutually exclusive in spatial terms, but as horizontal stages or building blocks they converge, if only by inference, in a temporal line that advances cumulatively towards true happiness.

However, the horizontal aspect of Pascal's three orders gives no sense of a direct progress in time *through* each, as if mere mortals were achieving

---

[49] Pascal, *Pensées*, 372. [50] Broome, *Pascal*, p. 122.

salvation by their own bootstraps. 'We are incapable of attaining the good by our own efforts.'[51] Just as concupiscence is the obstacle in the order of the flesh, and intellectual enjoyment indulged merely for its own sake is the obstacle in the order of minds, so the order of charity carries its own specific obstacle which is an even stronger indicator of lapse – namely, pride: claiming, if only to oneself, to know that one is chosen. (Claiming to know what only God can know had been the cardinal original sin in the Garden of Eden.) Linear time was not yet a journey with an expected arrival as in modern developmentalism; there was only a vague aspiration one dared not even confess to.

Another developmentalist hint in the temporal aspects of Pascalian Order was his approach to the concept of *potentiality*. Aristotle's rigorous metaphysical distinction between the potential and the actual was taken up by scholastic philosophers who distinguished between a 'potential' and an 'actual intellect', a relationship that as we saw in Chapter 2 was proximal rather than temporal. Pascal elided the distinction. This elision is key to modern notions of childhood and development. How does one categorize and measure an invisible interiority, using psychological criteria, other than by predicting people's future 'potential' on the basis of certain 'actual' abilities presently observable in them? Pascal, attacking the old medieval distinction, uses the example of prayer. We cannot say that someone has a potential ability to pray and yet does not actually (i.e. actively) do so. If lapse were evidenced by *choosing* not to pray, this would imply that it was due to the individual's lack of effort, and thus that effort was a valid mode of the religious existence, independently of prior election. So, no: 'those who do not have the *act* of prayer do not have the ability [= potential] to pray either'.[52] Lack of potential thus comes to be identified as developmental failure, an absence of 'counterweight' or pushback.

The horizontal linearity of time is apparent as much in Pascal's writing about the human species and society as about the individual. The idea of a 'communion of saints' living and dead, mentioned in the Apostles' Creed of early Christianity, inspired his vision of a Christian Republic of the elect, which in some ways anticipated Rousseau's political republic.[53] Pascal's vision of community in the order of charity remained rather less precise. As the wide range of Rousseau's nineteenth-century political endorsements (conservative, liberal, socialist) would demonstrate, his was closer to

---

[51] Pascal, *Pensées*, 148.
[52] In (ed.) Chevalier, *Oeuvres*, pp. 266–8. See also Moriarty, 'Grace and religious belief', p. 153.
[53] On this, see Keohane, *Philosophy and the State*, p. 280ff.

a concrete project. Nevertheless, Pascal started off as Rousseau would from the willing self, whose self-interest the vision has to take into account so that one may discover one's true self in the whole. In the working out of the personal destinies of the elect individual, God participates by using the machine-like habituation of common church ritual to coax us to a point where 'happiness' consists in all particular members of the elect community having 'one will and conform[ing] it to the body ... of thinking members'.[54]

Forward movement became the essential characteristic of Order, including its social aspects, because forward movement was what Order now had to cope with in the existing world. This was not yet the idea of social progress, introduced into the discussion by Pascal's countryman Turgot a century later. But seeds of Turgot's idea are visible when Pascal says:

> By a particular prerogative, not only does every man advance daily in knowledge, but all men together make a continual progress to the extent that the world grows older, because the same thing happens in the succession of men as in the different ages of an individual man. So that the whole course of man over so many centuries should be considered as a single man who continues to exist and continually learns. Hence respecting antiquity for its philosophers is unjustifiable. For just as old age is the age farthest from infancy, who cannot see that the old age of this universal individual should not be sought in time that is close to his birth but in time that is further off in the future?[55]

Once again, we need to ask ourselves who 'man' is here, or rather who is modelling 'all men'. Man in general may be defined as a 'rational animal' (by contrast with the rest of the animal kingdom) whom 'nature' has endowed with a 'limited perfection', but Pascal's reference to a 'particular' prerogative elicits the idea of elect individuals only: elect merely by imputation (it cannot be otherwise) but lifted nevertheless out of their native reprobation. Man's 'limitless' acquisition of knowledge, his 'progress', says Pascal, is because he has been 'brought forth for nothing less than infinity' – but we must always remember that progress belongs to the elect alone. Their foreseeable end is to be with the rest of the elect in the communion of saints, living and dead, in Pascal's 'Christian Republic' whose actual location was neither here nor there.

It would become increasingly clear in the following two centuries that if the goal itself *is* on earth, or at least if the route to perfection lies across

---

[54] Pascal, *Pensées*, 370–1.
[55] Pascal, 'Préface pour le traité du vide', in (ed.) Chevalier, *Oeuvres,* p. 533.

a single continuous terrain where the abyss between time on earth and time in heaven seems to have been lost sight of, then such an aspiration might expand the elect to include perhaps many more people. For the Jansenists, however, sainthood was still not for the majority, and possibly not even for some of their own number. There would be no point if everyone responded to Christ's act of atonement and were saved, any more than if everyone were damned. Either way, it would make Christianity redundant. Yet we can see in Jansenism certain intimations of equality that would enable the later expansion of the category, from the in-group represented by the elect towards an in-group that does not even see itself as an in-group because it claims today to represent a universal humanity. Political thought calls this 'the people', biological science 'the species' and psychology 'the normal' as an aggregate of perfected or matured individuals.

Pascal wrote that 'the true and unique virtue is to hate the self and to seek for a truly lovable being to love; but since we cannot love that which is outside ourselves, we must love a [supreme] being which will be in us and yet not us.'[56] But it would not have occurred to him to ask, in how many of us? He simply continues here, 'This is true of each and every man.' What any seventeenth-century thinker meant by 'every man' or 'all mankind' is never clear. Pascal meant no more than what Augustine or Calvin probably did when they used the word 'all' about the possibility of being saved: that is to say, people from *all* walks of life but only *some*, indeed few, walkers. Any wider interpretation was 'heresy'.[57] Augustine had not overtly restricted the scope of the word. Pascal was clearer. 'The elect of God make a universality which is called *a world* because they are spread throughout the world, *all* because they form a totality, *various* (*plusieurs*) because they vary among themselves, and *few* because they are few in proportion to the totality of the abandoned'; moreover the variety is specific ('sex, age, [social] condition, complexion, from all countries, all times, and finally of all sorts'). 'The abandoned', on the other hand, 'form a totality which is called a *world*, *all*, and *various,* [but] never *few*.'[58]

The one true leveller in the Jansenist scheme was the unavoidable possibility of lapse. Pessimism on this score had the potential to see everyone as damned – either by remaining stuck in their original reprobate status or (in the case of the elect) by lapsing – and, again, there would have been no point to the Creation: hence again the need to push back. Many writers in the Calvinist tradition (and notably Locke), less mired in

---

[56] Pascal, *Pensées*, 564.   [57] Pascal, *Pensées*, 571.
[58] Pascal, *Ecrits sur la grâce*, in (ed.) Chevalier, *Oeuvres*, p. 966. Italics in original.

pessimism, were moving in the same proto-developmentalist direction.[59] Both traditions had in common a new approach to categorizing natural kinds in general. In his picture of what it is to be human, Pascal is often described as an 'extreme nominalist',[60] for whom there is no 'real essence' of man. There is only a nominal label that one has chosen to affix to the species, along with its descriptive characteristics: 'a man does not lose humanity by losing both legs, and a chicken does not acquire it by losing its feathers'.[61] But the question then arose: if not physical characteristics, then might there not be other criteria? Perhaps non-physical ones? Pascal (again like Locke) uses his surface scepticism about the existence of real essences to smuggle in a new and covertly real essence of his own: not the 'rational animal' of the scholastics, where 'rational' implied some element of participation in divine reason, but 'man' defined by a species-specific interiority to which *time* is of the essence.

The Jansenist version of God's saving grace, seen as a temporally structured force pushing back against the elect individual's tendency to lapse into the corruptions of 'natural' man, made it possible for that force itself to be seen as equally natural. The corruption of human nature is inseparable from nature's role as a redemptive cure: 'Let [man] love himself because there is in him a nature capable of good; but for all that, let him not love the baseness in him. Let him despise himself because this capacity is unrealized (*est vide*); but for all that, let him not despise this natural capacity.'[62] In the long view this was not so different from the Jesuit idea that man has a continual natural aspiration towards the good. The two rival dogmas, Jansenist and Jesuit, would finally achieve compatibility in the following century, at the point where they yielded to an increasing emphasis on natural religion: that is to say, the idea that there are 'principles of morality common to the human race' which can be rationally attributed to a divine being, and which do away with the need for appeals to Revelation.[63] Natural religion would inform the way in which the next two generations handled the developmental idea, as we shall see shortly.

---

[59] See Goodey, 'From natural disability to the moral man: Calvinism and the history of psychology', *History of the Human Sciences*, 14/3 (2001).
[60] Monique Cottret, *Jansénismes et lumières* (Paris: Albin Michel, 1998), p. 79.
[61] Pascal, 'De l'esprit géometrique', in (ed.) Chevalier, *Oeuvres*, p. 579.   [62] Pascal, *Pensées*, 119.
[63] Voltaire, *Oeuvres* 1883–85, vol. 22, p. 419, cited in Carl Becker, *The Heavenly City of the Eighteenth-Century Philosophers* (New Haven: Yale University Press, 2003 [1932]), p. 44.

CHAPTER 5

The Normalization of the Elect: Locke to Montesquieu

This chapter discusses some major writers of the period immediately prior to the Enlightenment, in all of whom the theory of election can still be observed. It is not a matter of simply collating disconnected bits of primary sources and seeing how far they match up to the modern developmental idea. Most of the texts discussed here, written within the two decades around 1700, were circulating and discussed at the time. Their authors were thereby, if unwittingly, co-creators of the idea as a joint product of the Western intellectual enterprise.

Many historians have acknowledged that the eighteenth-century *philosophes* owed more to their personal religious upbringing than they liked to admit, and conversely that their theological contemporaries were capable of participating in enlightened rational debate.[1] However, the same historians have shown no great interest in the theory of election. Perhaps this very fact is part of the historical legacy I am writing about. Today, give or take the occasional self-deprecatory flourish, most of us have a subliminal awareness of ourselves as the chosen simply by virtue of our status as adults (cognitive, emotional, moral, but especially the first of these), which thereby constitutes us as the group of the normal. As the theory of election gets caught up in that of normal development, the elect go from *leading* society to *being* it, and (in the human sciences) to being the species. One difference from the seventeenth century, then, is that today's elite is simply larger in number: it is by definition everyone who has achieved a normal development, or what is judged to be a satisfactory degree of it, over their lifespan.

The Enlightenment thinkers are said by Becker here to have 'demolished the Heavenly City of St Augustine only to rebuild it with more up-to-date

---

[1] Robert Palmer, *Catholics and Unbelievers in Eighteenth-Century France* (Princeton: Princeton University Press, 1966). For a more recent account, see (eds.) Sarah Mortimer and John Robertson, *The Intellectual Consequences of Religious Heterodoxy 1600–1750* (Leiden: Brill, 2012).

materials'. In the case of the mind sciences, though, we can go further: the engineering was new perhaps, but the original bricks have been used. Inasmuch as psychology is a type of sacralization – crudely, a secular religion (like the belief in progress) – its deepest roots lie in the theological ambiguities around interiority, which was seen *both* as having potentially a divine element *and* as a specifically human property, but only in *some* human beings.

So far the theory of election may have seemed to the reader like a fly in amber, trapped in the past. But if past ways of classifying interiority were different from our own and thereby proved to be short-term entities, in the medium term, that of the whole Christian era, there is another sense in which these ways are also continuous. Disparate categories of interiority do arrive out of the blue and later vanish, but there is also a continuous reconfiguring of certain continuous and irreducible elements. One opposed pairing of conceptually included and excluded groups may disappear and a new one emerge, but it does so only through that longer-term reconfiguration process which has its own historical patterns. 'Normalization of the elect', as I shall call it, happened as a part of a chain reaction that did not replace just any old hierarchy of categories with just any new one. Hence it is just what the phrasing implies: the active conversion of one category into its successor, not its abandonment and replacement by something entirely novel.

When we come across generic 'man' in pre-modern texts of a psychological bent it clearly does not mean absolutely everyone born to human parents; only for logicians was this the case, and even then precariously. Paradigmatic 'man' in most early modern contexts implies a social elite, signifying externals such as land, inherited title or political power: but it was also a matter of interior status. Anabaptist revolts on the Continent and political revolution in England had thrown up socially upstart preachers claiming to know they were chosen, but on the whole elite meant elect (the words are etymologically the same). This continued to be the case with Pascal, Malebranche and Leibniz, and would remain so even with some who might at a surface level be thought to have rejected the whole theory of election: Locke, Montesquieu and Rousseau among others.

How the Reprobate Became the Abnormal: Social Context

Normalization of the elect coincided with new ways of associating order and justice – once largely static conceptions – with time. The stadial structuring of the human interior was partly the accompaniment to an increasing recognition that any theory of order in the external, sociopolitical world must have a temporal dimension. As we saw with Pascal, it was a way of coping with the unpredictability and evident chaotic mutability of linear time in external affairs. This meant starting with the human agents of disorder: the developmental failure of reprobates represented them as the harbingers of social chaos, sown by the Devil. And just as today we rely on cognitive disability to tell us what cognitive ability is, it is reprobation that can ultimately tell us what election was and what it then became.

How did reprobation get turned into a cognitive category? For it would become one conceptual marker of the 'idiots' of nineteenth-century psycho-medical anxiety, of the socially disrespectable and psychologically abnormal, and thence of the modern 'developmentally disabled' person. Such idiots are not simply one more item on the list of supposedly inferior out-groups in general (class, gender, race etc.), they are the successor to a very particular kind of out-group: that which was and is defined precisely by the challenge to its actual species membership. Medieval authorities had deposited and sometimes invented a range of types in this very specific slot: heretics, Cathars, Jews, sodomites.[2] The modern era, with its vision of human cognitive abilities tracking a universal and scientific path into an Edenic future, is rooted in the anxiety created by just one category. This category, signifying cognitive deficit, spawned minor variations ('imbeciles', 'morons', 'the feeble-minded' etc.) that fed subsequently into countless expert specialisms in psychology, but they have all retained the core notion previously definitive of reprobation: that of *an absence of interior change*. And the anthropological thread that links these categories over centuries is fear of contamination.

It is easy to see how the quite different medieval 'idiot' group – that is, the majority of the population, those who were simply illiterate or vocationally unqualified but nevertheless in that period fully human – gradually shrank in size, through changes in socioeconomic organization and therefore in public perception, into a small pathological minority. More complicated, however, is the historical role of reprobation.

In the last decades of the seventeenth century the concept entered a burgeoning public arena. As we shall be starting our chain of texts with John Locke, an English example may be appropriate. Within a few months of publication of Locke's *Essay Concerning Human Understanding*, the Society for the Reformation of Manners was founded on the wild eastern

---

[2] On this, see Moore, *The War on Heresy*.

fringes of London, claiming divine foundation (by proxy of William III). Its criteria of respectability targeted outward misbehaviours and mundane pollutions such as sodomy and prostitution (these were also symbolic of the threatening political resurgence of an entire tranche of reprobates – that is, the recently overturned Catholic monarchy). The corralling of this area's ungoverned mass of casual labourers – associated in any preacher's mind with reprobation – into borderline respectability, and the co-option of aspirational locals in their moral policing, was necessary for the preservation of social order.

At the same time, cognitive criteria were muscling in on the moral ones. There were changes in the notion of what happens in hell, where the notion of physical torment was ceding to the torment of the soul, a notion of interior suffering that would later be attributed by psychology to the cognitively disabled person. The reduction of social idiocy involved the expansion of a lower middle class together with increased education and literacy. However, these were still meaningless without also the elimination of moral deficiency, by religious criteria such as regular church attendance and the taking of Communion. The quest of the famous social and educational reformer Hannah More (1745–1833) for improvement of the lower orders would be sparked by her enthusiasm for the Jansenist Pierre Nicole's *Moral Essays*, widely known to English readers through Locke's translations from them. She may have promoted the value of human agency, over-interpreting Nicole as saying that you are more likely to get to heaven if you can read; nevertheless her writings, like those of the Arminian mass educator John Wesley, retain a latent predestinarian substructure. Literacy, achieved over time, may be a sign of election, without necessarily guaranteeing it; illiteracy, to which time is irrelevant because no learning develops, is a much surer sign of reprobation.

Although nineteenth-century psychology would invent alongside the cognitive idiot a parallel subcategory that had its own moral connotations, the 'moral imbecile', it is not the case that a direct historical line runs from reprobation seen as a moral phenomenon (as just described) to moral imbecility in particular. The relevance of reprobation was more general. The transition of reprobate status into clinical cognitive idiocy was fuelled by the rise of the *developmental* idea and developmental failure. In the seventeenth century a reprobate's everyday cognitive abilities in the narrow sense had not been in question. Neither cleverness nor well-intentioned moral behaviour guaranteed elect status. Calling someone 'reprobate' might betray your class-based intellectual disdain, but if you were a landowning magistrate your landless servants were as likely as yourself to be elect – at least in theory. Correspondingly, neither low social class nor low intellectual ability could (again, in theory) be a proxy for reprobation. If at first sight reprobation shared no actual conceptual content with modern idiocy, what then did it infuse into our modern clinical categories?

The Theology of Reprobation

For an answer, we need to know some of the important theological details. First of all, increasing belief in human agency from the late seventeenth century – whether cognitive ('the understanding') or moral ('good works') – was to start with a rhetorical device rather than a matter of principle. It encouraged the masses to behave, being a plea against the despondency that might result from not being able to know whether one was personally elect. Despondency risked sliding into unbelief. This led writers like Baxter, who was also a part-time doctor, to medicalize it and give it a psychiatric profile as 'melancholy'. The constant, core belief had to be belief in one's own elect status. Even when more ostensibly non-predestinarian doctrines did start to gain traction, they were not necessarily more inclusive. The question remained, how logically can some be 'chosen' unless some others are not? If More or Wesley were to be elect and certain of it, someone else had to be damned, regardless of any effort they might make. Predestination did not simply fade away.

Secondly, the expanding early eighteenth-century interest in natural religion dispensed with the absolute necessity of Revelation (though it often retained a secondary role), and this made it possible to overlap divine explanations for human interiority with rational ones. The developmental idea straddles both of these explanatory possibilities. Causes from an external (divine, genetic etc.) source may have an existence beyond time, but they only take effect within the human individual's timed nature, a nature now endowed with its own stadial determinism. This made it possible to speak of human nature as a condition that is phased; it created a certain type of creature, the infant, for whom fully human status is a matter of 'catching up' on the adult state. Infants, all born reprobate, were saved no longer by the triggering miracle of baptism alone but by an automated self-propulsion – at first in the form of grace accrued over time but thereafter in the developmentalist form of cognitive ability. In linear time, the child who will never catch up occupies the place which the reprobate held before.

And finally, from here on a very important distinction must be borne in mind, between 'single' and 'double' predestination. Double predestinarians maintained that election and reprobation were opposite and equal: that God had already determined who was saved *and*, directly, who was damned. You had to be fairly tough like Jansen or his Protestant equivalent Franciscus Gomarus (1563–1641) to stomach this, because it ruled out human agency absolutely. Among other things, it might lead to those who believed they were elect thinking that on earth they could do no wrong. When people rejected predestination, it was usually only double predestination they actually meant. The fact that they mostly did not feel a need to spell this out has led to much modern misinterpretation which assumes that the abandonment of predestination was total.

Single predestination had a much longer historical shelf life. The large majority of religious writers saw the salvation of the elect as determinate, but the damnation of reprobates and God's part in this as less so. There were many ways of explaining this. One was that whereas God directly wills the salvation of the elect, he simply knows in advance the damnation of reprobates and is therefore not responsible for their fate: it is the consequence of original sin.[3] Such evasions, in placing the deterministic spotlight on election alone, thereby left reprobation to gradually fade from discussion. But if the large majority of predestinarians were single ones, it was also true that the large majority of Christian thinkers were still predestinarian. To stop talking about something does not necessarily mean that the underlying motive for conceiving human interiority in terms of a fundamental divide had itself subsided.

For double predestinarians causality was all. Their determinism had an essential simplicity: either you were gifted with saving grace or you were refused it, and God was the determinate cause in both cases. Single predestinarians too were determinists. For them, time and the temporal structuring of interiority were features of election alone; election had development ('growth in grace') imputed to it whereas reprobation was a straightforward absence. They doubted only God's direct, interventionist role in it. Criteria for observing and assessing reprobation among actual individuals could not be clearly discerned by mere mortals; but it had to exist, otherwise there would be no hell; and without hell, no Christianity.

In both cases, single as well as double, the presupposition linking reprobation to modern pathological idiocy is precisely its causal, deterministic element, which looks forward to genetics (if the Almighty exhibits one kind of arbitrary harshness, genes exhibit another). The conceptual transition from one kind of cause to the other belongs to the history of the

---

[3] See Chapter 2, '2: Interiority'.

relation between interiority and time. Conventionally, reprobate status lay *outside* of time, and described all human beings. It was unalterable unless by an external, providential source – namely, the grace and foresight of God who cancelled that status in a few by 'justifying' them (rendering them just, in other words pardoning them). Everyone else's souls remained stuck in the original state, and so temporal descriptors did not apply to them. Hence they did not develop.

The historical importance of this seemingly arcane distinction between single and double predestination will become clear further down the line, reaching as far as Francis Galton (see Chapter 8). Single predestinarians, by rejecting the idea that reprobates were determined to the same degree as the elect and being vague about the alternatives, opened up a space for explanations that could eventually accommodate individual effort and what we now call 'nurture', and thereby for the elect to become a majority. Double predestinarians, by upholding the idea of God's direct determination of reprobates as of the elect, were simultaneously opening up a space in which direct determination of the biological sort might apply equally to the majority and the minority, to normal and abnormal. Modern psychobiology is the descendant of both theories.

John Locke (1632–1704) on Election

If during the seventeenth century the theory of election took centre stage in European doctrinal battles (and in devastating actual wars where it featured heavily as propaganda), by 1700 the gradual marginalization of theology as a whole within intellectual milieux meant that the discussion was less fraught. But to say that belief in the theory was in decline is the wrong way of putting it. For one thing, even if it was sidelined from high philosophy, it retained a noisy presence in the popular religious culture of the following century. Rather, at this latter level, we can speak of a conceptual overhaul. Locke's *Essay Concerning Human Understanding* and his discussion of how species are defined can be read as the preface to it. In his definition of the human species he substituted (using Calvinist and Jansenist precedents) interior, psychological criteria for those of bodily form. He proposed replacing the 'rational man' of the scholastics with what he calls the 'moral man', which unlike the former is not exactly a universal since it corresponds partly with the restricted group of the elect and similarly suggests an out-group. The out-group are 'changelings', creatures who resemble humans physically but whose humanity is questionable because they are unable to acquire reason empirically over time. This descriptor could equally be used of modern developmental disability. Close textual inspection, however, reveals that he took much of the content of these new definitions from certain texts of predestinarian predecessors including Baxter and others, simply substituting the label 'elect' with 'moral man' and 'reprobate' with 'changeling'.[4] Thus his theory of the human understanding did not throw election out of the window; rather, it helped to reshape the theory of election in terms suited to an empiricist version of the interior timeline.

This is evident from a letter to his friend William Molyneux, the one place in his entire output where he discusses predestination directly.[5] Molyneux had spotted the conceptual equivalence between reprobates and Locke's changelings. He complained: 'This thread seems so wonderfully fine spun in your book that at last the great question of liberty and necessity seems to vanish, and herein you seem to make all sins to proceed from our understandings . . . Now it seems harsh to say that a man shall be damned because he understands no better than he does.' Locke's answer is not dismissive but evasive:

> I own freely to you the weakness of my understanding, that though it be unquestionable that there is omnipotence and omniscience in God our maker, and I cannot have a clearer perception of any thing than that I am free, yet I cannot make freedom in man consistent with omnipotence and omniscience in God, though I am as fully persuaded of *both* as of any truths I most firmly assent to. And therefore I have long since given off the consideration of that question, resolving all into this short conclusion, That if it be possible for God to make a free agent, then man is free, though I see not the way of it.[6]

He has not completely rejected either the belief that man's destiny is predetermined, or that man is free; nor does he think the idea of 'consistency' between predestined status and personal effort (the Jesuit/Arminian notion of 'congruence') is any kind of solution. He claims only to have given up. His own 'understanding' is too 'weak' to stretch to it (we shall see shortly what a 'weak' predestinarian might look like). Possibly he is being ironic. Nevertheless, he preserves intact a binary template, while redirecting the focus of the 'liberty and necessity' question ('agency' and

---

[4] See Goodey, *A History of Intelligence*, p. 313ff.
[5] Letter to John Locke, 22 December 1692, in (ed.) E. S. de Beer, *The Correspondence of John Locke* (Oxford: Clarendon, 1979), vol. 4, p. 625.
[6] Letter to William Molyneux, 20 January 1693, in de Beer, *Correspondence*.

'omnipotence' in his letter to Molyneux) to cognitive ability, exactly as his correspondent had pointed out.

Nicolas Malebranche (1638–1715): Order, Election and the Child

Locke is often seen as the chief source of Enlightenment thought, but Malebranche was equally so. In his writings, the theory of election is implicit but also substantive, while the temporal nature of human interiority is more sharply defined than it was in Pascal. We shall look at several aspects of this, but some context is needed first. Malebranche belonged to the Oratorian order of priesthood, which had reacted against the worldliness of the French church; it had also inspired the first Jansenists, though it advocated peace and was wary of their combativeness. Malebranche's work prompts certain interlinked questions relevant to our topic. If most people are predestined to everlasting torment, how does that square with the idea that the universe is built on Justice? If what we need in order to be saved is faith, how does that square with the increasing importance of reason in explaining religion? And if all human beings without exception are conceived in the concupiscence of the sexual act, how do the elect in particular free themselves from this unavoidable taint in their natural origins?

As we shall see, these questions could not be answered without a concept of natural human development. Drawing on Pascal, Malebranche associated the concepts of Order and Justice with that of Time; and in a departure from the previously universal view that human nature was merely dispositional and that necessity (determinism) lay in predestined grace rather than nature, he started to elide the difference between the these latter two. His *Treatise on Ethics* of 1684 starts with the premise that 'Love of Order is the only virtue': in human beings the love of rational, logical Order is no different from 'charity', the love of God.[7] And Order hinges on Justice, which has to be rationally explicable. The paradigm in this case is God's punishment of reprobates. God, being good, would not be just if he abandoned all of them to their reprobate state. Is the damnation of reprobates just, or is it pointlessly harsh? After all, the theory implies God is laying down a rule which he knows people will not be able to obey even if they try.

Why goodness should have *justice* as its main marker at this historical point, in the late seventeenth century, was a question that intersected with

---

[7] Nicolas Malebranche, *Traité de morale*, in (ed.) André Robinet, *Oeuvres complètes* (Paris: Vrin, 1962), vol. II, p. 28.

contemporary shifts in political theory and its questioning of justice on earth. If nothing else will convince today's reader of how central the theory of election is to the history of the human sciences, its association with *justice* will, because that is the topic from which the most influential political thought of the Enlightenment era springs. The Enlightenment's concern with social justice derived directly from the anguished question the previous century had asked of a God who sends people to hell on an arbitrary basis. The question was not whether hell exists, which went without saying. Rather, the question was how an all-knowing and all-powerful God who damns people arbitrarily can also be all-loving. David Hume, though influenced by Malebranche, would hint at a way of cutting this contradiction short: write God out of it. For his predecessors like Malebranche and Leibniz who could not have even conceived of throwing the baby out with the bathwater, election remained at the core of the solution.

The first important thing to note about all this is that, in keeping with his fellow Oratorians' mildness of demeanour, Malebranche's avoidance of overt disputes about election did not mean he had abandoned it. His instinct was to cover the endless quibbling with a pacificatory rationalism. His rational explanation for the existence of God was rooted in the concept of Order. Others thought the very attempt to justify rationally the ways of God to man was blasphemous, because it implied equality between the two parties: to justify meant to excuse. Mere mortals were being asked to make excuses for God; thus they were already accepting his role in the creation of evil and disorder. Malebranche, however, saw the emphasis on Order and rationality as a way of making God's justice cognitively intelligible: it had to be seen to done.

His concept of Order elided the distinction between physical explanations and those arising in the 'moral' realm (i.e. that of man's personal relationship to God). Necessity plays the same role in both. Conduct can be assessed as 'just' with the same degree of certainty as the sides of a triangle always making 180 degrees. Even God cannot violate the mathematical rules he himself has laid down, so likewise the fact that he wills a moral action does not make it just; on the contrary, he must will it *because* it is just.[8] In Malebranche, then, the operations of Order are primary. Its demands transcend both nature and grace. This goes part way to explaining how he could tend towards amalgamating the two, to the dismay of many

---

[8] See Andrew Pyle, *Malebranche* (London: Routledge, 2003), p. 211. For Locke in the same sense, see *An Essay*, 3.11.16.

of his co-religionists (and sure enough, nineteenth-century biology and psychology would muscle grace aside). From the late Middle Ages onwards, the idea of interior grace had become encrusted with so many endlessly fine distinctions that the only workable, if radical, solution seemed to be to homogenize them all; and one way of doing so was for them all to shelter under the umbrella of 'nature'. Categories of human interiority and their deeper causality could be explained in religious terms by the higher, unwavering general lawfulness of a merged nature and grace.

A second important thing to note is that Malebranche worried about how election can be imputed to naturally concupiscent individuals. The cure for his anxiety was their ability to grasp 'clear and distinct ideas', in the sense proposed by Descartes. This cognitive element in Descartes could be reconciled with the idea of election as the means to salvation. How did this work? The idea of God's General Will – the original example of it being his will *to save* – could be extended beyond election to make it responsible for nature in general,[9] so that God would thus be 'not only [nature's] originator but also its executor'.[10] In this respect 'God acts by general wills when he acts as a consequence of general laws which he has established,' and 'Nature is nothing but the general law which God has established.'[11] We can see here therefore the kind of thinking that might eventually allow interior status (election) to become a natural kind (cognitive ability). The generality of God's will in the realm of grace was in a position to connect up with Descartes's theory of a generality of laws in the realm of physical nature and hence, one day, in the realm of psychological nature.

Malebranche's insistence on an ordered generality overrides certain 'particulars', including the particularity of human individuals. God has to operate through the simplest means, not get bogged down in the complex detail of individual cases. For example, he would not match a proportionate amount of grace to the particular qualifications or needs of each separate sinner.[12] If suffering in hell simply means reprobates getting what they deserve (the elect deserve it too but have struck lucky), suffering on this earth is likewise explicable by the theory of a General Will. People suffer physically: there is the 'malformed' child, for example, whose head grows out of his chest. This was a conventional case (taken from the Roman naturalist Pliny), but it now has a new application. Monsters like

---

[9] Malebranche, *Recherche de la vérité*, éclaircissement 1, in *Oeuvres*, vol. 3, p. 17ff.
[10] Alberto Postigliola, 'Da Malebranche a Rousseau: le aporie della volontà generale e la rivincita del "ragionatore violento"', *Studi filosofici*, 1 (Naples: Istituto Universitario Orientale, 1978).
[11] Malebranche, *Traité de la nature et de la grâce*, éclaircissement 1, in *Oeuvres*, vol. 5, p. 147.
[12] Malebranche, *Traité de la nature*, in *Oeuvres*, vol. 5, pp. 49–50.

this had, for medieval writers, been an allegorical display of nature's sheer exotic range. Now, in being associated with suffering instead, monsters are explained in terms of a nature that becomes a system of general, determinate lawfulness. Instead of the *existence* of anomaly, it is now the causality, the *birth* of particular anomalous children, that has to be explained. For Malebranche, the answer is straightforward: the exceptionality of malformed children is there to demonstrate precisely the generality of God's laws, since he loves his own wisdom 'more than all his [particular] works'.[13]

This could then be applied to a concept of anomalous interior states. Suffering in the form of physical disability is ready to be wafted across the Cartesian mind–body divide and bracketed with modern cognitive disability. Malebranche makes just one mention, alongside bodily malformation, of newborns who are 'not of sound mind' (*fou* – the French word having a wider remit than 'mad').[14] Their condition is explained by the original sin in the mother, whose imagination during pregnancy was full of monstrous objects. This was frequently how medical writers explained physical disability in a newborn, and Malebranche exports the discussion to a parallel mental category. However, it is not yet developmental. Even in such a case, he implies, the *enfant fou* can undergo a 'regeneration'; this is not developmental, it is merely providential.

Thirdly, when dealing with the relationship between faith and reason, Malebranche elevates the role of the latter. By contrast with the primacy which Pascal had appeared to give to faith, Malebranche says that 'Faith will pass, but intelligence will exist eternally.'[15] Too much that is modern can be read into such a statement. Words like 'reason' and 'intelligence' (the latter being the active aspect of the former) still did not clearly demarcate between human and divine aspects. When human beings reasoned, they were in some sense sharing in a quality that belonged to God and the angels. For Malebranche, reason was still positioned vertically, high up on the chain of being and closer to God, where it gives expression to the law of Order.

He nevertheless hints at a temporal dimension in this context. Humankind's earthly task is, over time, to re-establish Order and logic as the supreme authorities on earth, as they had been before the Fall. Hence his remark, 'Let us set ourselves to know, love, and follow Order; let us work for our perfection' (even while recognizing that with regard to

---

[13] Malebranche, *Traité de la nature*, in *Oeuvres*, vol. 5, p. 47.
[14] Malebranche, *Recherche*, in *Oeuvres*, vol. 1, p. 232.
[15] Malebranche, *Traité de morale*, in *Oeuvres*, vol. 11, p. 34.

our – afterlife – happiness, we should 'leave it in the hands of God, upon whom it solely depends').¹⁶ So whom does Malebranche mean by 'us' here? Faith, seeded by baptism, is a possession of the Society of the Spirit (*la société spirituelle*), by which he means the small group of the imputedly elect. Even if a perfect, reasoned Order can only exist above, such persons can at least become divine participants in Order through their love of it: 'The virtue that renders those who possess it truly virtuous and just [that is to say, justified, hence elect] is precisely a ruling love of immutable Order.'¹⁷ With hindsight we can see this love of Order reflected in the idea of working for social progress over time, on earth; and since 'reason' is the ether in which such a prospect floats, we can also begin to see in outline a means to the sacralization of a secular, specifically human intelligence.

The fourth and final relevant aspect of Malebranche's work brings us back to children. In one section of *The Search after Truth* (1675) he had explained that changes in the womb occur as the result of 'communication between the brain of the mother and that of her child ... such that all the traces and motion occurring in the mother's brain are excited in the child's'.¹⁸ His 'clarification' of this, made in response to the book's critics, makes it evident that by 'children' he means the small number of *elect* children. The fact that he does not explicitly term them 'elect' is because he assumes everyone knows who he is talking about; after all, the parents – among them his readers – of such children are themselves the imputedly elect. This becomes clearer still in his otherwise conventional-looking remarks about their schooling.¹⁹

And it is not just election as such that is predetermined: so too is the timed process by which the elect are diverted away from the mass of humanity during their life on earth. Their interior status has somehow to be switched over from its default reprobate condition. Election allocates to interiority its specifically temporal character. What possible interest could there be in the detailed condition of the damned? Do they even have

---

[16] Malebranche, *Traité de morale*, in *Oeuvres*, vol. II, p. 24.
[17] Malebranche, *Traité de morale*, in *Oeuvres*, vol. II, p. 41.
[18] Malebranche, *Recherche de la vérité*, in *Oeuvres*, vol. I, p. 238. Malebranche does not refer specifically to election, but here as elsewhere the text is incomprehensible without it. The standard English translation usefully interpolates here the adjective 'righteous' (i.e. justified and elect) in front of 'child', in order to clarify what a contemporary reader would have taken for granted and what the modern reader will otherwise find confusing: see Nicolas Malebranche, *The Search after Truth*, translated by Thomas Lennon and Paul Olscamp (Columbus: Ohio State University Press, 1980), p. 583.
[19] Malebranche, *Traité de morale*, in *Oeuvres*, vol. II, p. 228ff.

interiors? They are simply a mass, a shapeless incorrigible blob. Therefore Malebranche is not interested in notionally damned children – themselves the children of reprobates – because they are already beyond redemption. Time, and the eventual escape from time through a structured and ordered linearity that arrives eventually at salvation and then infinity, pertains to the elect and no one else.

Malebranche's failure to spell out election may also be partly because he simply did not want to sound dogmatic, in this case about human category differences. Likewise, for example, he describes higher levels of the human in terms merely of their natural 'dispositions' – a concept with a less determinate feel. Nevertheless, the question remains as to who – elect or reprobate – is likely to have the required dispositions in the first place. Like Pascal, who was himself less of a dogmatist than hardcore Jansenists like Arnauld, Malebranche and the Oratorians were against doctrinal rigidity because it aroused the passions, specifically anger. But this softness around the edges of his discussion does not dilute the sharpness of the category divisions whose causes remained as deterministic as any in today's psychiatric or behavioural genetics.

Malebranche noted one causal problem in particular about children. If communication between the mother's brain and the child's is 'necessary to the formation of the foetus', the elect child therefore cannot be born 'innocent' since this would mean that the initial mother–child communication, occurring as it did through the inevitably concupiscent body, had somehow been 'suspended'. In short, the child could not have been conceived in the first place. (That was presumably why Jesus's conception had to be immaculate.) The inevitability of the sexual act on the part of their parents means that all children are born sinners. It is even 'just' for them to be born so. They are 'in a state of disorder', with the result that 'God, who loves order, hates the child' – at least in this state.[20] (Here he is echoing Cardinal Bérulle, founder of the Oratorian order, who had deemed childhood to be 'the most vile and abject state of human nature, after that of death'.)[21] The fleshly 'communication' between mother and child 'has to be excused (*justifié*) so as to remove from all reproach the conduct of Him whose every volition necessarily conforms to order'. Malebranche's whole explanation here is based on what must *subsequently occur* in the children's brains and concupiscent bodies to demonstrate that

---

[20] Malebranche, *Recherche*, éclaircissement 8, in *Oeuvres*, vol. 3, p. 77.
[21] Pierre de Bérulle, *Opuscules de piété*, 69, cited in Colin Heywood, *A History of Childhood* (Cambridge: Polity, 2001).

they have, despite God's 'hatred', been chosen. Election occurs 'in spite of themselves' – that is, in spite of that carnal relationship. It can only do so in such a way as to prove God's conformity with Order: and that way lies over time.

Since election is initially triggered by just one instantaneous miracle, 'the grace of baptism', further miracles according to Malebranche would be superfluous. Gradualist elements come to the fore instead. Subsequent to baptism are the familiar stages of regeneration, justification and sanctification. He is rather offhanded about them: 'it is not necessary to know precisely how they work', he says here. But rather than reverting to Aquinas's non-temporal view of them, he allocates them to the individual's *natural disposition*, in which sense they form a temporal continuity of stages. Baptism may be the 'single instant' or trigger, but the ensuing 'disposition' merges nature with grace and unfolds over time, constituting the ordered identity of the individual interior. This identity consists in the child's (gradual) abandonment of disorder for an order that corresponds with and is integrated with the overall order of the universe.

Despite his insistence on the pointlessness of the attempt to know the minds of other people (only God knows), the whole of Malebranche's *The Search after Truth* is steeped in it. The fact that baptism is the trigger for subsequent interior processes in the elect child which are natural and dispositional creates a near-Freudian sense of buried time: 'Only a single instant [baptism] is needed to perform His act of love that changes the heart. And since this act can be formed in the soul without traces of it occurring in the brain, you should not be surprised if children never have any recollection of it, for we have no memory of things whose traces are not preserved in the brain.' The individual child's truly developmental 'disposition' begins only thereafter. Regeneration, justification and sanctification are non-instantaneous phases rather than events, and are subsumed under the heading of the dispositional and gradual. They form an objective mechanism, an 'ordinary means' of ongoing salvific operations within the elect, and they lead to 'acts of charity', thereby fulfilling the aspiration to Order. Moreover they are attached to other dispositional phases – cognitive, affective and volitional – which constitute a temporally ordered growth that is goal-oriented and 'ever stronger and more perfect'. It is precisely when Malebranche applies his concept of Order to elect infants that its prevailing sense is temporal.

In the final analysis, however, Malebranche is not one of those who would draw from the notion of temporal order the modern conclusion that childhood is a separate phase within it. Precisely the opposite. In the remarkable conclusion to this passage he attacks the 'prejudices' of those who do so, and who deny the ability of infants to 'think' or to 'love' as adults do, or who assert that 'if they do have certain inclinations, these are in no way of the same nature as our own'. Infancy is just part of a continuous movement over time from disorder to order that transcends calendar time. Something similar applies with 'stupid' and 'feeble-minded' people. These may be defined by their failure to emerge from the disordered state over time;[22] but they are not strictly demarcated or pathological exceptions to the rule that man is a rational creature. Like the child who is *fou*, they are defined merely by '*ignorance* of order',[23] and this broadly cognitive phenomenon is visible among all human beings to some extent, as a failure of the 'animal spirits' and the will. Some men may be exceptionally stupid 'like children and women', but disobedience to God is the default condition of the whole species regardless of age and gender. Despite the linearity of human time, he warns us against seeing the childhood condition as different in kind from adulthood.

Gottfried Wilhelm Leibniz (1646–1714): Election and Pre-established Harmony

Leibniz focused like Malebranche on God's Justice, and on the need to explain it rationally by its connection to Order. Where is Justice when his creatures suffer? Leibniz too tried to square suffering with the idea of an all-loving and all-powerful God. In his most discussed work, the *Theodicy* of 1710, he wanted among other things to demonstrate that there must be a systematic order in the universe. This had to have a rational explanation, capable of meeting the objections put forward by sticklers for Revelation alone. Leibniz's answer lay partly in giving it a temporal character. The only alternative to the principle that the world operates through continual miracles whose source lies beyond time is that it unfolds naturally, and in a structured way, over linear time. Consequently rational means developmental, and developmental means rational.

Some such suggestion lay at the core of Leibniz's famous Panglossian principle that where God exists, all must be for the best in the best of all possible worlds. This was famously mocked by Voltaire in *Candide*, whose satirical aim is often seen as the gateway to a modern rational atheism. However, it misrepresents Leibniz. Voltaire's assault on the fluffiness of Leibniz's optimism was based on the fact that one surely cannot justify

---

[22] Malebranche, *Recherche*, in *Oeuvres*, vol. 2, p. 107.
[23] Malebranche, *Recherche*, éclaircissement 15, in *Oeuvres*, vol. 3, p. 203ff. My italics.

natural disasters. The chief example was the Lisbon earthquake. If a God exists who by definition is all-powerful and all-loving, he would not allow such tragedies to happen. But earthquakes lead to earthly suffering and it was not earthly suffering that preoccupied Leibniz; it was the afterlife. Not flood, fire, famine or pestilence but the suffering of the damned in hell, and how few were saved. Whereas earlier pictures of hellfire presented it as physical torment, Leibniz was among those who now saw its suffering as interior, a disembodied mental state. But this reinterpretation scarcely mitigates the anxiety he voices about it. Election and reprobation were the hobby horse of the households and cultures in which he, as well as Pascal, Malebranche and Locke, had all grown up. Like Malebranche, he sometimes hedges his bets, saying that the predestined elect might contribute to their salvation by their 'disposition' (penitence was advisable, for example).[24] But its effect remained secondary. Overall, Leibniz was a predestinarian.[25] He did not even claim to be confused about it like Locke. There must be eternal suffering for some, or how could others like himself be saved?

Voltairean scepticism obscured the picture by focusing on external events. If any 'event' needed justifying, thought Leibniz, it was what happened before the beginning of time when God decided to abandon most of his creatures to hell. It is on damnation, not earthquakes, that God's justice and the need for evil to exist stands or falls. For Leibniz, it stands. God remains just, and that is because the good is infinite whereas evil is merely finite. Evil has no positive or 'efficient' cause of its own; it is mere absence or privation. The good of salvation for a few therefore trumps the evil of damnation for the many; for God to give someone grace is a just act, but to damn them is not an unjust one. In the *Theodicy* Leibniz sets out a textbook summary of the range of denominational views on predestination, which the book was partly designed to reconcile. This has led some to maintain that he stood outside the theory subjecting the whole of it to critical analysis. But Leibniz's critique is chiefly of *double* predestination, the Manichean-style theory that election and damnation are symmetrically opposite and therefore equally weighted.

Before the *Theodicy* Leibniz had also written a *Dissertation on Predestination and Grace* (c.1701).[26] Between them, these were the chief

---

[24] See Gregory Brown, 'Leibniz's moral philosophy', in (ed.) Nicholas Jolley, *The Cambridge Companion to Leibniz* (Cambridge: Cambridge University Press, 1995).
[25] For extended discussions of Leibniz on predestination, see (eds.) Larry Jorgensen and Samuel Newlands, *New Essays on Leibniz's Theodicy* (Oxford: Oxford University Press, 2014); Gaston Grua, *Jurisprudence universelle et théodicée selon Leibniz* (Paris: PUF, 1953).
[26] Gottfried Wilhelm Leibniz, *Dissertation on Predestination and Grace*, translated by Michael Murray (New Haven: Yale University Press, 2011).

works of his that were widely read during his lifetime, and damnation was the central concern of both. This has consequences for those whom he influenced in the early period of the Enlightenment. The *Dissertation* arose from his official role as the Holy Roman Emperor's chief international diplomat in the 1690s, when he was trying to establish unity between the Catholic and Protestant churches across Europe. Following the failure of this mission, he was reduced to the less promising one of establishing unity just among Protestants. The *Dissertation* was his response to an overview of predestination set out by the English Protestant bishop, Gilbert Burnet, a confidant of William III.[27] In short, the *Dissertation* was a political text. But this does not mean Leibniz believed any the less in predestination itself. And although he occasionally refers the contemporary theological dispute upstairs to its more lofty philosophical context – that is, to the question of freedom versus necessity, which is, he says, 'older and deeper' – neither text is merely a theological hook on which to hang this.[28] We have to credit Leibniz with believing what he says.

First, says Leibniz, 'the predetermination I admit is such as always to predispose, but never to necessitate'.[29] However, this statement turns out to be ambiguous. He writes about a 'concurrence' between the individual's prior, predestined status and their dispositions or actual choice of actions.[30] The Jesuits had argued something similar with their theory of 'congruence' (see Chapter 2), and were met with the objection: if God already has foreknowledge of men's actions, is this not tantamount to determining them? The Jesuits' answer was that what happens necessarily is not the same as what happens contingently. Leibniz's is fairly similar.[31] He even hints at an element of proportionality: if individuals are subject to 'different circumstances' and some are therefore more able than others or more inclined to the good, this is all 'in conformity with God's plan' and their agency does not usurp divine authority.[32] Though Leibniz was obliged to distance himself from the Jesuits, his version of 'concurrence' resembles

---

[27] Gilbert Burnet, *Exposition of the Thirty-Nine Articles of the Church of England* (London: Richard Chiswell, 1699).
[28] See Hélène Bouchilloux, 'Le jansénisme dans les *Essais de théodicée* de Leibniz', in (ed.) Raymond Baustert, *Le jansénisme et l'Europe* (Tübingen: Narr Verlag, 2010), p. 226.
[29] Leibniz, *Theodicy: Essays on the Goodness of God, the Freedom of Man and the Origin of Evil*, translated by E. M. Huggard (London: Routledge, 1951), Preface.
[30] I have made a literal translation here (most translators render it as 'concomitance' or 'correspondence') because it shows the possible link back to Pascal (see Chapter 5), and even back to the medieval theory of a twofold natural causation that is 'concurrently' divine and human.
[31] Leibniz, *Theodicy*, p. 145ff.
[32] Leibniz, *Theodicy*, p. 123. On this, see Donald Rutherford, 'Justice and circumstances: theodicy as religion', in Jorgensen, *New Essays*.

theirs at least in the broad sense that he was seeking a middle way between freedom and necessity.

Secondly, as a single predestinarian, Leibniz differentiated between the divine act which leads to election and that which leads to damnation. We are all born reprobate through original sin, so if some of us are rescued it must be regardless of our personal merits or demerits, abilities or disabilities; rescue can only be an *act of grace*. But if most of us remain reprobate and not rescued, this by contrast is an *act of justice*.[33]

Both the above arguments were explicit: they answered, first, whether there could be any connection between human agency and one's afterlife destination, and secondly, whether God's damnation of the reprobate is the same kind of act as that which saves the elect. And in both respects Leibniz took the milder position: agency has some role albeit a secondary one; and reprobation is not the direct antithesis of election.

However, there is a third, unwitting distinction cutting across the first two that can easily be overlooked: namely, the urge which a writer feels to foreground predestination (by whatever version) in relation to other issues. This third distinction is key to our whole discussion in this book. The Reformation had laid down doctrine on the topic, but for neither Luther nor Calvin was predestination the central issue. It was later Reformers who foregrounded it; to put it another way, their anxiety levels were high. On the Counter-Reformation side Ignatius Loyola, the primary inspiration behind the Jesuit order, had already issued a warning against letting anxiety take over; it was a 'rule' that 'although it is very true that no one can be saved unless he is predestined and has faith and grace, we must be very careful in our manner of speaking and treating of these subjects', for fear of debate getting out of hand.[34] In this third respect Leibniz is not at all the mild sort: he was the offspring of a generation that could not stop harping on it. Although not a double predestinarian, then, he is certainly what must be called in this sense a *strong* predestinarian. He attacks 'vague indifference' on the topic.[35]

There is also optimism, however. He speculates about the prospect of a universal jurisprudence, and of a confluence between grace and subjective ability.[36] He hinges almost everything on 'the education of the human race' (the title of one of his essays). However, by 'education' he clearly means something that currently takes place only in the City of God, where the

---

[33] Leibniz, *Dissertation*, p. 147.   [34] Ignatius Loyola, *Spiritual Exercises*, rule 14.
[35] Leibniz, *Theodicy*, p. 324.
[36] See Patrick Riley, *Leibniz' Universal Jurisprudence: Justice as the Charity of the Wise* (Cambridge MA: Harvard University Press, 1996), p. 89ff.

elect alone belong. True, heaven is not static. It has an element of process, with values and norms continuing on from those on earth. Crime and punishment take place there, since there is 'a jurisprudence for the City of God', just as there is penance in hell.[37] He sees this, moreover, in historiographical terms: 'natural religion' is something that arises in due historical course, and he envisages it attaining public authority. In other words, the relationship between the present earthly life and the City of God is a concrete historical and developmental connection, not a merely analogical one.

This optimism highlights and complements the anxiety. The former cannot exist without the latter. Leibniz's foresight is one thing, his feelings another. The grim fate of reprobates in hell saturates the *Theodicy*. The 'strong' tendency in Leibniz's predestinarianism contrasts with Locke and Malebranche. Locke is weak in the sense that he prevaricates about it; any anxiety is displaced to non-developing 'changeling' infants, for whom he seems to recommend infanticide. The weakness of Malebranche's tone, born of the Oratorian desire for calm, comes from his being so certain about it that he takes it for granted, seeing no need even to reference it. It was vulnerable for a different reason: that calmness leads to neglect. And neglect was in fact what happened after a while. Rather than being defeated in battle, God's determinism about the human interior would go underground, only to resurface as biological determinism.

Leibniz's tone meanwhile, despite his justifiable reputation as a reconciler, echoes the defensiveness that had provoked incessant argument throughout the previous century. In order to understand the rise of a modern psychology as well as of modern moral and political philosophy, we must get inside the one strong presupposition which Leibniz would have felt unable to doubt: 'the infallibility of divine election'.[38] The question 'How do I know I am saved?' directly inspired the late seventeenth-century turn to epistemology, both rationalist (Leibniz) and empiricist (Locke). The problem of certainty in modern psychological knowledge was in part stimulated by the need for certainty over one's personal election. Leibniz seems to set great store by this convention, and refuted the Jansenist belief that one can lapse from saving grace after it has been bestowed. 'One is never justified in believing oneself reprobate,' he says, or at least – the sting in the tail – 'not as long as one is alive.'[39]

---

[37] On this, see Grua, *Jurisprudence universelle*, p. 375ff.   [38] Leibniz, *Theodicy*, p. 101.
[39] Leibniz, *Dissertation*, p. 149.

Leibniz's discussion of freedom and necessity, so important to the history of political ideas, stems from this same need for ontological certainty. The *Theodicy* only pursues that wider philosophical question in so far as it will advance his version of the predestination theory that forms part of it. His need to maintain that God is just would be a key source, alongside Malebranche, for eighteenth-century views on social justice. And if God is just, it is above all damnation and the eternity of hellfire that must be justified. That was the whole aim of the book, which as his preface states came into being in order 'to remove these difficulties'. He explicitly says that the predestination of events (earthquakes, for example) is secondary to that of souls:

> [God] knows all that which will come to pass, if, having created man, he places him in such and such circumstances ... Thus the world will be brought into a strange confusion, by this means death and diseases being introduced, with a thousand other misfortunes and miseries that afflict the good and the bad alike ... so that it will scarce appear that a providence governs affairs. But it is *much worse* when one considers the life to come, since but a small number of men will be saved and all the rest will perish eternally.[40]

Historians commenting on these texts seem to prefer earthquakes to hellfire as their evidence base, possibly because we know today that earthquakes actually happen whereas hellfire probably doesn't. But for the conceptual historian there is always tension between a presupposition that is absolute but also obsolete and a modern one that has grown out of the first even if it now has its own new content. And in order to grasp how this works, one must be prepared to acknowledge that the modern theory of development itself is just that, a presupposition, like election.

The attempt to explain away Leibniz's core predestinarian beliefs began with the later Enlightenment. The German theologian Johann Augustus Eberhard (1739–1809), arguing now against the eternity of hell, claimed that for Leibniz it had been a mere metaphor. By this period, optimism about the happiness of the majority via infinite rational progress and pessimism about their damnation were seen simply as opposites. In Leibniz's time the relationship between them had been not oppositional but mutually supportive. Any optimism about the members of the Society of Minds or General Republic of Minds (Leibniz),[41] as of the Christian Republic (Pascal) and the Society of the Spirit (Malebranche), had been

---

[40] Leibniz, *Theodicy*, p. 125. My italics.
[41] Leibniz, Letter to Arnauld, 9 October 1687, cited in Grua *Jurisprudence*, p. 380.

dependent for its very existence upon the norm of mass damnation for non-members.

The very idea of the elect as a 'society' that did not distinguish between its living or dead members filled in the cleft, previously marked by death, in the linear trajectory; thus it helped to align the heavenly goal of perfection and happiness with an earthly one. This is clearly relevant to the rise of the developmental idea. Leibniz's concept of justice created a straight line from time on earth to time as it is in heaven. 'Divine justice and human justice', he says, 'have common rules which can be reduced to a system', a unitary one.[42] In this continuity from life to afterlife, time is no longer (as it had been for Augustine) something to be overcome. It continues in linear fashion after death, and involves values and norms that are continuous with and equivalent to those on earth, since souls can still do wrong even when they are in heaven or hell. This resonates with the temporal and concrete historical continuity which Leibniz the professional diplomat had in mind when he envisaged the renewed unity between Protestants and Catholics as a 'republic' or 'commonwealth of Christian Nations' on earth that would lead to the City of God itself.[43]

When he writes about 'the human race' as being the republic's inhabitants, however, Leibniz can still see little more than his own social class. The 'spiritual disposition' of justice belongs only to a minority of people, because only a minority has the ability to understand 'the harmony of the physical world upon which a true love of God, and hence a universal love of man, supervenes'.[44] Most people are incapable of true justice – and precisely because of their lack of cognitive ability. The intellectual bar is set so high that Leibniz's view of education as central to the ethical life means that justice is the moral inclination of a small elite, albeit one that could expand in number (and later did). There is an aspiration for the elect to become the majority, and for the religion of the wise to become the natural, rational religion of the many. But it remains very vague.

Consequences of Jansenism: Pierre Nicole (1625–1695)

If writers of a philosophical bent like Malebranche and Leibniz were steeped in the theory of election, it goes without saying that their more

---

[42] Leibniz, *Opinions on the Principles of Pufendorf* (1706), cited in Riley, *Leibniz' Universal Jurisprudence*, p. 16.
[43] Leibniz, *Codex Juris Gentium* (1693), cited in Riley in *Leibniz' Universal Jurisprudence*, p. 165; see also p. 184.
[44] Brown, 'Leibniz's moral philosophy'.

strictly theological contemporaries were. Yet there is no particular distinction to be drawn between the two types of writer. The theory was deep-rooted in both cases. In theology too, which one might assume to be the more conservative discipline, the belief itself started to change into something else. First, there was a blurring of the boundaries between 'special' or 'saving' grace on the one hand and the universal or general graces, among which earthly abilities also belonged, on the other. Secondly, there was an expansion of the numbers of the elect. And thirdly, there was a clearer parallel between nascent concepts of social progress and the progress of the individual. We can see all three in the works of the widely known Jansenist theologian Pierre Nicole.

Nicole's part in these changes is particularly interesting in that he was old enough to have belonged to the Jansenist founding generation. As the changes just described are detectable mostly in his later work, it is the period (late-century) as much as the personality that must be significant, and here some background is required. The Jansenists' original raison d'être, emphasizing purity, had been to challenge the church hierarchy's worldliness and political manoeuvring. Louis XIV's denunciation of them as heretics coincided with the political defeat of French Calvinism and the Fronde rebellions. Under the ensuing absolutist peace Jansenists were nevertheless still persecuted or exiled. Typically under these conditions, factional disputes broke out within the movement itself, as the coterie of a few marginalized noble families grew into a broader, politically engaged movement under pressure from the state.

The political outlook of the first Jansenists had been that of a professional class within the minor nobility, 'feeling itself slighted and undervalued, but having a concern for the preservation of a social order which . . . it believed to be divinely decreed'.[45] Their focus on 'saving' grace and election, and with it the assumption, however precarious, of their own elect status, had the flavour of caste resentment against their just-a-bit-betters, which made the group at least incipiently political. By the end of the century interpenetrating currents of Jansenist and Oratorian thought would stand in overt opposition to church and state. The Pope, under pressure from the Jesuits, issued a papal bull in 1713 proclaiming Jansenism to be heresy. The definition of such an '-ism' consequently became a receptacle for almost anything not Jesuit- or state-approved. It turned into a political movement because its victimhood was a focal point for the

---

[45] E. D. James, *Pierre Nicole, Jansenist and Humanist: A Study of His Thought* (The Hague: Martinus Nijhoff, 1972), p. 138.

many others opposing the decrepit Louis. This gave it an increasingly diffuse character, which was later channelled into a nascent public opinion and notions of citizenship. The transitions taken by election into normality began in this context, at a level that impacted on the everyday culture.

Roots of this 'political' Jansenism can be detected in Nicole's work. Nicole had co-authored with Arnauld and with Pascal's help the Port Royal *Logic*, helped to publish Pascal's *Lettres provinciales* and the *Pensées*, taught at the Jansenists' schools and then in his own *Moral Essays* of 1671–8 gave practical advice on how Christians should behave in public life. The *Essays*, widely read across Europe, drew from Pascal's 'three orders' certain political implications about order in general, and gave it a more naturalistic cast. Although he did not create a fully fledged temporal model, he did give it goal-oriented and utilitarian tendencies. For Nicole the 'lunatic' selfishness of the individual that had alarmed Pascal actually benefits the collective because it is precisely the grounds upon which absolute obedience is rendered necessary.[46] Obedience, that is, both to God and to the state (Nicole did not question the idea that the monarch who had exiled him was head of the body politic as Christ was of the church). At Nicole's hands, Pascal's three orders – flesh, minds and charity (love of God) – become also social descriptors. Where Pascal's emphasis had been ultimately on their mutual exclusivity, Nicole reinforces the sense of them as social vocations, in which individuals can progress from one to the next over the lifespan. In this way moral improvement involves individual and society in tandem.

Out of all the Jansenists Nicole did most to revive Irenaeus's early Christian principle of recapitulation, in which the elect aspire to become a 'second Adam', both as individuals and as representatives of the species. Indeed, for his pen name Nicole chose Paul Irenaeus. Referencing the early Church Fathers had been a regular practice in theological discussion, but the name of Irenaeus rarely features until the Jansenists get hold of him. Why was Irenaeus's seminal concept of a human timeline uppermost in their minds, or at least in Nicole's? One possible reason was the problem of reprobation. Nicole and his fellow first-generation Jansenists started taking issue with each other precisely over this.[47] He himself evolved towards a less harsh vision of the human destiny than Pascal or Arnauld. The latter two had kept to a straightforwardly Augustinian account of grace: a general

---

[46] Pierre Nicole, 'Des moyens de conserver la paix avec les hommes', in (ed.) Laurent Thirouin, *Essais de morale* (Paris: PUF, 1999), p. 171.
[47] See James, *Pierre Nicole*, p. 7ff.

or habitual grace is common to all, alongside but completely distinct from the 'special', saving grace available only to the few elect. Nicole, however, was prepared to grant that even special grace was in some sense available to all: even if God foreknew that most people were not actually going to put it to use, he still actually supplied it to them.

Colleagues complained that this was going too far. Not only did it make concessions to the Jesuits' idea of a 'congruism' between what was foreknown and what was predetermined, it might even lead to assimilation between the two forms of grace, general and special. Arnauld opposed Nicole chiefly on the grounds that this might lead to contamination of the special by the general and therefore of the whole community of the elect. The two men thus differed above all in the strength of their concern about the strictness of the conceptual boundary that had to be drawn around reprobates. Again, the issue is as much the relative strength with which the doctrine is held, as its actual content. As with Malebranche, the fact that Nicole is in this sense a *weak* predestinarian does not mean he believes any the less in election; he was simply trying to calm the quarrels between Jansenists and others. Although the interminable cross hairs in these quarrels always appear to concern a specific point of doctrine, they always boil down to something along the lines of: 'You can't say that, because if you did, you would be saying there is no fundamental distinction between different categories of the human.' Nicole was not saying this. He took election and reprobation for granted. For Pascal and Arnauld, to generalize 'special' grace would be to override the elect/reprobate distinction and thereby open the possibility of redemption for all, when the very basis of Christian redemption is the need for it, the fact that it is *im*possible for all.

Nicole agrees that such a distinction is necessary. However, his version differs from theirs precisely in those respects that emphasize interior movement and change. First, like Malebranche, he blurs the distinction between 'special grace' in the elect and their 'natural dispositions'. The latter, as well as the former, can help the already elect Christian to ward off the threat of pollution from the reprobate mass and confirm his sanctification.[48] Secondly, he proposes certain 'graces of Providence', a kind of *gradual* Providence or 'concatenation' that allows for 'continuous ascent' from the universal attribution of habitual grace to the numerically restricted 'special' one of being saved.[49] And thirdly, like Leibniz, he hints

---

[48] Nicole, 'De la soumission à la volonté de Dieu', in *Essais*, p. 106. On this, see James, *Pierre Nicole*, p. 104.
[49] Nicole, *Instructions théologiques et morales sur le symbole* (Charleston SC: Nabu Reprints, 2011), vol. 2, p. 394ff.

that God might excuse original sin in the elect *proportionately*, by bestowing only that amount of special grace which is necessary to overcome it in any one individual. This novel element of proportionality illustrates how obscure theological arguments can be significant to the rise of modern ways of thinking about the mind: today's overriding principle of meritocracy becomes a visible prospect, standing as it does on deep historical foundations.

As an example of what Nicole means by a general or habitual grace he gives the power of 'reason'. There are instances, he says, where reason comprises *both* a divine illumination of the soul *and* a dispositional, specifically human understanding of nature and natural law. Such a possibility illustrates the osmosis by which presuppostions about election might slip into those about cognitive ability. But we must beware of too hindsighted a reading. On the one hand, it is true that Nicole 'forms a bridge between Jansenist rigour and the rationalism of the *philosophes*' of the Enlightenment.[50] On the other hand, when he connects man's 'true interests' to 'right reason', the former does not mean Enlightenment self-interest and the latter does not mean cognitive and moral ability; rather, he means 'the salvation of [one's] soul' and 'the reason which guides us on the path to that salvation', respectively. An even greater caution against thrusting Nicole ahead of his time is that for him the source of potential corruption is still, as for Pascal, the human will, to which the role of human reason in salvation is secondary. Nicole does, however, see reason and human knowledge (*la science*) as a progressive force, and psychology as a component of natural law: 'One sees [since the Creation] a perpetual progress of the world similar to that of a man emerging from infancy and passing through subsequent ages.'[51]

Consequences of Jansenism: Jacques-Joseph Duguet (1649–1733)

Although the Papacy named Pasquier Quesnel, the Jansenist leader after Arnauld's death, in its 1713 denunciation of Jansenism, its real target was Jacques-Joseph Duguet. His output, though little known, is important to the emergence of a secular normality out of election because it begins to reconfigure the religious account of human interiority in a manner appropriate to the reconfiguration of contemporary political alignments. In other words, this conceptual shift had cultural roots. An open-minded

---

[50] See James, *Pierre Nicole*, pp. 99–107.
[51] 'Preuves naturelles de l'existence de Dieu', cited in James, p. 60.

parish priest would not have had Malebranche or Leibniz in his study, but might have had Duguet. He held an important position within the new Jansenism, tempering its Jesuit-baiting urges with a mentality of reasoned opposition. Even more than Nicole, he emphasized the importance of the will as distinct from reason.[52] But like Pascal, he found reason already occupying the social and intellectual space of that period and impossible to budge.

Duguet's writings went further than Jansenism's first advocates could have imagined. In his later life the movement was organized enough to bring out what was probably France's first regular journal of reasoned opposition to absolutism, *Les nouvelles écclesiastiques*; this was launched in the wake of the Pope's denunciation of Jansenism as heresy and was influential up until the Revolution. Duguet had mentored its founders, though he was soon forced to distance himself from some of their manic enthusiasms (by now there were even 'Jansenists' who testified to incessant miracles or had convulsions, which hardly squared with the Pascalian aspiration to Order in the interior life).

Dating Duguet's works is difficult, but the relevant ones seem as if they belong to the first two decades of the new century. At some point in his career he abandoned his Jansenist predecessors' ahistorical approaches to biblical exegesis and saw the past, including biblical prophecies such as the conversion of the Jews at the millennium, as 'the model of the future': in short, he advanced a philosophy of history.[53] In his *Explication du livre de la sagesse*, overtly a commentary on the wisdom of the biblical Solomon, one prominent strand (as with Pascal, Malebranche and Leibniz) is his attention to Justice and its relationship to Order. Justice is that which is 'stable and immortal' by contrast with the hurried movement of animal-like creatures unable to look beyond their present needs and thus insanely intent on reaching their own doom.[54] Intertwined with Justice is 'Intelligence'. Justice is about the ultimate goal of human lives, but Intelligence is the most important principle God can lend to our everyday actions. The status of the elect on earth comprises both at once; justification (removal of guilt) consists in Intelligence, and vice versa.

Duguet says that when the elect die early, they are well off – not because they have avoided earthly suffering, but because their chances of lapsing, and thus their anxiety, are less. God has 'relieved them of the fear that they

---

[52] Jacques-Joseph Duguet, *Lettre sur la grâce générale*, (Utrecht: n.p., 1737).
[53] Catherine Maire, *De la cause de Dieu à la cause de la nation: le Jansénisme au XVIII siècle* (Paris: Gallimard, 1998), p. 173.
[54] Duguet, *Explication du livre de la sagesse* (Paris: François Babuty, 1756), p. 19.

might have been corrupted by malice, and that deceitful appearances have seduced their souls; for … restless concupiscence overthrows the mind itself.' The evil they avoid is thus not the foolish, concupiscent act as such but the lack of certainty about their elect status. However, in a letter from the 1690s criticizing Nicole, Duguet takes the opposite tack, with a more optimistic emphasis that would increasingly characterize the eighteenth century. Optimism as much as anxiety is appropriate, because 'God could, in causing his elect to live a long time, endow them with a strength proportionate to the duration of this life's temptations.'[55] In other words, interior status is not only staged but cumulative. Dying young with less opportunity for succumbing to temptation no longer has to be a joyful prospect for the elect.

Duration, on this earth, is therefore now important enough to be the common denominator uniting (a) the growth of certainty in the elect and (b) certainty as a cognitive phenomenon (rather than an intermittent or providential gift from the Almighty). And so, although he does not actually discount the medieval assumption of an overlap between human and divine reason, he sets it aside. Instead, he expressly argues, first, that a specifically human reason exists, and second, that if this is the case then all the quite separate 'cognitive'-type terms bandied about by scholastic philosophers – *la sagesse* (wisdom, the lofty principle), *la prudence* (practical reason) and *l'intelligence* itself (the active process of thinking) – must in fact all be the same thing. This kind of species-specific synthesis would clearly be adaptable to modern theories of cognitive ability. But even more importantly, given the relationship between reason and election, such a theory can only be arrived at by already having a developmentally linear notion of cognitive *growth* over time.

Duguet's work hovers tentatively around the distinction between the habitual grace granted to all and the saving grace of the elect in-group. The possibility of development among the elect, and of education as the means to preserve their purity, begins to look rather Rousseauian. 'Desire' for wisdom, and the 'love' which consists in the observation of its laws, reinforces the vulnerable order of charity and can 'lead to the eternal kingdom'.[56] Moreover he strikes out on a radical path with a further plea, for *beaucoup de Sages*: that is, an expansion of the elect on the grounds of their wisdom.

However, Duguet's urge to expand the numbers of the elect does not mean that he has given up on reprobation. Two-thirds of the way through

---

[55] Duguet, *Explication*, p. 87. [56] Duguet, *Explication*, p. 144ff.

his exegesis on Solomon, he suddenly remembers it, then promptly drops it: 'The whole intent of [Solomon's Book of Wisdom] is to lead us to the knowledge of the origin of Justice and salvation ... and to show us the relationship of all [biblical] events to the Predestination of some and the Reprobation of others.' On the one hand, Duguet says that reprobation is Solomon's main concern; on the other, he (Duguet) mentions it only once. Yet the existence of reprobates is no less essential to him. In ducking the question of whether God himself can be 'just' in condemning them to the flames, all he does is identify himself as a single predestinarian: only election is actually predested, not reprobation. However, his call for the wise to be many at least might lead to the possibility that only a minority end up in hell.

The fact that Duguet announces reprobation to be key while hardly mentioning it indicates once again, not that it is in retreat, but that as the negative category it is taken for granted and residual. The concepts not only of Justice but also of Intelligence are schematically dependent on the continued existence of a fundamental intra-human division. On the one hand, he writes about 'the need all men have to be saved, to be made participants in the Wisdom of the Father, or of that essential and primal Justice which lives in his breast, and which must one day become flesh and live among men'; since it is a 'need', 'all' really does start to sound as if it means all, rather than (as we saw with Augustine and Pascal) a few men from all walks of life. On the other hand, the world would not make sense if there were no exceptions to the rule. Optimism about oneself and one's destiny, and one's certain knowledge of it, may increase; but anxiety about the out-group, its absences and its static character, still forms the impassable bedrock of any concept of the mind and of interiority generally. If intelligence here starts to resemble a specifically human but also sanctified cognitive ability (that is to say, the modern model), Duguet remains ambiguous. Wisdom has also its miraculous, instantaneous, non-developmental forms. It can make the dumb speak and can cause the feeblest infant to become instantly eloquent. When it arrives, 'no one can resist' – an acknowledgement of Providence – even though elsewhere his eye is on general laws in a sense that prefigures the Enlightenment and Montesquieu in particular.

A similar ambiguity arises when Duguet asks what is the more important goal: perfection and happiness in this life, or in the next. While his conventional answer is the next life, by juxtaposing them he creates a discursive context in which earthly perfection may, at least hypothetically, have parity. Although the Eucharist can only act on the mind through the corrupt body, even in the present unwholesome earthly environment it can still '*gradually* reform and change' the person: 'It is partly this that Irenaeus understands by the ideas of *perfection* and *growth*' in this life. Having got the saint's endorsement, Duguet then scuttles back to first base: 'But principally Irenaeus has resurrection and immortality in mind ... The growth and perfection he is talking about happens in the future life [in heaven] rather than this one.'[57] It is nevertheless significant that Duguet sees the need to clarify himself. He anticipates a readership already capable of misinterpreting him.

Duguet writes with similar ambiguity about original sin. There was always one naturalistic possibility buried away in the predestinarian insistence on God's authorship of election and reprobation: namely, that the children of the elect are themselves elect. This furtively hereditarian principle was held in check among Jansenists by the possibility that they or their children might lapse or degenerate. Duguet asserts the hereditary principle much more strongly: 'Often one wonders why some children are so incorrigible, so inclined to evil; it is the frightening incontinence of their mother and father that has drawn this perversity upon them; by contrast, benediction quite commonly remains for a long time over the children of saints.'[58] This 'benediction', in which grace and nature seem to merge, acts as a prophylactic against lapse into original sin. Duguet was thus Rousseau's predecessor in dealing with the intellectual problems around original sin not so much by abandoning it as by rerouting it.[59]

In a vein simultaneously probed by Malebranche and Leibniz, Duguet also writes about God having established 'natural laws' in the relationship between soul and body, 'between the actions of the one and the organs of the other',[60] a relationship that is not only 'mutual' but also 'necessary'. Here, 'nature' and 'necessity' are compatible if not yet coterminous in a modern sense.[61] If we align this thought of an internally located natural causality with what he terms the 'gradual' character of the Eucharist's salvific effect, we can see the sacralization of the developmental idea. Both the tone and the substance of this kind of thinking would enter the new arena of public debate and oppositional thought, and contribute also to the Enlightenment idea of progress.

---

[57] Duguet, *Dissertations théologiques et dogmatiques* (Paris: Jacques Estienne, 1727), p. 35. Italics in original.
[58] Duguet, *Dissertations*, p. 84.
[59] On this see J. Alberg, *A Reinterpretation of Rousseau: A Religious System* (New York: Palgrave, 2007).
[60] Duguet, *Dissertations*, p. 268.   [61] Duguet, *Dissertations*, p. 259.

Election and Enlightenment: Montesquieu (1689–1755)

Today the sharp distinction between old-time religion and Enlightenment reason, with Montesquieu and Voltaire leading the charge, is mere cliché but still needs closer scrutiny. These men's formative years coincided with the reconfiguration of the most contested of the previous century's religious issues, described in this chapter. The sacralization of a specifically human reason by virtue of its staged temporal character took place in an Enlightenment which, though retrospectively seen as secular, coincided with a still largely undiminished religious culture.

By 'reconfiguration' I mean a medium-term transitional phase within the longer-term principle, generated by monotheism, of classifying absence/presence in terms of a presupposed human interior growth. Enlightenment figureheads like Montesquieu are not rational twenty-first-century minds that have courteously travelled back in time in order to create for us the conceptual framework for appropriately modern social and human sciences. The Montesquieu of that period did not *reject* election and reprobation, as if ideas about human interiority were or are freely chosen intellectual commodities on offer in a transhistorical marketplace. He absorbed their existing profile within his response to changing political and cultural conditions, at the point where a public sphere for intellectual debate was rapidly coming into being.

Montesquieu kept Jansenists and Jesuits alike at a distance, and famously bemoaned the ill effects of the predestinarian idea – or at least of its tendency to become 'dogma'. Believing you could not alter your fate induced mental 'laziness' and thus made you vulnerable to political despotism. But being dogmatic and intolerant about the idea was one thing, belief in its actual content was quite another. Although Montesquieu thought being intolerant about one's religion missed the point of it, this did not mean that the patron saint of *laïcité* did not believe in elements of predestination theory himself, or that he saw it merely as a social phenomenon.[62]

True, in his discussion of determinism he raises the possibility that human agency can have an effect irrespective of God's foreknowledge.[63] It supported his observations of the everyday world, which told him that people do seem to act according to their own inclinations. Such a thought would also have reinforced his political anti-absolutism; and if only because of this, his general reputation seems as if it ought to have been

---

[62] Montesquieu, *De l'esprit des lois*, 2.5; 25.9–10.   [63] Montesquieu, *Lettres Persanes*, no. 69.

anti-predestinarian too. After all, he was genuinely a pioneer of modern freedoms, theological as much as political. However, this ex-pupil of the Oratorians also seems to have held on to a belief in salvation as predestinate, and that this was the sign or even guarantee of divine Order. It was not necessarily incompatible with his more characteristically Enlightenment principles – for example, that God does not intervene in the course of nature, which has its own causal mechanisms. Both are instances of a more general determinism; either way, it showed that there was always a way of relating effects to causes.

In Montesquieu, history's long-term fundamental division within humanity remains in play. The 'dogma' he attacks is, in fact, double predestination. Single predestination remains possible. For example, he writes, in a private correspondence not subject to ecclesiastical scrutiny and therefore to be taken at face value, 'If it happens sometimes that God predestines (which happens only rarely, because God rarely deprives us of our freedom), he can only predestine us to salvation. Those who are predestined are saved. But it does not follow that all those who are not predestined are damned.'[64] This is exactly the language of single predestination we saw in Leibniz and others. Vagueness or silence about the causes of damnation, born of the need to defend God against the charge of cruelty, seems finally to permit a 'Pelagian' belief that the individual can scramble clear of universal reprobation by personal effort. But this only applies to a particular group of people. Here again not everyone, nor even most, have the ability to do so.

This, in conclusion, is further evidence of the broad historical shift I have described. There is movement towards a concept of law-governed natural causation of human interiority, within which a certain exclusiveness is preserved, the condition of being selected out of the mass. The letter just referred to comes under Montesquieu's heading of 'Doubts'. The doubt is not so much about the existence of election itself, however, as about where election stands in the wider order of things. He does not doubt that a fundamental intra-human division exists: obviously there must be one, whatever it is. Rather, there is a theoretical displacement. The saved are now merely a subset – one example – of a larger one: namely, the set of all things that are determined. A point in our history has been reached where to be elect means to belong to this more general order of the *naturally* determined – a natural order into which (for example) psychological development and genetic causes might also one day enter.

---

[64] (Ed.) Louis Desgraves, Montesquieu, *Pensées* (Paris: Laffont, 1991), no. 1, 945.

CHAPTER 6

The Coining of a Developmental Theory: Leibniz to Bonnet

Obviously no participant in the piecemeal discussions so far described could have foreseen where they were actually heading, and in putting together this picture of a conceptual transition from the elect to the normal I have had benefit of hindsight. But since these discussions would one day end up in developmental psychology, it must be assumed that some kind of explicit *theory* was emerging with them. Physical development was an externally observable fact, for which theoretical explanations were already available. The question then is, how did such explanations get transferred from body to mind? And how in the process did causal determinism of a modern psychobiological kind replace the divine sort that lay at the core of the theory of election? The answer, which occupies much of this chapter, lies in certain theories about bodily growth from that period. In the twentieth century developmental psychologists continued to resort in extremis to models drawn from biology. This was the case both for Piaget with his 'genetic epistemology', and for his chief critic Lev Vygotsky (1896–1934), for whom the very definition of developmental disability lay in the continuing dominance of biology as the 'primary function' while a child's 'normal' development was defined by its increasingly sociocultural character.

The important point for us is that modern psychobiology and psychiatric genetics are predicated on the historical shift that took place from divine to genetic determinism: instead of God causing deficiency or absence (as in reprobates), genes do (as in the developmentally disabled or, at first, in children). The theological and biological theories share a certain common ground. The very possibility of associating biological with psychological development demonstrates how at this historical stage the mind was starting to be seen as if it were a fully *natural* entity, albeit within divine creation. The theological and the biological were both marked by the underlying anxiety about causes, itself a historically specific phenomenon that had been gathering pace in the seventeenth century. In this latter respect, the early modern and the modern theories have at least a motive in common. If you are focused on causes above all, the epistemological status of the thing caused may be lost sight of. To put it another way, you only seek causes if you are anxious about the (notional) thing that is caused.

However, psychobiology is by no means the whole story of determinism in the mind sciences. The developmental idea is informed also by *stadial* determinism; in other words, a deterministic element operates not only via material biology but equally *within* the psychological realm itself, thanks to its temporalization. A link between the two kinds of deterministic approach can be found in the theory of preformationism. This, the dominant theory of physical growth for most of the eighteenth century, was found at a certain point to be capable of explaining mental growth on its own terms.

Preformationism in Biology

In the relevant (mainly French-language) texts the arrival of *développement*, as a quasi-technical term, signalled the start of a coherently developmentalist theory. The verb *développer* was already being used by Malebranche and Leibniz, as we shall see, but the noun broke surface in the 1740s when at least three of Rousseau's leading Enlightenment contemporaries – the Lockean philosopher Etienne de Condillac and the naturalists Charles Bonnet and the Comte de Buffon – started using it occasionally, in a psychological sense. Their work influenced and blossomed in Rousseau's groundbreaking, ubiquitous role for it in *Emile*.

In order to understand how this came about, it is preformationism in biology that we must first look at. According to this theory all living beings ever since Creation have existed prior to conception, folded up in preformed 'envelopes' in the female egg. After birth the envelope unfolds ('de-velopes', so to speak) in distinct phases of growth, phases structured by determinate points in time that are also points of transformation (e.g. caterpillar – pupa – butterfly).

Preformationism encountered two rival theories. One was epigenesis, according to which the living creature grows by gradual differentiation from originally undifferentiated matter conceived by both parents.[1] For the

---

[1] Particularly the version in William Harvey, *Disputations Touching the Generation of Animals* (Oxford: Blackwell, 1981 [1651]). See also Janina Wellmann, *The Form of Becoming: Embryology and the Epistemology of Rhythm, 1760–1830*, translated by Kate Sturge (New York: Zone Books, 2017).

epigenesist, change was a more or less smooth *continuity*, whereas for the preformationist the notion of *order* had to be prior, consisting as it did in the 'lawful regularity' or structured and phased character of bodily events.[2] The other rival theory was that of spontaneous generation, which could occur even out of non-living matter; dung, for example, generated flies and maggots directly out of itself. Preformationism arose in opposition to both theories, which it saw as denying religion. Jan Swammerdam (1637–1680), the Dutch experimental biologist who in 1669 had been first to observe the preformed stages of the butterfly, called spontaneous generation 'atheistic' and a 'great danger' because it seemed to be a chance occurrence, and a world ruled by God would not be so chaotic.[3] Epigenesis came under similar scrutiny; a world ruled by God had to have order, and in living beings linear time would need to be ordered by a temporal structure.

The verbal form *développer* had long existed (in English it was 'to disvelop'). Originally it meant to unfurl or unfold: the unrolling of a scroll with written characters, or of a flag with heraldic devices. (The OED unearths, as early as 1659, a usage of 'disvelope' that refers to human interiority and the unfolding of thoughts and feelings, though this seems to have been an isolated and self-consciously metaphorical usage.)[4] The act of progressive unfurling reveals what was once folded, whether the physical item or the meanings of the heraldic characters. Whereas in the modern developmental idea, both physical and mental, it is the goal or point of arrival that is all-important, those initial usages of the verb were neutral: there was a balance between the end revealed by the fully unfurled state, and its starting point in the original furled state. (In this sense it echoed the still dominant Aristotelian account of causation, in which a thing's final goal is already present in its original essence.) Any use of the verb 'to develop' therefore would at first have been ambivalent. Unfurling could expose an initial pristine glory to the contaminating dimension of time (man is born free and everywhere he is chains), or it could reach over time a full glory that had previously lain hidden (man that is born to die can be redeemed).

Early eighteenth-century science saw also the start of the verbal usage in geometry, where it referred to changes in the outline of a plane that

---

[2] John H. Zammito, *The Gestation of German Biology: Philosophy and Physiology from Stahl to Schelling* (Chicago: University of Chicago Press, 2018), p. 113.
[3] Jan Swammerdam, *Bybel der Natuure sive Historia Insectorum* (Leiden: Herman Severinus, 1737), p. 28.
[4] Anon, *The Unhappy Marksman* (London: R. Clavell, 1659), published in Thomason Tracts E972(1). The author uses the word several times.

'develops a curve'. As the French historical dictionary, *Le Grand Robert*, notes, this has a 'spatial' significance, by contrast with the 'biological' usage whose significance is temporal. When Bonnet recorded the first use of the word 'evolution' in a biological context, he stated explicitly that he was using it as a synonym for 'development';[5] by it, he said, he meant the unfolding of individual creatures among 'the host of microscopic beings' according to 'determinate' laws of preformation.[6] (He also writes of the 'evolution' or unfolding of physical deformity in the children of deformed parents.)[7]

Swammerdam and Malebranche: A Window of Theoretical Opportunity

Preformationism's sense of a sharply *phased* linearity avoided the naïve gradualism of epigenesis and the chaotic instantaneousness of spontaneous generation. Its sense of structure might prove that God, having created the universe, could then step back and allow it to run lawfully, and thus would help to justify the harsh fate of the damned by distancing him from it.

In the 1660s Swammerdam, like Bonnet a devout Calvinist, had already used the preformed phases of the butterfly to illustrate how original sin gets to be hereditary, in a quasi-biological sense: today's human beings sin 'through' Adam because every single upcoming human being was already preformed and had been in Adam's loins at the Creation. When Swammerdam linked his experimental biology to Christian doctrine in this way, he used it to deny the miraculousness of the resurrection. Miracles are disordered things by definition. His science confirms instead the primacy of a 'natural and comprehensible' order in God's works, so that even Jesus's rising from the dead was a natural event[8] – a principle foreshadowed in the book of Revelation itself and the seven seals of the apocalypse:

> So very wonderful is God with regard to these little bees, that I venture to say that concerning the insects God's ineffable wonders are sealed, and that those seals are opened when one diligently comes to leaf through the book of nature, the Bible of natural theology, in which God's invisibility becomes visible.[9]

---

[5] Charles Bonnet, *Palingénésie, ou Idées sur l'état passé et sur l'état futur des êtres vivants*, in *Oeuvres* (Neuchâtel: Fauche, 1779–1783), vol. 7, part 9.
[6] Bonnet, *Palingénésie*, p. 249.
[7] Bonnet, *Considérations sur les corps organisés* (Amsterdam: Mark-Michel Rey, 1762), vol. 2, p. 313.
[8] Swammerdam, *Bybel*, p. 28.   [9] Swammerdam, *Bybel*, p. 394.

This is more than mere metaphor. In this passage the book of Revelation, whose seven seals are on the scrolls unfurled by the Lamb of God, and the staged biological revelation expressed by unfolding forms of the insect, are integral to each other. The problem of the Pascalian God, who remains hidden during the earthly lifetime, is solved by God's re-emergence before our very eyes as nature itself.

A few years later, in the 1680s, Malebranche endorsed Swammerdam's observation of caterpillar, pupa and butterfly, as a result of his own experiments that showed the flower of the tulip to be already present inside the bulb. But to his botanical discoveries he added, unlike the Dutchman, a theoretical framework. Where did this come from? The answer is that it came from the fact that Malebranche was interested in the metaphysics of change first, and only secondarily in its biological expression. If a tree comes from a seed, the tree must in some sense have been there from the start: its production cannot be explained epigenetically – that is, by simple laws of motion.[10] According to the seventeenth-century 'mechanical philosophy' of nature, even if the planets were created once and for all, plants and animals were being created all the time. To explain causes for every individual creature would thus be impossibly complicated. Rather, as we saw in the previous chapter, God rules by 'general laws'. Malebranche wondered how precisely these general causative laws might operate within the particular individual (including individual human beings). Citing Swammerdam, he answers that their 'parts' must already exist. These parts have been in place since Creation, but 'boxed up' (*emboîtés*). They merely need to unfold (*se développer*):

> It is necessary that every seed should contain the whole species which it can produce, that every grain of corn contains in miniature the ear which it will eventually produce, every grain of which in its turn contains its ear, all the grains of which again can always be just as fruitful ... These simple and general laws should suffice to cause the silent growth and appearance *at their due moment* of all these wonderful works of God, produced in the first days of the creation of the world.[11]

He also coins for *développer* an transitive sense. He writes here, for example, about 'the fecundity of ways in which God conserves and develops ... the infinite number of his various works'; he 'develops them before our eyes, following exactly certain very simple and very productive general laws'.[12]

---

[10] Malebranche, *Recherche*, in *Oeuvres*, vol. 1, p. 82.
[11] Malebranche, *Entretiens sur la métaphysique et sur la religion*, in *Oeuvres*, vol. 12, pp. 228–9, 252–3. My italics.
[12] Malebranche, *Entretiens*, pp. 223, 233.

Malebranche uses *développer* infrequently and only in very general contexts. Nevertheless, in using it to suggest a theoretical framework for Swammerdam's empirical observations, he was extending the ground over which one might look in a new way at individuals and indeed at individual souls or minds, whose features might likewise unfurl 'at their due moment' over the course of a human life. And in a theological context at least, this move had already been made. The Catholic moralist Jacques-Bénigne Bossuet, Louis XIV's court preacher who would later become an enthusiastic preformationist, had already applied the verb to human interiority as early as 1649, in respect of faith. We know *true* faith, he says, by its 'seeking to unfold itself (*se développer*) from the dark shadows around it'.[13] It is characteristic of the developmental idea that its application to interiority is detectable first in the context of faith rather than of the 'reason' that would later come to dominate.

Leibniz Again: The Preformation of the Interior Realm

To see how the theory of preformation crossed over from biology to psychology and became a model for timed cognitive and moral development, we must return to Leibniz. If Malebranche had supplied preformationist experimentation with a theory that was sufficiently general to accommodate, further down the line, a nascent science of psychological development, Leibniz nailed it in place.

First there was his theory of 'monads', the quasi-atomic irreducible substances that make up the universe. Whereas Hobbes, on a similar quest for infinitesimal atoms, had only conceived of material ones, Leibniz found his in the realm of minds, and defined them in terms of time as much as space. His indivisible substances form a hierarchy in which the highest form is the 'rational soul', found in God and the angels, and sometimes in small numbers of human beings.[14]

Secondly, we looked in the previous chapter at Leibniz's temporal conception of the soul and its continuity as it crosses over the threshold of death. He was wrestling like so many others with the Cartesian problem of how soul and body interconnect. Time was central in his rejection of double predestination, that is, that election and reprobation were diametrical opposites: the elect experience change through grace; the reprobate do

---

[13] Jacques-Bénigne Bossuet, *Oraison funèbre de très-haut et puissant seigneur Messire Michel Le Tellier, Chevalier, Chancelier de France* (Paris: Sebastian Mabre-Cramoisy, 1686 [1649]), p. 55.
[14] Leibniz, *Monadology*, para. 82.

not experience change at all. This emphasis on time reflects his objection to the static, Manichean-style representation of good and evil as equally balanced forces.[15] He emphasized it in order to reinforce the solution he had come up with, namely, that body and soul have a pre-established harmony; it was 'one of the rules of my system of general harmony that the present is big with the future'.[16] And so linear time – the relationship between the present and a changed, better future – lay at the core of that solution.

It helps explain why Leibniz took to preformationism. He wrote how Swammerdam's experiments 'helped me the more easily to acknowledge that the Animal and any other organized Substance does not start at all when we think it does, and that its apparent generation is only an unfolding (*développement*)'.[17] He endorsed Swammerdam again in the *Theodicy*, where he went further and, crucially, transferred the notion of development from the body across to the human interior. As he says, 'I would have added [to Swammerdam] that nothing is better qualified than the preformation of plants and animals to confirm my system of an established harmony between the soul and the body':[18]

> Considering that so admirable an order and rules so general are established in regard to animals, it does not appear reasonable that man should be completely excluded from that order, and that everything in relation to his soul should come about in him by miracle. Besides ... it is of the essence of God's wisdom that all should be harmonious in his works, and that nature should be parallel with grace. It is thus my belief that those souls which one day shall be human souls, like those of other species, have been in the seed, and in the progenitors as far back as Adam.[19]

So here we have it in black and white. True, this conscious transfer of preformation theory from the physical to the interior realm came about for secondary reasons. In general, Leibniz preferred not to think of the activities of body and soul or mind as being comparable: the 'harmony' between them did not mean that analogies should be drawn from one to the other.[20]

---

[15] Leibniz, *Monadology*, Preface. See also Catherine Wilson, 'The reception of Leibniz', in *Cambridge Companion to Leibniz*.
[16] Leibniz, *Theodicy*, p. 341.
[17] Leibniz, *Système nouveau de la nature*, in (ed.) Paul Janet, *Oeuvres philosophiques de Leibniz* (Paris: Alcan, 1900), vol. 1, p. 638; this was first published in the 1695 volume of *Journal des Sçavans*, the French equivalent to the Royal Society's *Philosophical Transactions*. For an English translation see (eds.) R. S. Woolhouse and Richard Franks, *Leibniz's 'New System' and Associated Contemporary Texts* (Oxford: Clarendon, 1997).
[18] Leibniz, *Theodicy*, Preface.   [19] Leibniz, *Theodicy*, p. 274.
[20] See, for example, Leibniz, *Monadology*, para. 80.

It was just that sometimes he 'looked to empirical life science for empirical corroboration of his prior metaphysical principles' (e.g. the soul's pre-existing the body).[21] And true, Leibniz means here only the 'sensitive' or 'animal soul' (he uses these interchangeably) – that is, that aspect of interiority which is capable of sensation, perception and feeling, and not the 'rational soul' with its divine moral and cognitive resonances. Nevertheless, we should note that the harmony between body and soul occurs *within* the biological seed. With this, the possibility of a modern causal (e.g. genetic) explanation for psychological phenomena heaves into view.

It should also be noted that once preformation took on this interior role it was in a position to displace the theory of innate ideas, which said that human individuals' knowledge is 'preformed' only in the quite different sense that we are born with ideas already complete. The two theories are not incompatible, and in fact Leibniz championed innatism. The point is rather that the theory of innate ideas ceded its former historical importance to the developmentalist one, which allocated the key role to temporal *structure* over the detachable *content* of ideas as such.

Election and the 'Unfolding' of the Rational Soul in Leibniz

Leibniz's importance to the developmental idea lies partly in his reworking of the medieval convention of the rational soul. Nature, he says, is 'parallel with grace'. How then does the rational soul, which his predecessors had set apart from nature, fit into this picture? On the one hand, Leibniz says that the 'preordained' and 'harmonized' body–soul relationship is itself natural, which might suggest a kind of universal human; on the other hand, this relationship still had to find a place for 'saving' grace, and the very existence of the latter was predicated on its being absent in some people. Leibniz's notion of harmony led to a reframing of that fundamental human division. In theology the division had belonged within the conceptualization of grace itself; it lay between the saving grace of a few and the general grace of everyone. It could not lie between possession and privation of a rational soul, because this soul was the defining property of every human being. The rational soul was genuinely universal because it defined the 'substance' of man qua man; whatever the shortcomings in the

---

[21] Justin Erik Smith, 'Leibniz's preformationism: between metaphysics and biology', in (ed.) Anna-Teresa Tymieniecka, *The Creative Matrix of the Origins: Dynamisms, Forces and the Shaping of Life* (Dordrecht: Kluwer, 2002), vol. 2, p. 165.

rationality of this or that individual, the universality principle was stuck fast in the presuppositions of scholastic logic.

Moreover, the basic divide that did exist – that is, between saving and general grace – operated only at an abstract level; as far as individuals were concerned, its existence could only be guessed at. A few medieval writers, notably William of Ockham, had suggested that saving grace might be measurable, and vary from individual to individual; but the mainstream did not see it as something distributed across the aggregate of individual rational souls. However, once Calvinist and Jansenist accounts of predestination arrived, the focus shifted to the *individual receipt* of saving grace, and to the recipient's elect or reprobate status.

While this marked a break with scholasticism, a certain continuity remained. Something of scholastic logic seeped into the theory of election. In the sixteenth century, for example, we find the leading Calvinist Girolamo Zanchi mapping the category of the elect on to that of the rational. The propositions, 'Every man is a creature endowed with reason' and, 'All the faithful are elect to eternal life,' he says, are equivalent.[22] He was merely drawing an analogy, to illustrate the utility of logic for framing theological proofs; he knew very well that (according to the scholastic formula) every human being has a rational soul, while not every human being is elect. Nevertheless, analogy can lead to osmosis.

Leibniz, like Locke, did more than merely draw analogies. Both were raised in predestinarian Protestant households. As philosophers, both came to see the fundamental intra-human divide in the individual's *acquisition over the lifespan*, or not, of the vital ingredient once called 'saving' grace which now begins to take on a 'natural' profile, thus priming it to turn into cognitive ability. They went about it in different ways. Locke dismissed the vocabulary itself, that of a universal 'rational soul', on the grounds that rationality was absent in idiots and cognitively disabled 'changelings'; he replaced it with a new vocabulary of 'the moral man'. This substituted a different set of beliefs about a natural division among human beings, one which he nevertheless derived from the theory of election and grace, as we saw in the previous chapter. His theory of empirical learning assumed a smoothly gradual acquisition of abilities and ideas; if he had drawn an analogy from physical to mental growth, it would have been epigenetic rather than preformationist. Empirical learning was unproblematically gradual, rather than structured into stages.

---

[22] In William Perkins, *A Brief Discourse, Taken out of the Writings of Herr Zanchius* (London: John Legat, 1595), p. 23.

Leibniz, by contrast, retained the original vocabulary of 'rational souls'. However, he defined these, as the scholastics had not done, by their exclusive possession of 'saving' grace. Only some people, he suggests, are saved and/or have rational souls. One question for Leibniz then was, how do they acquire them? By an external lightning strike from God, or by a staged process, which God merely initiated? Though he sometimes wavers, Leibniz emphasizes the second option. Once again, there arises the metaphysical question underlying the relationship between difference and time, as to how change occurs at all. When the rational soul arrives, says Leibniz, it is a 'new perfection'. But if it is new, how then does it emerge from its previous condition? Leibnizian development or 'unfolding' involves transformative structural *stages* drawn by analogy from biological preformationism; but these stages cannot consist of 'leaps', as they occur in tulips and butterflies, because it is 'hard to imagine ... a *natural* means of raising a sensitive soul to the degree of a rational soul'.[23] Therein lies the problem. In the interior realm, can change only happen miraculously? And how can miracles be natural?

The puzzle arose because of the 'parallel' (or even fusion) between grace and nature. Scholastic convention had said that the rational soul arrives via a 'special operation' by God, pre-natally. Leibniz rewrote this. It arrives, he said, as 'a middle way between creation [of the rational soul] and [its] entire pre-existence' or preformation – that is, between instantaneous miracle and natural stages. He coined a word for this middle way: 'transcreation'.[24] On the one hand, the rational soul's arrival is still miraculous (though later in the book he would claim to have 'dispensed with miracles in God's generating of man').[25] On the other, although the rational soul is thereby more 'perfect' than the sensitive or animal soul, it too is quite capable of sin on its own account, thus suggesting that it has roots in the natural man. Consequently the soul or mind still needs to be 'operated on', and 'specially', at some point along the human timeline. Leibniz calls this operation 'regeneration',[26] which conventionally had meant the first stage in the series of changes in the elect individual as he receives saving grace. Election remained a divine addition; to be saved, rationality was not something you simply *possessed*, as (for example) you possessed bodily attributes.

As so often in the history of psychology, it is exceptions to the rule that can throw light on the puzzle. What becomes of the necessary and

---

[23] Leibniz, *Theodicy*, p. 173. My italics.
[24] On transcreation, see Larry M. Jorgensen, 'By leaps and bounds', *The Leibniz Review*, 23 (2013).
[25] Leibniz, *Theodicy*, p. 361.   [26] Leibniz, *Monadologie*, para. 82.

fundamental elect–reprobate divide among human beings when grace starts to overlap with nature in this way? The premise was that God 'uses his creatures in the manner most consistent with order' and 'with the fewest exceptions possible'.[27] Whereas Malebranche simply thought it was 'better to admit [individual] defects and monstrosities than to violate general laws', Leibniz went further and asserted that 'even monstrosities are part of order'.[28] He explained this by analogy with developmental curves in geometry: 'A line may have twists and turns ... so that one sees neither rhyme nor reason therein ... and yet it may be that ... a geometrician would find the reason and the fittingness of all these so-called irregularities.' One might indeed seek a whole science of interior monstrosity, since (as he had once remarked) 'it seems hardly rational that [any] souls should remain uselessly in a chaos of confused matter'.[29] Locke too had proposed a science based on 'exact observation' of the various different 'ways of faltering' exhibited by 'idiots'.[30] What was demanded in both cases was a science of psychological abnormality, no less.

Order, then, hinges on 'the *duration* that must be attributed to the material *soul*' – and, as we shall see, to the rational soul as well. The reconstitution of order is a natural, not a supernatural process. The relationship between soul and body 'is supernatural' – that is, beyond nature and time – 'only in the beginning of things', at 'the original constitution of pre-established harmony between the soul and the body'. Harmony having thus been established at the first moment of Creation, all consequent events including 'the formation of animals and the relation between soul and body ... are something as natural now as the most ordinary operations of Nature' and therefore dependent upon time.[31]

Another problem that required a natural and temporal solution was how the soul separates from the body at death. Since 'what we call death is not a destruction' but rather a blip in linear time, Leibniz's solution is to see death as a 'folding up' (*enveloppemens*) of the human creature into an infinitesimally small state, from which it expands again into renewed life. 'The Animal conserves its organic machine, and by the destruction of the grosser parts of this machine the Animal finds itself reduced by death to such a small state as to render it ... imperceptible.' This allows the creature's 'least gross' material elements to survive (that is, the 'animal spirits', which were conventionally supposed to cause the movements of the animal soul).

---

[27] *Theodicy*, Preface.   [28] *Theodicy*, p. 276.   [29] Leibniz, *Système nouveau*, p. 638.
[30] Locke, *An Essay*, 1.11.12.   [31] Leibniz, *Theodicy*, Preface. My italics.

As a solution to the problem of how the soul separates from the body at death, Leibniz prefers this to the 'absurdity' of the transmigration of souls:

> Since there is thus no first birth nor entirely new generation of the animal, it follows that there will be no final extinction, nor complete death, in the strictly metaphysical sense, and that consequently, instead of the transmigration of souls, there is only the transformation of one and the same animal, according as its organs are variously folded (*pliés*) and more or less unfolded (*développés*).[32]

He would add later that 'there is neither generation nor coming to life, ever, in the strict sense of a separation from the soul. And what we call generations are unfoldings (*développemens*) and growths, just as what we call deaths are envelopments and diminutions.'[33] 'Unfolding' in this sense constitutes natural growth as such, and at this point he is talking only about the human being's animal soul, concerned with sense impressions. But the vocabulary is preformationist, and the preformationist structure of human interiority, indeed the very principle of change itself, only applied to the elect; so surely this 'unfolding' or natural development must also apply to elect, *rational* souls, concerned with moral and cognitive activities? In which case, might not predestinate election be a natural phenomenon, played out over the course of one's time on earth? The linear development of elect 'rational souls', once these have been operated on or 'regenerated', follows much higher (temporal) laws:

> They are exempt from everything which could make them lose their status as citizens of the society of minds (*esprits*); God has provided for them so well that no changes in matter can ever make them lose their moral qualities; and we can say that everything tends to the perfection, not only of the universe in general, but also of these created beings in particular, for they are [pre]destined for happiness.[34]

However incomplete such 'created' elect natures still are at any one point on the timeline – 'no [individual] soul can unfold (*développer*) completely' – they are nevertheless in a state of 'progress towards the infinite' which is in heaven.

The obscure theoretical problem of how the soul's identity is conserved when separated from the body at death, along with the solution (its temporal continuity), was actually the trigger for Leibniz's more famous dictum about the pre-established harmony between them. It was in this

---

[32] Leibniz, *Système nouveau*, p. 639.   [33] Leibniz, *Monadology*, para. 73.
[34] Leibniz, *Monadology*, para. 61.

precise context – that is, the need for and primacy of temporal extension in the soul of elect individuals – that the pre-established harmony theory arose. In short, it is a harmony that exists only in the elect. From here, over the next two centuries, the elect – the limited group defined by possession of a Leibnizian rational soul in the realm of grace – would be decked out with quasi-universal features, centred on the acquisition of natural psychological capabilities. Thus the secularization of psychological nature was also its sacralization.

It was not, then, the relationship of body to soul/mind in universally human terms so much as that relationship in the elect alone which gave rise to Leibniz's theory of pre-established harmony. This theory also opened up a new perspective on the wider relationship between freedom and necessity. For predestinarians who sought an accommodation between the two, their relationship as we have seen was one of 'congruence': the elect were free to choose their behaviours but God necessarily foreknew what these would be. Divine foreknowledge did not trump divine causation. Leibniz claimed to be doing something new about this question. Always the diplomat and reconciler, he defined free choice in such a way that it could be predestinate without ceasing to be choice,[35] and so determinism starts to become a recognizably modern issue. The old dispute as to whether God has foreknowledge of and thus a responsibility for sin and reprobation is sidelined. Instead,

> Why might not God give to a [human] substance, from the beginning, a nature or internal force that could produce, by order (as in a spiritual or formal automaton; but free in the case where that substance participates in reason), everything that will happen to it? All the more so inasmuch as the nature of the substance necessarily requires and essentially implicates (*enveloppe*) progress or change, without which it would have no capability of acting.[36]

The term *la force* implies here, within the individual, both a subjective capability and its objective unfolding over time in a pre-arranged form. On the one hand, Leibniz's ontology of substances already seems to include the subjective sense of capability.[37] On the other, the objective sense of the term evokes a second, equally long-standing aspect of 'predestination' which we have only touched upon so far in this book: predestination not

---

[35] Julia Jorati, *Leibniz on Causation and Agency* (Cambridge: Cambridge University Press, 2017), pp. 133–4.
[36] Leibniz, *Système nouveau*, p. 642.
[37] See Jorati, 'Leibniz's ontology of force', *Oxford Studies in Philosophy*, 8 (2019).

of the *soul* and its afterlife destiny but of *events* in the external world. Before, the two aspects had for the most part been discussed separately. Now, evidently, external 'events' might be seen as embracing, alongside all other kinds of externality, individual human behaviours too. We get a sense of this in Leibniz's assertion that the rational soul is itself 'a primitive *force*' or capability, to which the body 'adapts', 'for the occasions when we think of the soul as acting externally' via willed actions. The actions or behaviours may still be foreknown by God, but with Leibniz this fact is starting to recede in importance; instead, the determinism of the causes of election as such has spread to an equally deterministic causation of the relationship between the individual's elect status and his behavioural interventions in society and nature.

Expressly, this applies 'only to minds (*esprits*) capable of entering into association with God' – that is, the elect.[38] 'Each of these minds should always play its part in a way most fitted to contribute to the perfecting of the society of all minds, which constitutes their moral union in the City of God.' The word 'all' in this phrase would once have meant the 'communion of saints', that mystical union of all the elect in heaven together with all the elect on earth, past and present. However, this still elitist Leibnizian definition of interiority is no such fluffy abstraction. It denotes real people in earthly situations where grace and natural (cognitive) 'force' or capability overlap; and just as the pre-established harmony in the relationship between nature and grace is not a static but a developmental conception, so the society of minds itself is temporally conceived and structured.

Its task is to 'lead things to grace through the very paths of nature', thus implying a role for nurture and education.[39] But Leibniz was not hopeful about the numbers who might even be in a starting position to be led. At best, 'simple' people not up to 'understanding by ordinary means' may benefit by their will and 'the warmth of a sincere love for the true good which is God's'.[40] For 'weak' predestinarians it was enough to assume that hell exists and most people end up there; denying God's responsibility for the damnation of reprobates led eventually to ceasing even to worry about them. The 'strong' predestinarian anxiety of Leibniz, however, focused on the suffering of that group which turns out to be unchangeable, ineducable and therefore unable to contribute over time to the society of minds. This

---

[38] Leibniz, *Système nouveau*, p. 642.   [39] Leibniz, *Monadology*, para. 88.
[40] Leibniz, Letter to the Landgrave Ernst of Hesse-Rheinfels, 25 March 1688, cited in Grua, *Jurisprudence universelle*, p. 495.

too points towards elements in modern psychology and its pathological view of certain people.

Condillac and Buffon on Development

Use of the word 'development' by Condillac (1714–1780) and Buffon (1707–1788), both of whom knew their Leibniz, accompanied the secularization of scientific investigation. This provokes the thought: could the developmental idea have taken on the aspect of a whole theory of modern science only by having its religious components filleted out, through unbelief or at least the marginalization of religion? Condillac in particular has often been singled out as an ancestor of the atheistic and mechanist theorists of the developmental idea such as Hippolyte Taine (1828–1893) and Herbert Spencer (1820–1903), whose views of psychology were permeated by the idea.[41] But as the next chapter will suggest, the source of such scientific psychologies may equally have been a more intuitively religious, even romantic one: namely, the deep cultural impact which Rousseau had made on European intellectual life in the meantime. Meanwhile, for a biologist like Buffon, seen today as one of the shapers of the modern discipline of biology, nature was 'God's second book'. The identification between nature and grace – endowing the natural world with an independence from God but simultaneously worshipping it – was not new, though you had to be careful how you phrased it (Spinoza's version of it had been condemned as atheistic across late seventeenth-century Europe). In the right context it was quite compatible with established belief. Indeed, it could actively *preserve* Christianity, because it was woolly enough to stifle the captiousness of the previous century's predestinarian debates.

For the moment, let us position ourselves in the eighteenth-century mind, not the nineteenth and after. When a modern atheist 'sees the light', they know what they are letting themselves in for: there is a two-thousand-year-old Christian culture already laid out for them to connect with, which they will have unconsciously absorbed prior to conversion. Enlightenment thinkers making the jump in the opposite direction could not 'know' atheism in this way. It had no systematic backstory or theoretical base of its own. Unbelief may well have always existed, more so than we suppose, and maybe the number of people who believed in hell was no greater than those who merely wanted the masses to believe in hell in order to prevent them from sinning.

---

[41] Hippolyte Taine, 'Les débuts de l'intelligence: Esquisse biographique d'un petit enfant', *Revue philosophique*, 1 (1877); Herbert Spencer, *Principles of Psychology* (London: Longman, 1855).

But among lay people, 'I don't care' (lack of anxiety) may have been more usual than 'I don't believe'. At an intellectual level, atheism meant various things. It could be a hypothesis advanced by philosophers for the sake of argument, although the argument sometimes led to suspicions that they were taking the hypothesis a bit too seriously. Or it could indicate belief in a rationalist explanation of the universe that does not need God for its operation (even though he is still needed to set it in motion). Or it could simply express despair about one's fate in the afterlife by exhibitionistic displays of defiance to one's maker. What atheism was not, or not yet, was an off-the-shelf rational belief system premised on the prior absence of God.

Modern commentators often suppose that both Condillac and Buffon had lost their belief (Bonnet was clearly devout). Condillac pioneered his mechanist description of the human mind while in post as Abbé de Mureau. Buffon's botanical career was by appointment to the divinely appointed Louis XV. So were their professions of faith mere lip service? Condillac met objections to the atheistic implications of his mechanical system by simply blanking them and reasserting his faith, in an appendix to his most offending text, the *Treatise on Sensations* (1754). Moreover, the opening words of his first book, which had been inspired by Locke, point again to a motive that conserves lingering anxiety about election and turns it in an epistemological direction: 'Whether we rise to heaven, or descend to the abyss, we never get outside ourselves – it is always our own thoughts that we perceive' – in short, we cannot know whether we are saved.[42] As for Buffon, his private correspondence reveals a worldly cynicism about ecclesiastical affairs, though not about the basis of belief as such. Even if their claims to belief had been an expedient fake, that is not the point. Their question was rather, is the universe and hence human life itself ordered, or is it random? Belief in order sprang from anxiety about randomness and chaos, and it led to the question of how order, internal as well as external, is structured. In this sense, Condillac and Buffon were model pupils of Père Malebranche.

In his *Essay on the Origin of Human Knowledge* (1746) and the *Treatise on Sensations* Condillac confines the term 'development' and the less novel one of 'progress' chiefly to his introductions and summaries. This indicates that they describe his broad metaphysical framework, rather than pointing to empirically observable aspects of the mind. This is despite his claim to have eschewed the involvement of metaphysics in his theory of the mind.[43]

---

[42] Condillac, *Essai sur l'origine des conoissances humaines* (Paris: Pierre Mortier, 1746).
[43] On this, see Isabel F. Knight, *The Geometric Spirit: The Abbé de Condillac and the French Enlightenment* (New Haven: Yale University Press, 1968).

Although he contrasts this latter, Leibnizan approach with his own empirical and Lockean one, his use of 'development' here echoes Leibniz's sense of a preformed, 'unfolding' grace. This lends a sense of order to Condillac's text. However, he does not use it to roll out a whole temporal theory. When Rousseau got hold of it, the word's temporal sense instantly flooded the psychology; and even Condillac himself, by the time he came to write about education a few years after *Emile*, started using 'development' and 'progress' in the main body of the text.[44]

The case of Buffon is more complicated, and to understand it we must return to biology. In one of his sporadic observations on human interiority he writes that the passions, by interfering with reason, give rise to 'injustice', a realm of 'illusion' and 'shadows' that 'extinguishes the [divine] light in our souls'.[45] Neither Jesuit nor Jansenist could have faulted him for this, but the point for him was that the ultimate choice was not between religion and atheism but between order and chaos. And in that case, the core problem was how to account for change. Change does not have to mean chaos, but it can be threatening. That was why preformationists sought order in biology. Buffon was sceptical about preformationism. That was because he was uncertain about notions of time in general,[46] seeing nature as fixed and species as fixed. But on the occasions when he is forced to accommodate time, he deploys exactly the word *développement*, in a sense analogous to that of the preformationists. The passages in question lie in his 1749 *Natural History*, which Rousseau admired. Rousseau's coining of 'perfectibility' and Buffon's 'development' belong with each other. When Rousseau states that 'perfectibility' is exclusive to man, he is imagining readers 'whose reading of Buffon has already prepared them not to be surprised by such a neologism'.[47]

Sometimes there would be a topic that forced Buffon to deal with his diffidence about time. For example, when he discovered that the layering of sediments in geology occurs in chronological stages, he claimed that this was still compatible with a static view of the universe. On the one hand, the history of the material earth has neither beginning nor end. On the other hand, it is 'the history of man' that really matters, and this 'is only one

---

[44] Condillac, *Cours d'études pour l'instruction du Prince de Parme* (Paris: François Monory, 1776).
[45] Buffon, 'Histoire naturelle', in *Oeuvres complètes* (Paris: Furne, 1842), vol. 3, p. 437.
[46] See P. J. Bowler, 'Theories of generation and the problem of species', *Journal of the History of Biology*, 6/2 (1973).
[47] Jean Starobinski, 'Buffon et Rousseau', in (ed.) Comité national pour la commémoration de J.-J. Rousseau, *Jean-Jacques Rousseau et son oeuvre: problèmes et recherches* (Paris: Klincksieck, 1964), p. 139.

point in the history of nature', thus occupying a whole sector of time. Time *is* important in this one respect, and human development's linear trajectory is the model for the whole of living nature.[48]

Buffon uses the word 'development' as an overarching abstraction that can slide into metaphor – for example, when he writes (in a way that seems novel for the period) about 'developing an argument'. But he also employs it in a more specific sense. In a section on the 'development and growth of the foetus', he uses it to attack a variant subbranch of preformationism. This said that living beings come not from the ovum but from the sperm, which houses a miniature but fully formed human, 'an infinitely small man, whose figure and form are absolutely the same as those of the adult man' – that is, a homunculus that grows whole in the womb. When Buffon used 'development' here, it was precisely in order to counter this spermist theory. He did so by citing diversification over time: there can be no homunculus or mini-man in the womb, he says, because different parts of the foetus unfold at different speeds. It is true that over time their respective growths tend to become proportional to each other, but only after actual birth does a creature's growth start to be a unitary process.

Buffon does not have a consistent vocabulary for change. On the one hand, he uses non-temporal terms for the variety and complexity of the variations among different parts of one foetus; he talks here not about phases, only about 'degrees' and 'types' (*espèces*). On the other hand, while the unfolding of a folded piece of paper reveals 'only ... a change in position among the various parts', in the 'unfolding (*développement*) composed by the body of an animal, the relative position of the parts changes as well as the volume and mass of those parts'. And it is precisely here, in his descriptions of variety and differentiation, that he does talk about 'different *times* of development', which are empirically observable (in birds' eggs, for example).[49]

Such talk is not so far from preformationism, and is enough to suggest links to the little he does say about human interiority and development. His writings on humankind are dominated by the body, the 'external man', and in this part of the *Natural History* there is only a stray, conventional reference to 'internal' and 'spiritual sensibility'.[50] Physical nature and the workings of the human mind exist in entirely separate realms. However, in a retrospectively written introduction to the whole work he does write

---

[48] See Jacques Roger, *Buffon: A Life in Natural History* (Ithaca: Cornell University Press, 1997), p. 409ff.
[49] Buffon, 'Histoire naturelle', in *Oeuvres complètes*, vol. 3, pp. 206–7. My italics.
[50] Buffon, 'Histoire naturelle', p. 224.

about 'development' in a psychological sense. The context here is pedagogical, and anticipates Rousseau. There is an exact moment in the young person's life, he says, when 'natural history ... should be presented to him ... and precisely at the time when reason begins to develop in him'.[51] In other words, the science of making natural classifications encompasses a classification of human beings as developers. If such an education *is* appropriately ordered, then success follows.

At the point where young people start to classify nature for themselves, their taste for knowledge will be born, and they must be helped, in a way that again anticipates Rousseau:

> This taste, so necessary for everything, but at the same time so rare, does not arise by precepts: it is in vain that education would seek to supplement them ... ; they will only ever lead them to a point common to all men, to that degree of intelligence and memory sufficient for society or for ordinary matters; it is to nature, rather, that we owe this first spark of genius, this germ of taste we speak of, which develops thereafter to a greater or lesser extent, according to differences in circumstance.

'Genius', meaning here the inner light of a natural instinct for knowledge of nature, is defined simply by *adulthood*. This is a further step in the normalization of the elect. Election is not yet 'ordinary', and the elect are still a minority. But its sacredness is rooted firmly in the earthly realm. Buffon does not mention reprobates, but he does offer his own example of the exceptions to this truly human nature: namely, 'imbeciles'. His definition of imbeciles as unable to compare and contrast 'ideas' is lifted wholesale from the account of 'idiots' in Book Two of Locke's *Essay*, and unwittingly evokes the doctrine of reprobation still lurking there. And in fact *most* human beings still come under the imbecile heading:

> The majority have so little life in their soul and are so apathetic in their thinking that they compare and combine nothing ... These men are more or less stupid and seem to differ from animals only by that small number of ideas which their soul has so much trouble producing.[52]

Their 'habits' are 'puerile' and resemble 'the attachment of ... a child for his toy'. The temporal model circumscribes more tightly the concept of childhood itself, 'puerility', as a mental incapacity. Children form here a subgroup under the imbecile heading, an imbecility modelled by the developmental idea.

---

[51] Buffon, 'De la manière d'étudier et de traiter l'histoire naturelle', in *Oeuvres complètes*, vol. 1, p. 2.
[52] Buffon, 'Histoire naturelle', in *Oeuvres complètes*, vol. 3, pp. 52–3 and 84.

Charles Bonnet: Human Development as the Fulfilment of Revelation

Unlike the patrician Condillac and Buffon, or the deracinated and peripatetic Rousseau, Charles Bonnet (1720–1793) came from a provincial lawyer caste in Geneva where he remained for his whole life. Bonnet was a scientist – the discoverer of an eponymous syndrome in ophthalmology and a pioneering entomologist with a preformationist outlook – but also a philosopher of religion, and the two activities were one. The biggest influences on him for our purposes were Leibniz and the latter's pupil and copyist, Christian Wolff, whose *Psychologia naturalis* and *Psychologia rationalis* of the 1730s contributed much to psychology's being seen (at least formally) as a separate discipline from philosophy.[53] The interest for us is his influence on the developmental aspects of *Emile*, which was more direct than Condillac's or Buffon's, and because Bonnet's 'preformationist psychology', so to speak, stands midway between Leibniz and Rousseau.

Whereas Condillac and Buffon had wheeled the word 'development' out only for special occasions, Bonnet deploys it across various aspects of his work. First of all, he sets out like Leibniz to reconcile necessity and human agency. In this respect his work marks another important phase in the overt abandonment of election and its covert rerouting into cognitive normality and subjective capability. Salvation, the goal of the linear route, was at that time increasingly being replaced by 'happiness', which to start with had been a merely terminological rather than a conceptual shift. Bonnet rejected the Jansenists' concept of 'pre-established' election. Happiness, he says, comes about proportionally, as the result of '*degrees* of moral perfection' and suitability for election[54] – something Leibniz and the more adventurous Jansenists such as Nicole and Duguet had only hinted at. But even in this respect, Bonnet keeps referring to the 'sufferings and recompenses of the life to come' as a 'System of necessity'. In the back of his mind is still God's determination of destinies. There is no paradox. It is simply that the language of necessity and order is being adapted to a more strictly developmental schema. He asks:

> What do I hear? Bitter complaints, piercing cries sent to heaven by a multitude of sinners and unfortunates who were, are, and will not be

---

[53] On the German connections here, see Fernando Vidal, *Les sciences de l'âme XVIe-XVIIIe siècle* (Paris: Honoré Champion, 2006).

[54] Bonnet, *Essai de psychologie, ou considérations sur les opérations de l'âme*, in *Oeuvres*, vol. 8, p. 112. My italics. The *Oeuvres* were published in quarto and octavo editions simultaneously, but the contents do not exactly correspond. All references are to the quarto unless otherwise stated.

[elect] unless by virtue of pre-established Order. No, these cries do not alarm me at all. Out of this valley of misery I turn my attention to our stay in Eternity. There, I see all Men enjoying happiness, but in a proportion relative to the degree of moral perfection they have here below. All of them advance ceaselessly, from perfection to perfection. All of them are content with the place they occupy, because all of them see distinctly that this is the one appropriate to them, and that wherever they have been placed they can always have the ambition of higher places, the distance between the finite and the infinite being itself infinite. In a word, those who are less Happy cry that they prefer their state to that of non-existence ... The soul will perfect itself ceaselessly.[55]

To be chosen, we must be judged by what we do in life and even after it, but this is only on top of what has been ordained for us pre-natally. Nevertheless, agency can now also incorporate ambition. The soul's progress towards its goal of perfection consists not in a vague gradualism but in preformed stages of *appropriateness*, or relative degrees of preparedness. And (echoing Leibniz) any 'advances' occur over a terrain whose temporal dimension levels the earthly trajectory with the heavenly one. Development being a principle that transcends earth and heaven, its sacralization follows.

Bonnet thereby opens out a whole new field for investigation in which necessity and freedom combine. In the opening salvo of his *Essay on Psychology* (1755) he identifies his topic as a scientific description of the temporal advance of the reasoning mind, all within a Christian framework. 'Christianity is the better philosophy, because it is the perfection of reason: but reason only perfects itself by the means allotted to it.'

What are those means? It is here that Bonnet defines psychology as 'the Economy of Grace', a phrase that needs explaining briefly. In this book we have been looking at texts concerning one particular thread in the theory of election, an ethical one ('theodicy') designed to justify God's apparent harshness. Here we are dealing with a second, much less noisy discussion.[56] The phrase 'the Economy of Grace' comes from Paul's Epistle to the Ephesians 3.2. The word *oikonomia* in Paul's New Testament Greek meant the rules of household management; Aristotle had used it in his *Politics* for the relationship between the master of a household and its slaves, children and womenfolk. Paul then applied the word metaphorically to grace: the 'Economy of

---

[55] Bonnet, *Essai de psychologie*, p. 121.
[56] For a fuller discussion, see Gerhard Richter, *Oikonomia: Der Gebrauch des Wortes Oikonomia im Neuen Testament* (Berlin: De Gruyter, 2005), p. 80; Giorgio Agamben, *The Kingdom and the Glory: For a Theological Genealogy of Economy and Government* (Stanford: Stanford University Press, 2011), pp. 21ff, 137.

Grace' referred to God's plan, his ordering of the interior lives of human beings in this world as a preparation for the next. In the Latin (Vulgate) Bible, *oikonomia* was rendered as *dispensatio*, a word that even then carried the sense of a *special* dispensation, an exemption from deserved damnation. For Paul, this dispensation was 'the mystery of His will', and did not require justifying. It was also 'the dispensation of the fullness of times' (Ephesians 1.9–10), by which he meant the completion of a period in historical time, marked in this instance by the atonement and redemption. The sense of linear time was therefore already embedded in the idea of the Economy of Grace, because it suggested God's governance of time via a planned future for humankind.

Bonnet's account of it goes back to Leibniz. The latter, aside from his ethical treatment of election, had also discussed election in the neutral sense of the 'efficacy' of its operations. This part of his account focused (a) on how grace actually works within each individual, and (b) on how to explain the fact that it affects different individuals differently. He too called this latter the 'dispensation' of grace;[57] and given the harmony between grace and nature which he was keen to establish, it was also a dispensation of nature.[58] Bonnet takes this a step further. He asks himself how such an 'Economy of Grace' in all its efficacy might be defined. We would, he says, have to call it 'psychology' (*la psychologie*). And this comes precisely at the point where he decides to call himself a psychologist (*psychologue*), probably the very first French usage of the term.

The principle of proportionality – of different degrees of chosenness, so to speak, alongside secondary differences in personal ability and effort – replaces the qualitative sense of election with a quantitative, almost epidemiological one. The focus on God's direct allocation of grace has given way to a focus on its effects – that is, on the interior differences among humans. These differences exist in the realm of nature, even if the discussion's overall framework is an explanation for divine justice.[59] Bringing the concept of grace down to earth for dissection in this (to us) rather mundane-sounding form of 'efficacy' reveals its newly developmental character: reason, being necessary but not sufficient for grace, has to perfect itself before there can be salvation. And, foreshadowing *Emile*, that must mean there was an earlier stage in the natural life of the individual when

---

[57] See, for example, Leibniz, *Theodicy*, p. 283.
[58] On this, see Agustín Echavarría, 'Leibniz on the efficacy and economy of divine grace', in (eds.) L. Strickland et al., *Tercentenary Essays on the Philosophy and Science of Leibniz* (New York: Palgrave, 2017); Ansgar Lyssy, 'Nature and grace: on the concept of divine economy in Leibniz', *Studia Leibnitiana* 48/2 (2018).
[59] Bonnet, *Essai analytique sur les facultés de l'âme*, in *Oeuvres*, vol. 13, p. 51.

reason as such was imperfect. It had its own infancy, and is graded across individuals from imperfect infant reason to an adult 'right reason' (still substantively equivalent here to divine reason).

In a short undated essay on education supplementing the 1783 edition of his collected works, Bonnet writes about *la psychologie* as a distinct discipline for study purposes, as already suggested by Wolff. Here he fills out the mundane 'economic' template of grace with pedagogical advice. It has a Rousseauian tone, though it is unclear whether it was written before or after *Emile*:

> In the order of the mind's advance, which runs naturally from the concrete to the abstract and from the less abstract to the more abstract, it will be good to finish with Ontology or the Science of Being in general, and to position it after the other parts of rational philosophy. This order is ... opposite to what the majority of writers prefer; but at least it is the one that is most appropriate to the infancy of Reason. The tutor should adapt himself to the needs of an emergent Reason: notions that are too random, too distanced from sensible Objects, strongly deter the mind of a beginner.[60]

He announces the salvific premise: 'Happiness is thus the great End of Man. Reason is the means to this End.' This reflects a historical tipping of the balance of emphasis from where the timeline starts (its origins in Eden) to where it is heading (happiness, its utilitarian goal). And anticipating Rousseau again, it enhances the prospect of perfectibility over the course of life on earth: 'Of all terrestrial Beings, Man is uncontestably the most perfectible.'

What then happens to the reprobate, who is damned and non-perfectible by definition? Bonnet did not tackle this question directly. However, he did discuss the old and classic question of whether pagans are necessarily damned.[61] This led him to start eliding the distinction between election and intellectual ability. Although 'the [pagan] Hottentot would seem a Brute [and] Newton an Angel', nevertheless 'the Hottentot participates in the same Essence as Newton and placed in other circumstances would have been able himself to *become* a Newton'.[62] All 'circumstances', both Newton's and the Hottentot's, are relative and synchronic. The old quandary had been diachronic and historical: what to do about Aristotle, for example, who, even though Christian theology

---

[60] Bonnet, *Idées sur l'art d'étudier et sur l'ordre et le but des études de philosophie rationelle*, in *Oeuvres*, vol. 18 octavo, pp. 179, 181.
[61] On this, see John Marenbon, *Pagans and Philosophers: The Problem of Paganism from Augustine to Leibniz* (Princeton: Princeton University Press, 2015), p. 281ff.
[62] Bonnet, *Palingénésie*, in *Oeuvres*, vol. 7, p. 415.

could not have existed without him, had died before Christ's atonement and so could not logically be declared elect. In Bonnet's view, Newton and the pagan Hottentot are of comparable perfectibility because they lie at a contemporaneous point on the developmental timeline of the human species. The 'faculties ... down here ... are developed to the same extent and susceptible to the same degree of growth'; it is a principle that applies to humankind in general.

If the residues of election and single predestination remain in Bonnet, it is for the same reason as they do in Malebranche. They prop up the sense of Order. He writes: 'The Author of Man, in recalling him to the moral Order, recalls him at the same time to reason ... This is the relation of cause to effect: a seed sown in the earth develops there.' This 'Man', however, is not unitary: 'God speaks to the Wise with the voice of Wisdom; to the People [the multitude] with that of Feeling and Authority. Great and generous Souls can conform to Order by love for Order. Souls of a weaker temper can be directed towards the same end by the hope of recompense or by the fear of punishment.' Thus in proposing, as Bonnet so often claims, to clear up the mess created by predestinarian debates, he shares their common presupposition of a fundamental intra-human division.

As for the debate over freedom and necessity, Bonnet transfers the notion of moral necessity from the realm of external, direct determination by God to a place within the internal realm of the human mind (*l'esprit*) itself. The endless debates about divine determination and personal responsibility have 'caused so much confusion in something that is very simple ... Determination in respect of Minds is a *moral* necessity, because it depends on the Mind's Faculties. A Mind is not determined to act in the way that a Body is determined to move. A Mind *determines itself* and is never *determined*.'[63]

Bonnet's account of *la psychologie* and the developmental idea is steeped in his religious beliefs, and centred on the resurrection.[64] Invoking the book of Revelation, he himself reminds us that his primary aim is to prove Christianity: 'Could one forget that the author of the *Psychologie* is also the author of the *Recherches sur les preuves du christianisme!*'[65] Leibniz had already seen a continuity between an earthly and a post-mortal interiority, but in order to do so he had conceived death as a re-enveloping of previously developed minds. Bonnet disliked this idea because it seemed

---

[63] Bonnet, *Palingénésie*, in *Oeuvres*, vol. 7, p. 635.   [64] Bonnet, *Essai de psychologie*, Préface, p. 8.
[65] Bonnet, *Essai de psychologie*, Avertissement, p. xi.

to involve a phase of retrogression and therefore a buckling, so to speak, of linear time.⁶⁶ He sought a smoother continuity of line. However, that continuity in the timed structure of the soul itself relied on the existence of preformed stages, which Bonnet surely got from his own experimental biology. (In his *Treatise on Insectology* of 1745, he had observed the pre-existence of future embryos in young aphids.)

In the *Essay on Psychology*, he went further and saw interiority as actually *constituted by* change: 'All is but change and development … The development of the soul is the consequence of its various modifications; and these modifications are the necessary effect of the play of the [bodily] organs, and of the circumstances that determine this – the number, the variety, the type of modifications determining the degree of perfection of the soul.' The language of necessity and determinism here encompasses both the experimental observation of bodies and their interaction with the largely predestinate condition of souls and minds.

We can see here the distance travelled from Augustine's definition of time itself as a regrettable 'distension' of mind, to the positive timeline characteristic of the eighteenth-century developmental idea. In a chapter of Bonnet's 1760 *Analytical Essay on the Faculties of the Soul* which clearly struck John Wesley, who translated and published it as a separate pamphlet, Bonnet writes again about a seamless continuity between the 'development' of the soul's terrestrial character and its existence and further development in the next. He invokes in passing the conventional idea of the ladder of nature, which is of course vertical and spatial, yet it is the horizontal, forward movement of the lives of both individual and species that catches the eye. Wesley's reliable enough translation gives a flavour:

> There is among men here on earth an almost infinite diversity of gifts, talents, knowledge, inclinations &c. The scale of humanity rises through innumerable steps from the brute man to the thinking man. This progression will continue no doubt in the life to come and will preserve the same essential relations: … the progress which we shall make here in knowledge and in virtue will determine the point from whence we shall begin our progress in the other life, or the place we shall there occupy.⁶⁷

This timeline that passes over the 'point' of death applies by definition only to an exclusive group of people. In addition to finding themselves willy-nilly

---

[66] Bonnet, *Palingénésie*, in *Oeuvres*, vol. 7, p. 209.
[67] John Wesley, *Conjectures Concerning the Nature of Future Happiness Translated from the French of Mons. Bonnet of Geneva* (Dublin: Dugdale, 1787), from Bonnet, *Essai analytique*, in *Oeuvres*, vols. 13–14.

in the right place at that point, they should have led earthly lives of progress in knowledge and virtue. They should be achievers. But even so this still seems secondary to the need for them to be *objectively* righteous. Bonnet grew up in a Calvinist environment where 'righteous' or 'justified' would have meant determinate and chosen, irrespective of any separately considered, 'congruent' personal achievements and morality. The development he describes is thus, at some underlying level, a necessary and thereby in some sense morally neutral development, one that would be the more easily adaptable in following centuries as the object of a neutral psychological science. If something gets carried over from the theory of election and reprobation to modern psychobiological explanations, it appears in the way Bonnet always manages to infiltrate a deterministic principle of causation into his description of merit and acquired skills.

The temporal structure of his preformationist psychology applies expressly now to 'the Individual', using the Christian model of resurrection:

> All the moments of our individual existence are indissolubly connected one with another. We do not pass from one state to another state without a sufficient reason. There are no *leaps*, properly so called. The *subsequent* state has always an *adequate* cause in the state which immediately *preceded* it. Death is not a *break* in the *chain*: it is the link that connects the two lives, or the two parts of the chain together.[68]

New 'states' of the mental realm arrive neither epigenetically (gradually and with no further explanation needed) nor miraculously (in spontaneous unexplainable leaps), but via a preformed temporal structure. Bonnet even speculates that some further 'senses', on top of the usual five, are currently 'folded up in infinite smallness within the location of the Soul ... [and] will unfold (*se développer*) once we are in heaven'.[69]

Into the theoretical space carved open by Malebranche and Leibniz, Bonnet inserts a concrete demonstration of precisely *how* one may infer from bodily to spiritual or intellectual preformation. He refers development specifically to the book of Revelation: each individual, he says, has an 'interior Revelation' that consists in the brain's 'developing in another life'.[70] It was from this kind of connection, as much as from Condillac's abstractions, that modern developmental science was forged.

Bonnet's most explicit attempt to synthesize biological and psychological development came in his 1769 *Palingenesis*. This word, drawn

---

[68] Wesley, *Conjectures*. Italics in original.   [69] Bonnet, *Essai analytique*, in *Oeuvres*, vol. 14, p. 351.
[70] Bonnet, *Essai analytique*, p. 232.

from the theory of the transmigration of souls, evoked notions of regeneration, recapitulation and spiritual rebirth. Attacking 'our epigenicists', he makes 'development', both physical and psychological, central to preformation: 'If everything has been *preformed* from the beginning; if nothing is *engendered*; and if what we inappropriately call a *Generation* is only the principle of a *Development* which renders visible and palpable what was invisible and impalpable before, then the germs were from the start boxed up inside each other.'[71]

Under the heading 'Explanation of Leibnizian development', Bonnet says he is happy to see 'our great Metaphysician [Leibniz] adopting so clearly an *organic preformation* and a correlative *pre-existence* of Souls',[72] but that he himself would go further. He would connect Leibniz's 'pre-established' harmony between body and soul concretely to the rest of the cosmos. Noting 'the pre-existence of a Soul in the Germ' in individuals, and linking this to the principle of temporal structure, he goes on to suggest it as a principle in the development of the universe as a whole:

> The Absolute Power could enclose within the first Germ of every organized Being the consequent Germs that correspond to the various revolutions which our Planet has undergone ... Our World has existed in the form of the Worm or Caterpillar: it is currently in the form of the Chrysalis: the last revolution will reveal to it that of the Butterfly.

Here, Bonnet's echoing of past debates over congruism (predestination with a secondary role for individual agency) is also the pre-echoing of a modern psychobiological argument (nature with a secondary role for nurture): 'The judgment which the Sovereign judge shall make concerning us, will have its foundation in the degree of perfection intellectual and moral which we shall acquire upon earth; or, *which is the same thing*, in the use we shall have made of our faculties and of the talents which shall have been committed to us.'[73] The picture begins to have a statistical appearance. 'The degree of acquired perfection' in the above sense 'will determine, in the life to come, the degree of happiness or glory which each individual shall enjoy'. Again, he invokes Revelation in support. 'Revelation also gives its sanction to these philosophical principles. It establishes expressly this gradation of happiness or of glory.' And even this gradation is not static: 'Because the distance between created beings

---

[71] Bonnet, *Palingénésie*, in *Oeuvres*, vol. 7, p. 151.   [72] Bonnet, *Palingénésie*, p. 202.
[73] Bonnet, *Palingénésie*, p. 191. My italics.

and the uncreated Being, between finite and infinite, is infinite, created beings will tend continually towards supreme perfection, without ever arriving at it.' And so we should 'insert the *resurrection* within the order of purely *natural* events',[74] whose determinism is physical (*une préordination physique*).

We should note here, finally, how in the developmental idea time is necessarily qualified by the relativities of speed. Fast, slow or mean? Again, Bonnet anticipates and perhaps instructs Rousseau:

> Would you make the sublime theory of infinitude enter into the brain of a child? This brain contains at present all the [preformed] fibres necessary to the acquisition of this theory: but you cannot yet put them into action. Every thing in the works of nature is done by degrees: a *development* more or less slow conducts all beings to the *perfection* that *properly* belongs to them. Our soul is only beginning to unfold itself; but this plant, so weak in its principles, so slow in its progress, will extend its roots and its branches into eternity.[75]

Not more or less fast, not even at a mean speed, but more or less *slow*. As Rousseau would repeatedly insist, excessive speed – the premature anticipation of adulthood – spells disaster. This too was inferred from physical development: Bonnet had already emphasized the importance of steady-as-she-goes when he wrote about the 'development' of the butterfly, out of which his portrayal of the mind arose.

To conclude, the fact that linear time extends into heaven suggests an unbroken line between the mundane and the sacred. In this sense, several passages in Bonnet's text (those which tend to belong with his engagement with Leibniz) come just short of being imported verbatim by Rousseau into *Emile*. Bonnet calls on his readers to abandon Leibniz's occasional and 'obscure' attributions of causality to miracles – that is, to the 'particular operation[s]' of God. There is now room for a general law of causality embedded within the psychological nature of human beings themselves. If Rousseau is *with* Bonnet on some of this, he is also possibly *from* Bonnet when the latter says, for example:

> Is not early infancy a state of pure Animality ... And yet is it not very true that Man raises himself by purely natural means to the most sublime knowledge of the intelligent Being? ... Does the effect not correspond here with its natural cause? Is not the state of the Soul exactly relative to that of the organs?[76]

---

[74] Bonnet, *Essai analytique*, in *Oeuvres*, vol. 14, p. 233. Italics in original.
[75] In Wesley, 'Conjectures', p. 4, and Bonnet, *Essai analytique*, p. 347. Italics in original. [76] Ibid.

The 'abject Animal', as he calls the infant, one day gets to be the 'exalted intelligent Being', the adult. Having identified the 'natural cause' of this as 'development' itself, Bonnet now sacralizes it and makes it fully identifiable with stadial determinism. As noted, he did not engage directly with the problem of reprobation. He did not need to, because a true science of development demands the abjection of the child instead.

CHAPTER 7

Emile: *Rousseau's Well-Ordered Developer*

From the perspective of the previous chapter, we can now see how Rousseau's *Emile* (1762) will lay the foundation for a whole theory of normal psychological and educational development as it finally emerges from that of election; the consequences of this for the debates about freedom and necessity raised by the earlier theory; its affirmation of a temporally structured notion of order within the individual interior; and the connection of all these things to Rousseau's sociopolitical thought.

Many commentators on this seminal work have focused on its effect on later writers, as if the value of studying early modern thought lay in its being modern rather than early. *Emile* is undoubtedly a key work in early modern conceptual history, but it is also where the developmental idea finally crawls out of its own chrysalis. Election and preformation retain subliminal presences: they are the unspoken basis on which Rousseau establishes the ubiquity of the word itself, 'development'. He uses it in two ways. First, he sometimes, like Condillac, uses it in a metaphysical sense, to describe the boundaries of a specifically human interiority; he had already used it in this way in the work that launched him on the world, the *Discourse on the Origin and Foundations of Inequality among Men* (1755). The second sense comes only with *Emile*, which is saturated by the word and assumes that the reader will understand it as something empirically observable. It and the word 'progress' are indicators of Rousseau's personal religious outlook. Failure to reconcile the era's doctrinal differences over predestination had led to a chemical reaction whose solvent was natural religion. In Rousseau's case this meant: a *religion* that can be explained by reason without the aid of scripture, and a *nature* that subsumes the idea of grace.[1] The latter is a word he rarely uses, but that is because he already

---

[1] On the sources of Rousseau's religious beliefs, see Jean Starobinski, *Jean-Jacques Rousseau, Transparency and Obstruction* (Chicago: University of Chicago Press, 1988); Jeremiah Alberg, *A Reinterpretation of Rousseau* (New York: Palgrave, 2007).

takes as read that it informs human nature, and the *reasoning* as well as the willing nature. The necessary divide between possession of grace and its absence has been transferred to this new picture.

As Rousseau's model pupil, Emile embodies a certain idea of Christian redemption while also being its first expression in modern developmental form. In Augustine, the goal of human interiority was to overcome time by achieving union with God in heaven; in *Emile* maturity, as the goal or ideal standard against which all child and adolescent development is measured, is also an overcoming of time – but naturally, here on earth. In the interim, the late seventeenth century had seen a growing tendency to centre the description of human interiority on natural dispositions. Religious writers across the board suspected that this might displace the siting of the developmental goal itself to nature, and on earth. Their suspicions were justifiable, as this would indeed become a core motive in Enlightenment thought.[2] The new version of interior status with a specifically human nature at its core, which Jansenists and Calvinists perceived as a threat and a rival to election, then became (thanks partly to their own noisy obsession with refuting it) an actual rival, and finally, over the course of the next century, would replace the now obsolete theory.[3]

It is only by incorporating the previous religious history within our understanding that we can grasp the modernity of the works by which Rousseau is judged to have been most influential on European thought: *On the Social Contract* (1761) and *Emile*. The latter has been slightly marginalized by posterity's engagement with Rousseau the social and political theorist, but Rousseau himself saw *Emile* as the centrepiece of his life's work and his optimal statement on the nature of man. On the one hand, the young Emile seems to epitomize all the potential of the Enlightenment. On the other hand, if we abstract from the fictional character and ask of the text 'Who develops?' the residual answer is: one of the elect. And if we ask 'What enables the young person to develop?' the residual answer is: a divine temporal order. The theory of election which Rousseau rejected at one level was at a deeper level re-theorized. In fact *Emile* may well have been the cure for Rousseau's personal anxiety about his own elect status. As a young adult in the 1730s, reared in the fiercely Calvinist environment of Geneva, he had accepted predestination. In his *Confessions* he recalls that his reason for

---

[2] For this aspect of Rousseau, see Lee Maclean, *The Free Animal: Rousseau on Free Will and Human Nature* (Toronto: University of Toronto Press, 2013), especially chapter 2.
[3] See Goodey, 'Exclusion from the eucharist: the reshaping of idiocy in the seventeenth-century church', in (ed.) Patrick McDonagh, *Intellectual Disability: A Conceptual History 1200–1900* (Manchester: Manchester University Press, 2018).

turning against it was his gloom about not being certain of his own election.[4]

His introductory remarks to the 1755 *Discourse on Inequality* still make passing reference to election. He intends to create a theory of human science on the basis of 'hypothetical reasonings' like those which, since Newton, 'are used by our physicists'. 'Let us begin by setting aside all the facts,' he says. It is no use 'pursuing historical truths' – by which he means here (a) facts about the inequality of grace between elect and reprobate, and (b) the truths of Holy Scripture, which has registered those facts. Is this mere irony? It may equally show that Rousseau still maintains a residually positive character for the theory of election, if only in order to relegate its importance by asserting how much more important are the distinctions of nature than those of grace (which in any case he has relocated *within* nature).[5] He was possibly also trying to outfox the censors. What is clear, though, is that he was not disagreeing with the theory because of its obsolescence, but because scriptural 'facts' and 'truths' are not to be cited against the Newtonian 'reasonings' he is proposing as an alternative. By 1761 and the philosophical novel *Julie*, its most sympathetic character fully rejects the idea that saving grace comes arbitrarily to some and not to others.[6] Another firm abandonment comes just after *Emile*, in which the reason given is no novelty: it is the old sentimental one, namely that the damnation of reprobates suggests a maleficent God.[7]

This was the context in which 'development', under precisely that label, became central for Rousseau. As we saw in the previous chapter, the term had begun to be used in the 1750s by contemporaries such as Buffon, Condillac and Bonnet, with whom Rousseau was intellectually and in Condillac's case personally acquainted. But when Condillac, for example, wrote about the mind having 'origins', he did not mean by this the developmental causes of psychological states; he meant only the immediate source for the mind's *ideas*: 'origins' were locational, not temporal, and were situated in the here and now of the sensations. Rousseau, however, sought the causes of psychological change and the origins of interiority in time, in the *history* of the first humans.

---

[4] Jean-Jacques Rousseau, *The Confessions* (Ware: Wordsworth, 1996), p. 236.
[5] (Ed.) Maurice Cranston, Rousseau, *A Discourse on the Origin and Foundations of Inequality among Men* (London: Penguin, 1984), p. 78; see also the editor's comment on this passage, p. 176.
[6] Rousseau, *Julie, ou la nouvelle Héloïse*, Letter 7.
[7] Rousseau, *Letter to Beaumont, Letters Written from the Mountain, and Related Writings*, (eds.) Christopher Kelly and Eve Grace (Hanover, NH: Dartmouth College Press, 2012), pp. 29, 204.

The eighteenth century was fascinated by the origins of society. Rousseau's *Discourse on Inequality* proposed a 'man of nature', antecedent to society, who might nevertheless become a part of the civil order as an equal member. When he came to write about the ideal education of the young Emile, he expressed this as an ordered natural growth that prepares the individual for citizenship and avoids the personal chaos that comes from failing to accord with the objective laws of timed interiority. Emphasis shifts away from the actual *content* of moral and cognitive interiority, as, for example, in medieval conceptions of innate 'common ideas', and towards its structured stages. These stages appear as natural kinds and are validated as such by analogies drawn with the preformed developmental stages of the bodily organism. Any departure from the temporal schema – failure to progress to the upcoming stage or, even worse, a premature anticipation of it – is due to and leads to a false representation of man (*l'homme de nos fantaisies*), by contrast with his true representation as the man of nature (*celui de la nature est fait autrement*).[8]

Rousseau's Adventures with the Word 'Development'

Rousseau's favoured terms for the linear trajectory of the young person's interior life towards his goal as a moral being are *le progrès* and above all *le développement*. 'Progress', the longer-established of the two, had begun life as a military term meaning to advance with inevitability, and later described formal processions at court; it expressed a sense of forward movement by external necessity. In addition, in the late seventeenth century it started to signify formalized time: a *staged* progress. Locke, for example, uses 'progress' synonymously with 'progression' in mathematics: the 'infinity of space' is 'a supposed endless progression of the mind, over what repeated ideas of space it please'. Thus a term originally specific to the externalities of mathematics adheres to interior progress, of a certain abstract kind.[9] Rousseau replaces this with more specific usages. Rather than the progress of the person in general, there is the progress of abilities (*les forces*), progress of the mind (*l'esprit*), progress of reason and progress of the affections or passions. He describes it, moreover, not only as *progrès naturel* but also *progrès ordonné*. This temporalization of order is such that when he writes about '*l'ordre et le progrès*' of knowledge the two words are synonymous.

---

[8] Rousseau, *Emile ou de l'éducation* (Paris: Flammarion, 1966), p. 51. [9] Locke, *An Essay*, 2.5.16.

7 *Emile*: Rousseau's Well-Ordered Developer

The word 'development' was more of a novelty. Locke does not use it ('development' in any sense is rarely found in English before the 1790s, and then only with an italicized French spelling – an exotic novelty). We have seen how early on Condillac had used 'development' and 'progress' in his psychology, but very generally, not as one of its substantive operational elements. There was a role for time in Condillac's psychology, but it involved only 'acquisition'; and what would be acquired, if the operations themselves were at optimal efficiency, was mere 'self-preservation', not the goal of actual 'happiness' or salvation itself. Rousseau does propose a goal: the formation of a 'moral being'. Although Condillac's use of 'development' surely influenced *Emile*, Rousseau absorbs the former's metaphysical notion within 'development' as a set of empirically observable mechanisms.

The first sign of this comes in the *Discourse*, where he uses the word to describe a quality of the mind's 'faculties' and 'operations' (a terminology still evoking scholastic psychology). In *Emile* it goes beyond this in being more varied and detailed. Its novel importance is hinted at in Rousseau's cryptic opening salvo: 'The internal development of our faculties and our organs is the education that comes to us from nature: the use which we learn to make of this development is the education of men; and the sum of our own experience with the objects which touch us is the education of things.'[10] Thereafter the word saturates *Emile*. The human constitution develops. Limbs and physiognomy develop. The sense of smell develops. The psychological faculties develop, and the faculty of reason develops as the composite of all of them. Conscience develops. Capabilities (*les forces*) develop. Curiosity develops. Knowledge (*la science*) develops. Intelligence develops. The mind (*l'esprit*) develops. Needs develop. Awareness of self in relation to others (*le moi relatif*) develops. The passions develop. Ability to control the passions develops. And the principle of development develops.

These usages already represent a whole world view. Once he had deployed the word, Rousseau's successors might have wondered how they had ever got by without it. The reason for its enthusiastic take-up was that it associated order with time (after 'development', 'order' is the second most important word in *Emile*). This becomes clear in certain passages that highlight chronological stages. In his triumphant ending to Book Two, for example, a key moment in the book's structure, Rousseau writes:

> I heard the late Lord Hyde tell how one of his friends, on returning from Italy after three years away, wanted to check out the progress of his son, who

---

[10] Rousseau, *Emile*, p. 37.

was nine or ten. One evening father and son went walking across a meadow with his tutor and Lord Hyde himself. Some youngsters were amusing themselves flying kites. The father said casually to his son, 'Where is the kite whose shadow we can see here?' Without hesitation, without raising his head, the child said, 'Back over the highway.' And indeed, Lord Hyde added, the highway was between the sun and ourselves. . . . What promise in [the] child! *The question is precisely that of age.*[11]

Translators sometimes render this final sentence of Book Two as, 'The question is age-appropriate' – that is, it asks where the kite is. But Rousseau's 'question' here is a much bigger one: age, he says, is the dominant factor. It is the *whole* question.

On the one hand, there is the boy's promise. This word still has the seventeenth-century resonance of election, often referred to as 'God's promise'; the boy belongs to the *nouveaux* elect, so to speak. On the other hand, promise is something that must not be tampered with – hence the father's assessment must 'casually' go undetected by the boy. That is because the site of its determination is beyond human control; it lies in the internal, ordered temporal 'nature' that has replaced divine Providence. Nature has taught the young heir and so should teach Emile, but this can only happen if no one tries to trigger prematurely the next innately natural stage. The stadial operations as such, fixed in and by time, constitute the ideal and essential nature of what it is to be human. They will function in any child who has not been spoiled by the inappropriate or premature intervention of teachers, or by being accidentally exposed to contamination from the unsuitable company and passions of others – a legacy of the Jansenist anxiety about preventing their own putatively elect children from lapse. (Rousseau would recall in his *Confessions* the beatings he got as a child from his beloved nurse, speculating that it was why he needed physical punishment for sexual arousal as an adult, and the shame he expresses about this seems a new phenomenon.)

Development and Progress: Theoretical Aspects in Rousseau

Malebranche, while recognizing temporal aspects of divine order, had regarded them as secondary. Condillac went on to make order the very axis of his theory of education, and gave it a crudely temporal character when he wrote that, in the skill set of the child, certain things must not come before others. Analysis (*la décomposition*), for example, must not

---

[11] Rousseau, *Emile*, p. 209. My italics.

precede 'observation'. The child starts off observing things in a certain order – but 'with the development of his faculties' they have to be *re-ordered*.[12] It is Rousseau, however, who introduces divine order directly into the temporal structure of human interiority. Emile, he says, experiences 'the profoundest indifference' when he hears things he does not understand, and 'when he begins to trouble himself with the big questions, it is not because he has heard them aired, but when the natural progress of his insights inclines his investigations that way'.[13] The tutor who fails to allow his pupil to develop as he should will be 'truly abandoning the order of nature ... The balance will be upset.' The terminology may seem ambiguous – balance has spatial connotations – but the surrounding context defines it in terms of time.

While Malebranche had on the surface dismissed psychology (knowledge of other people's minds is impossible, he said), Rousseau brought it to the threshold of a modern discipline: we *can* have such a science – but only if its order is temporal. His attribution of 'order' to chronological structure betrays an anxiety about the passions and the will as well as the intellect. True, he has gone well beyond Jansenism and has a positive view of the passions – but only as long as they are obedient to that structure. His anxiety is no longer about original sin as usually understood. He does not do away with it; he pulls it out of the past and extends it into the future, so that it becomes something to be avoided rather than (as in the theory of election) excused. 'If you wish to submit the nascent passions to order and regulation, extend the terrain over which they develop, so that they have time to arrange themselves as they emerge; your sole job is to let nature do the arranging.'[14]

This means: let an *interior, invisible* nature do the arranging. But it raises a problem. As a behaviourist might ask here, how can we know what is going on in the interior unless from external signs? Whereas predestinarian writers disapproved of trying to find out who was or was not elect (it was God's business alone), Rousseau posits an a priori necessity for the expert tutor to observe interiority directly. Even so, 'observations are difficult because, to make them, we must reject what is in front of our eyes and seek examples where successive developments occur according to the order of nature'.[15] To meet the difficulty, what he does offer is the negative example: he offers to show us how, why and in whom development does *not* happen as it should. And, as formerly with reprobation, it still seems to mean most

---

[12] Condillac, *Cours d'étude pour l'instruction des jeunes gens*, 3ᵉ ed. (Paris: Dufart, 1794), vol. I, p. 5.
[13] Rousseau, *Emile*, p. 338.   [14] Rousseau, *Emile*, p. 284.   [15] Rousseau, *Emile*, p. 285.

people. Few positive real-life examples of a developer appear in *Emile*, and of course the main one, as we saw, has to be the son of a Milord. From the many negative examples around us we can draw conclusions as to the right way of going about things.

The right way consists not in the knowledge of good and evil but in avoiding *premature* knowledge of them. Malebranche had already hinted at this:

> The ordinary conversation which children are forced to have with their nursemaids, or even with their mothers, who often have no education, ends up with their minds being abandoned and corrupted ... They only talk to them about things to do with the senses, and in such a way as to confirm in them the false judgments of the senses. In short, they sow in their minds the seeds of all their own weakness ... what happens is that not being accustomed to seek truth, nor to appreciate it, they eventually become incapable of discerning it, or to make any use of their reason.[16]

Rousseau writes that children obtain knowledge from a corrupt social environment that contaminates their biochemistry. Children (of a certain social class, as we must always assume) get it from 'shameless servants' and 'giggling governesses':

> A moulded, well-mannered, civilized child who is just waiting for the ability to put into practice the premature education he has received, never fails to seize the moment when this ability arrives in him. Rather than wait for it, he speeds it up, it gives his blood a premature fermentation ... It is not nature that stimulates him, it is he who forces nature ... The true pace of nature is more gradual and more slow.[17]

'Slow' here carries the opposite value of slow in the modern sense of retardation. For Rousseau slow is steady, meaning also properly structured. It wins the race. In this sense, although the modern developmental idea is already visible in *Emile*, such *développement* is still poised between 'progressing towards' and 'unfolding from'.

Development: Free or Necessary?

The sprawling intuitiveness of Rousseau's text gave later educationists latitude to see him *both* as the pioneer of an ordered science of education *and* as the liberator of the developing child. *Emile* may be the founding text of an emancipatory education, but is this young person really a free, autonomous

---

[16] Malebranche, *Recherche*, in *Oeuvres*, vol. 1, p. 259.   [17] Rousseau, *Emile*, p. 285.

decision maker, or is he his tutor's puppet and hence that of the author? He is both, but the puppetry is at least as much in evidence as the liberation. This ambiguity is clearly rooted in previous debates as to whether the elect individual might have a 'congruent' free will separate from God's predetermined will. As Pascal had said, even if the individual does have such a will, it is always subordinate to God's.[18] On the broader question of freedom and necessity, *Emile* remains undecided. Autonomous or automaton?

Emile's education, says Rousseau, resembles the principle of animation in an animated statue. This was a common modelling tool for early psychologists. It stands two-thirds of the way along the direct path that runs from the medieval monasteries' 'living statues' of Christ to today's AI 'thinking machines'. Medieval pilgrims had flocked to see Christ miraculously nodding his head on cue, a monk having discreetly slipped inside to operate the pulleys. From this folk memory, the thought experiment of the sentient statue was frequently invoked in the century before Rousseau. Malebranche invoked it to support his theodicy.[19] Leibniz resorted to the analogy of quasi-human automata to explain divine predetermination.[20] Buffon hypothesized 'a man who has actually forgotten everything or who wakes up innocent of everything around him' and whose sensations progressively organize themselves.[21] Condillac and Bonnet both fantasized about a statue that learns empirically along Lockean lines. All these statues in some way are harbingers of child development in its modern normative guise. Rousseau wrote that Condillac's version would not work because it presupposes a creature fully physically formed at birth, who would thus be equivalent to a 'perfect imbecile ... a statue lacking motion'.[22] Disability here comes to be defined precisely by lack of development. Conversely, the first two books of *Emile* establish that early childhood itself is now to be seen as a state of complete imbecility, after which (and only then) 'development' actually takes off,[23] with Emile the automaton being preprogrammed to think for him/itself.

Emile's tutor, in whose persona Rousseau operates the pulleys, embodies the nascent developmentalist expertise. Emile is free in the sense of being free to follow the one true path already laid out for him. There is here a residue of the Calvinist interpretation of freedom in which 'God made

---

[18] See Chapter 4, page 96.
[19] Malebranche, *Refléxions sur la promotion physique*, in *Oeuvres*, vol. 16, p. 85.
[20] Leibniz, *Theodicy*, I.63.66.   [21] Buffon, *Histoire naturelle*, cited in Roger, *Buffon*, p. 87.
[22] Rousseau, *Emile*, p. 69.
[23] On this, see Jørn Schøsler, 'La position sensualiste de Jean-Jacques Rousseau', *Revue romane* 18/1 (1978).

man with abilities to fulfil His commands'.[24] Man is born free, but everywhere he is in the wrong kind of chains. Here are some new ones, with the additional feature of a timer mechanism. Rousseau has removed miracles and 'particular volitions' from it, replacing them with a general lawfulness. 'The preoccupations of childhood amount to little: any evil that slips in is not irremediable, and there may be good to come later. But it is not in his first years that Man begins to live in the true sense.'[25] Even if the word 'development' still suggests an unfolding of something already there, the timer assumes a human being set initially at zero: 'born stupid', to use Rousseau's exact phrase.[26] Thus his reputation as liberator of the child is achieved at some cost: he 'can only discover the specificity of the child by denying him his rational capacity'.[27]

Not only that, but even once the state of childhood idiocy is past, Emile should still be prevented from turning into a man overnight. Again, biochemistry is involved. As the body grows, so too 'the spirits designed to calm the blood' are being formed; and if they get prematurely diverted – that is, if 'what is designed for the achievement of perfection serves [instead] for the production of another individual' – then 'nature's work remains imperfect'. Rousseau reduces Augustine's anxieties about lust to a coy, scientized prurience. 'The operations of the mind (*l'esprit*) are sensitive to this degradation', with the result that the soul (*l'âme*) becomes as feeble as the body: 'Generally one sees more spiritual vigour in men whose youth has been preserved from premature corruption than in those whose disorder began immediately they had the power to avail themselves of it.'[28]

He provides a link between the individual and the society here by continuing: 'and that doubtless is one reason why populations who possess moral conventions usually surpass in good sense and spiritedness those who do not'. This passage exposes the binary underlay without which no scientific knowledge of the human interior can be claimed. The second group may have 'vague qualities which they may call mind, astuteness, shrewdness', but only the first has the 'great and noble functions of wisdom and reason that honour Man by their virtues and their genuinely useful concerns'.

The salvific goal is located in what Rousseau calls Happiness (*le Bonheur*), which is now firmly located on earth and is made up of 'all

---

[24] Dudley Fenner, 'A Defence of the Thirty-Nine Articles of the Church of England', 10.2, in *The Artes of Logike and Rhethorique* (Middelburg: R. Schilders, 1584).
[25] Rousseau, *Emile*, p. 301.   [26] Rousseau, *Emile*, p. 37.
[27] Christine Quarfood, *Condillac: la statue et l'enfant* (Paris: L'Harmattan, 2002), pp. 232–61.
[28] Quarfood, *Condillac*, p. 301.

the rest of [Emile's] life', his maturity.²⁹ For Augustine the destination could have been nothing other than heaven. The nascent human sciences did not simply swap this for happiness in the sense of the earthly well-being of all. For Pascal and Malebranche as we saw, happiness lay in the company of the elect whether above or on earth; it was still (tautologously) *le Bonheur des bienheureux* – that is, the happiness of the elect.³⁰ Thus it would not be surprising if the population to which Rousseau's 'happiness' refers, though by now involving earthly well-being, were still in its own way a restricted one too. For example, 'it is manifestly against the law of nature ... that a child should govern an old man, that an imbecile should lead a wise man'.³¹ And these are only the extreme cases of a division that for Rousseau applies across society, which still needs a caste of 'great men'.

Be that as it may, the goal of Rousseau's educational theory is not strictly Utopian. It is not the ideal order or nothing. He suggests intervention when things are going wrong, especially in the relationship between the passions and reason. Whereas Augustine had seen this relationship in one lofty sweep, Rousseau envisages a separate but concurrent development of both, in stages over the human lifetime.

They must be jointly calibrated. 'We have seen', he says, 'how the cultivated human mind' achieves a mature capability for abstract thought:

> And I would willingly agree that it would only get there naturally, surrounded as it is by society, at a later age. But that very society inevitably causes an accelerated progress of the passions, and if one did not also accelerate a progress of the awareness that serves to rule these passions, then one really would be abandoning the order of nature.³²

The idea of temporal structures makes it possible to analyse this 'order of nature' further, at the level of faculty psychology. As he continues, picking up from Bonnet:

> If one has not mastered how to moderate an excessively rapid development, it is necessary to match that rapidity in the case of other, corresponding developments; so that order is not inverted, so that things that should be proceeding together are in no way separated, and so that Man, as a whole at every moment of his life, is not at one stage in one of his faculties, and at a different point in the others.

---

[29] Rousseau, *Emile, manuscrit Favre*, in *Oeuvres complètes* (Paris: Pléiade, 1969), vol. 4.
[30] Malebranche, *Recherche*, in *Oeuvres*, vol. 1, p. 86.   [31] Rousseau, *A Discourse*, p. 137.
[32] Rousseau, *Emile*, p. 339.

In the last resort, however, alongside direct tutorial intervention, the stadial determinism of a temporally structured order remains the dominant theme. In stadial determinism, the developmental idea orders the subject. Just as with the previous century's sequence of regeneration, justification and sanctification that marks the arrival of faith, the pupil's understanding of physical necessity must precede that of utility, which in turn must precede that of morality and religion. In the curriculum of nature, a series of points in time is prescribed before which certain things cannot happen and after which they ought to have happened or the next point will never be reached. As the developing individual goes through each prescribed chronological stage, he is warned not to eat of the tree whereof nature 'commanded thee that thou shouldest not eat' – at least, not until nature says he is ready.

Temporal Order and 'Mental Logic'

We saw in Chapter 2 that the late Middle Ages had created a separation between 'artificial' and 'natural' logic – that is, between logic as a set of formal propositions existing out there and logic as a feature of human interiority – but that it also assumed a correspondence between them. The Malebranchian idea of divine order, whether static or temporal, always incorporated logic, and this 'played a large role in Rousseau's *Emile*'.[33] As developmental time started to intrude into how we perceive order in the workings of the human mind, the presupposed correspondence between external and internal logics became a simple circularity. Logical consequences that worked perfectly well in a static picture of the cosmos became precarious, since time introduces the notion of unpredictable 'future contingents'.[34] Subsequently *Emile* was among the first major historical indicators of the modern presupposition whereby logic as system and the logical reasoning of the individual subject coalesce, underwriting thereby the human sciences' conception of the human species as a cognitive entity.

Rousseau's Emile, the fictional subject, and Rousseau's *Emile*, the prescriptive system, hold each other fast, as one day would psychological development and developmental psychology. The operations of logical order, conceived thus, were given a place within the internal, cognitive existence of the human individual in which order as a hierarchy of levels

---

[33] André Robinet, 'Lexicographie philosophique et paléographique: à propos d'ordre dans la *Profession de foi du vicaire savoyard*', in *Studie filosofici* 1 (1978), p. 39ff.
[34] A. N. Prior, *Past, Present and Future* (Oxford: Oxford University Press, 1967).

became order as a hierarchy of incremental states. (It should be added that Rousseau includes among these the emotions and the imagination.)[35] This adds a psychological content to Arthur Lovejoy's description of the eighteenth century's 'temporalizing of the chain of being'. Rousseau was securing for interior status the final shift of order from the *y* axis, the place of the human species on the ladder of nature, to the *x* axis, the individual reasoner's time on earth and its stadial make-up. Indeed, in the first draft of *Emile*, the sections were entitled 'Age 1', 'Age 2' etc., as if it were a textbook (*l'âge* can equally be rendered as 'stage'). Only in the published version did these become 'Book 1', 'Book 2' etc. Rousseau was trying to explain the problem of discontinuity and 'leaps' in time that we noted in previous chapters. Emile's pseudo-liberation can be seen as an attempt to solve the problem of how *structure* – a concept much easier to intuit in spatial terms – deals with temporal *change*.

This is indicated in Rousseau's injunction, *laissez mûrir l'enfance dans les enfants*: what should mature in the child is childhood, not adulthood.[36] The child's purity is an object of conservation; however, it can only be conserved to the extent that it also pushes forward, developmentally, towards the goal of reified adulthood, by fixed internal stages. Pascal and the Jansenists had launched this paradox, but for them and likewise for Malebranche the ability to abandon personal disorder was still dependent upon obedience to certain inbuilt dictates of grace, regardless of age. Grace lay behind, and was a given. In Rousseau, the obedience is to certain timed structures of nature, through which alone emerges grace: grace, in the form of perfected nature, lies ahead. In waiting for the pupil's disorder to be abandoned, one is also expecting a true nature to reveal itself. Gone are the time-defying miracles: the wise head on young shoulders, the *enfant sage*. Rousseau's dictum that advancing too quickly is more dangerous than advancing too slowly reformulates Pascal's anxiety about lapsing from elect status. His ideal citizen preserves his status and purity not so much by pushing back against the Devil as by following a properly timetabled curriculum.

Piaget would later replicate Rousseau's injunction by seeing development over time as forming the very substructure of a human 'mental logic': wrong test answers are now also 'age-appropriate' answers, the mistakes having their own consistent patterns, and are therefore also 'correct' in the

---

[35] See Michael Sonenscher, *Jean-Jacques Rousseau: The Division of Labour, the Concept of the Imagination and the Concept of Federal Government* (Oxford: Blackwell, 2020).
[36] Rousseau, *Emile*, p. 113.

sense that young children's cognitive processes are specifically different from those of adults. Piaget would go on to define the very 'structure' of 'mental logic', with its cognitive processes, as 'a system of transformations' which over time 'self-regulate' incrementally, so as to maintain their own 'stability' and 'properties of conservation'.[37]

The General Will in Rousseau: Psychological Aspects

To understand fully the relationship between the psychological and the social in Rousseau, we need to consider Patrick Riley's pathbreaking book *The General Will before Rousseau*. Riley describes how the general will had originally been a theological concept. It is not mentioned by Augustine; Aquinas mentions an 'antecedent' will to save, though he does not call it 'general'.[38] The phrase was coined by Arnauld, in order to justify the harshness of the fact that God's will to save only operates in favour of a few. Rousseau found in the religion of the Jansenists as well as Malebranche a vocabulary with which to elevate and sanctify the principle of a civic sphere. Just as God's choice of a few for salvation (*le salut eternel*)[39] had been a general rule that overrode the effect of their own agency, so the common welfare (*le salut de la Patrie*)[40] overrides the particular individual's self-interest. This substitution of society for God and of the common good for salvation came after certain key interventions by the Protestant Pierre Bayle in the 1680s and Denis Diderot in the *Encyclopedia*. What emerged from Rousseau's engagement with them was a whole theory,[41] and as Riley notes, this civic and political vision was 'integrate[d] ... into a developmental moral psychology', in which 'education cannot leap over the ideas and relations that are understood at different [calendar] ages'.[42]

Riley's passing insight is rich in consequences. Malebranche, endorsed by Leibniz,[43] had described God's general will as a general principle of lawfulness; Bayle suggested that such a principle could explain the divine determination of physical, material nature too.[44] This lent it a sense of objectivity which, as well as helping to tone down the conflicts over election and see them as mere 'strife about words', might also lead to the discovery of a 'lawfulness' in human behaviour too, and in its interior

---

[37] Jean Piaget, *Structuralism* (London: Routledge, 1971), p. 14.   [38] Aquinas, *De Veritate*, 23.2.
[39] Rousseau, *Emile*, p. 336.   [40] Rousseau, *On the Social Contract*, book 4, chapter 6.
[41] See Riley, *The General Will before Rousseau*, pp. 202–6.
[42] Riley, *The General Will before Rousseau*, p. 216.   [43] Leibniz, *Theodicy*, p. 170.
[44] Riley, *The General Will before Rousseau*, p. 98.

causes. Since the justice of divine order was a precondition of religious belief, its lawfulness then had to be relocated somewhere. That somewhere turned out to be a *general* theory of *human* justice. The general will Bayle had in mind was still of the divine sort, but when he gave specific examples of how it could be justified, they came less from election and reprobation than from the moral practices of people in this world. The common point, divine or civic, was to justify the authority of a general set of rules even when the undeserved consequences it has for any particular individual are bad. This is the world for which Emile must be fitted.

As well as justice, and connected to it, the other important principle involving general lawfulness was *causation*, an increasing interest in which was characteristic of the emergence of the human sciences from theology. Divine lawfulness was expressed in grace and nature at once, and this would open the way for physical and interior causation to come under the same joint rubric. It signalled a further step in the objectivization process marked by Bayle's recognition that 'there is nothing worthier of the greatness of God than to maintain general laws'.[45] It was this that led Montesquieu to underwrite his theory that a concatenation of general earthly causes can be moral, not just physical – a major step in the emergence of the human sciences.

Alongside this, as we saw in Chapter 5, Montesquieu's occasional references to the theory of election were not just some embarrassing residuum. True, earthly laws by their very existence reveal that the moral habits of a particular society belong to a certain time; there are particular laws, he says, which express the physical and cultural conditions peculiar to that society and its period, and they do not remain constant. Nevertheless, when he sought to illustrate how the concept of Order might accommodate change, his aim was still to prove that there is a more general lawfulness operating throughout the universe, including that regarding salvation. Order, even when displaced wholesale to the secular and temporal realm, still had to express God's place in nature.

It was just that particulars, and particular causes, were an increasingly popular field of investigation. Following Montesquieu's account of how particular societal and cultural laws arise, Rousseau discovered 'particular laws' of his own, which he reassembled into a general lawfulness concerning the human individual's internal developmental nature; and he did so in a way that corresponds with Montesquieu's way of accounting for change

---

[45] Pierre Bayle, *Various Thoughts on the Occasion of a Comet*, translated by Robert C. Bartlett (Albany: State University of New York Press, 2000), p. 78.

in social laws and customs. Its normativity transcends the mental states of particular individuals just as the divine general will had transcended the individual's internal religious status. A science of the human interior is the means (potentially a statistical one) by which one can measure particular individuals against general developmental norms.

Emile describes a generality that is neither religious (like God's general will in the theory of election) nor civic (like the general will in political theory). Rather, it takes on the one hand the form of an *abstraction* of the individual, irrespective of nation or earthly vocation; and on the other hand this *homme abstrait*, as Rousseau himself calls Emile, is representative of the social body only in so far as the latter will stretch to accommodate him.[46] From the medieval scholasticism which saw man as the prime example of a universal, with merely rhetorical exceptions who turn out numerically to be the majority (the beastlike 'multitude'), we arrive now at the abstract man, with scientific exceptions who are a beastlike minority.

The abstraction lords it over actual individuals. 'General' in Rousseau's socio-political thought still does not mean universal in a Kantian sense. Generality not only *can* exclude, it is dependent on the very possibility of exclusion – just as for the Jansenists God's general will stood or fell on the impossibility of his having rescued every last particular human being. In whatever historical application, whether *le salut* concerns this life or the next, generality can only be validated by the possibility of a priori exclusions. In *On the Social Contract* the general will is implicitly the collective will of broad-ish social strata – 'the people' – but still not that of everyone. In *Emile* it is '*le peuple* that constitutes the human species; that which is not *le peuple* is of little account'.[47] Who are these *non-peuple*? (The phrase has inevitably cropped up in French political discourse of the intervening centuries, indicating among other things those who do not qualify to pay taxes.)[48] It is possible that Rousseau's 'moral being', like Locke's 'moral man', excludes servants and landless labourers; and his political thought in this sense cannot be separated from his educational and psychological thought: 'the poor do not need education'.[49] Notoriously it excludes women, despite their primary role in the formation of a moral sense. Whatever the nature of human or simply political rights at a philosophical level, social participation is not for all.

---

[46] Rousseau, *Emile*, pp. 33, 42.   [47] Rousseau, *Emile*, p. 292.
[48] Nicolas-Louise-Marie Magon, *Le peuple et le non-peuple: Assiette des impôts* (Paris: Pihan-Delaforest, 1832).
[49] Rousseau, *Emile*, p. 56.

These exceptions are more than hypothetical. Rousseau is writing about the 'civilized' child with servants and governesses. The young Emile's tutor has to warn him that his 'development' will have to come without using the servants he is entitled to. He is certainly not some peasant child who, like some noble savage, might model a more positively 'natural' and moral development. Far from it: there is a lower social class that is disqualified a priori. Their static, unimprovable and ineducable nature does not need explaining, any more than the static, unchangeable status of reprobates had needed explaining. Rousseau's own five abandoned newborns were a case in point, having all been fathered with a maidservant. The 'society' that needs remodelling still carried its class-restricted sense. Rousseau imputed the prospect of psychological maturity to those who would be likely to read and benefit from him, and the great division in *Emile* between the purity of nature and the corruptions of civilization must be read in this light. The same ambiguity around certain social groups challenges what *On the Social Contract* itself calls the 'principle' of rights, since what unites the politics and psychology here is a specifically modern notion of competence. (Today, for example, the rights of children and developmentally disabled people, even in being asserted as 'human rights' to contrast with their former historical treatment, tend to be reinterpreted in terms of difference from the rights of 'competent' adults.)

While the relationship of the general will to the individual will in Rousseau's political thought may have been a whole *transformation* of the divine into the civic, as Riley puts it, Rousseau's work displays a mere *transition* of the divine into the psychological. From the divine to the civic involves a whole displacement. From the divine to the psychological, the displacement, though considerable, takes place within one and the same realm of interiority. Its core content – the individual's perilous route from imperfection to perfection – is common to both. In this sense the temporal structure of Rousseau's conception of interiority creates a category of disability which may well encompass many of the unskilled in general, but which definitely encompasses all children by virtue of their chronological incompleteness.

Emile, in this sense, is one of the chosen. He is plucked from a contaminating mass of creatures that develops physically without ever developing cognitively or emotionally, at least not sufficiently to arrive at 'happiness'. Whatever the historical gulf between Pascal's Christian Republic and Rousseau's society of nature, their 'blessedness' still excludes some.[50] Today's formal developmental psychology has imported determinism and intra-human division in a form appropriate to the

---

[50] On this, see Keohane, *Philosophy and the State*, p. 280.

emerging vision of social order found above all in Rousseau. Equality and rights, whether in eighteenth-century form or in the putatively 'inclusive' versions of today, only ever extend up to a certain limit. We have never lost the shamanic instinct for presence/absence. Today it is the developmental idea that creates the division and is decisive.

Religion as Modernity in Rousseau

Perhaps, rather than seeing Pascal and Malebranche as precursors of Rousseau, we should see Rousseau as inherently Pascalian and Malebranchian, and precisely in respect of the one thing by which he is also unmistakably modern: namely, the temporalization of order and its place in the developmental idea. The *sources* of Rousseau's religion must be taken seriously if we are to grasp its full importance to the modern human sciences. 'Natural religion' was not just a stepping stone to atheism, and it is no good jettisoning preceding, religious accounts of interiority as so much obsolescent and useless junk. That is not what history itself did.

Leibniz also made a contribution in this respect with his 'pre-established harmony' between body and soul/mind, which was providential. In Rousseau, the human being's harmony is reached over time, as a new explanation for God's justice: this was Rousseau's own theodicy, and it reinstated the role of Providence following Voltaire's rejection of it.[51] In this sense, it was a major contribution to the eighteenth century's 'temporalization of Utopia'.[52] Although it was a social blueprint too, it looks inwards, at the human individual's 'moral being' and 'perfectibility' over time. It produces a historically specific version of the relationship between society and individual in the modern human sciences, though Rousseau's picture of this remains complex and unsimplified. That is because its religious roots are still poking up on the surface.

He concludes the *Discourse on Inequality* with the remark that 'inequality, being almost non-existent in the state of nature, [has] derive[d] its power and its growth from the development of our faculties'.[53] Development thus has an ambiguous role. The task was to go back to nature and start again: for nature read the Garden of Eden, and for start again read the early Christian

---

[51] F. di Rita, 'Rousseau and Leibniz: elements of Leibniz's philosophy in Rousseau's theodicy', *Rivista della storia della filosofia* 70/1 (1984).
[52] Reinhart Koselleck, *The Practice of Conceptual History: Timing History, Spacing Concepts* (Stanford: Stanford University Press, 2002), p. 84.
[53] Rousseau, *A Discourse*, p. 137.

notion of 'recapitulation'. Emile's prospective perfection as a 'moral being' is like that of Jesus: the most perfect of creatures, given flesh and blood in order to set an example on earth. As well as being divinely fathered, Jesus was also 'Son of Man' and as such stood at the head of the line of the naturally born elect. Various earlier doctrines, not to mention Rousseau himself in one of his own personae (the 'Savoyard Priest' who appears in *Emile*), raised the possibility that Jesus was not in fact divine. Transposed to nature and society, he becomes the trailblazer for 'normal development'. The book itself represents a summation of the religious mindset at this point in its history; it shows us how the Saviour was embedded in the human sciences and their formal secular discourses from the outset.

Publication of *Emile* came at a time when the differences between Jansenism and Calvinism were finally losing significance; Rousseau belonged to the first generation capable of absorbing both traditions. His views on pedagogy owe something to the Jansenist focus on learning from experience, and on the value of a secular curriculum in preserving a pure internal and moral status. That is why Rousseau prevents Emile from going anywhere. He stays in the same place, locationally and socially. Morally too: if 'the pupil makes a single step on the earth, if he [then] goes down a single degree, he is lost'.[54] It directly echoes Pascal's and the Jansenists' emphasis on the prevention, through isolation, of lapse and contamination.

This echo has been noted as 'curious'.[55] It is more than that. It is evidence of the deeper-lying historical transition. The child's *static* place in external, geographical nature – Emile's pure Swiss mountain air being, like the Abbey at Port Royal, a form of laboratory isolation – was necessary to allow for the contrasting temporal dimension, that of interior *movement* towards moral being and citizenship. The interior 'path' towards these things was no less straight and narrow than the biblical one. Only in such an ideal isolation could Rousseau envisage, to put it in terms of modern pedagogical theory, 'the reconciliation of an education for autonomy with an education for community'.[56] The goal of perfectibility in both personal and social senses meant that it was the younger individual above all whose 'moral being' was at issue.

This takes us back to the passage in Rousseau's *Confessions* where he remembers abandoning the theory of election. In terms of religious autobiography this *abandonment* has a function equivalent to the *arrival* of the

---

[54] Rousseau, *Emile*, p. 42.
[55] Pierre Burgelin, *La philosophie de l'existence de Jean-Jacques Rousseau* (Paris: Vrin, 1973), p. 477.
[56] Geraint Parry, '*Emile*: Learning to be men, women and citizens', in (ed.) Patrick Riley, *The Cambridge Companion to Rousseau* (Cambridge: Cambridge University Press, 2001).

Calvinist's internal perception of being elect, or the 'night of fire' that told Pascal he might be saved. In Rousseau's picture of radical interior change, election represents not a new or regenerated self but the old one. Nevertheless, the very act of its abandonment simulates the former theory's representation of change from reprobate status. What the two have in common is their underlying sense of intellectual certainty. It is Rousseau's rejection of the former predestinarian picture of certainty that constitutes precisely the intellectual 'development' whereby his own status is affirmed. To put it another way: his abandonment of election gives him his sense of certainty about his membership of the 'elect' of a newly conceived type. In letting go of anxiety about his elect status, he let go of the developmental disability and immaturity he had perceived in himself up till that point.

The young Emile's upbringing seems much like a reconstruction of Jean-Jacques's own as he would like it to have been, and at some semi-conscious level this may have been his aim in writing the story. Moreover, he sees Emile as representing a whole society, and even a whole species, which also undergo development. This would make Emile and Jean-Jacques himself, between them, the Second Adam. They represent the human species as it starts from the beginning again in order to get things right at the second attempt and to rescue the first, failed Adam in the process. In early Christianity's theory of recapitulation the leader of this successful reprise had been Jesus himself. The good shepherd has now become the good hike leader, whom Rousseau clearly resembles. If nature for the eighteenth century was God's 'second book', *Emile* is its New Testament.

Emile on the one hand and *On the Social Contract* on the other mark between them the separation of political thought from the conceptualization of human interiority (whether religious or psychological), at least in a purely formal sense. Rousseau's developmentalist restructuring of the elect/elite individual in the first of those texts was aimed at their future moral being; the second text may not actually invoke 'progress' in the social sense pioneered a dozen years earlier by Turgot,[57] but *Emile* provided its psychological accompaniment. It is important for historians of ideas and political thought not to ignore this – as if psychology, development and interiority were not themselves, and at their very root, ideas. The question then is: should they, can they safely, continue being passed across to the history of science and its study of the external realm.

---

[57] Anne-Robert-Jacques Turgot, 'A philosophical review of the advances of the human mind', in (ed.) David Gordon, *The Turgot Collection* (Auburn: Ludwig von Mises Institute, 2011).

CHAPTER 8

Nature versus Nurture and Cognitive Ability Testing: Historical Sketches

The onset of the developmental idea as a self-consciously scientific theory, intervening in the lives of increasing numbers of people and especially children, dates from the mid-eighteenth century. There is already a large secondary literature on the history of psychology over the two and a half centuries since, covering a whole range of theories and historical figures.[1] This final chapter does not claim to be a summary; it simply points out a few incidents in this more recent history that arise directly from our previous themes. They focus on two of the largest inscriptions on modern psychology's totem pole: the 'nature versus nurture' formula, and its monozygous twin, cognitive ability measurement (IQ), which initially arose as a measurement of 'mental age'. Neither the inscriptions nor their authors, Francis Galton and Alfred Binet respectively, can be understood without a knowledge of the ideas discussed in previous chapters.

Hartley, Priestley, Galton

David Hartley (1705–1757) and Joseph Priestley (1733–1804) are important interim figures: Hartley because he made the decisive contribution towards establishing the empirical basis of a psychological science, Priestley because he found a place for it in the late eighteenth-century treatment of interiority in general, and in its broader study of human history.

To understand the arrival of 'nature versus nurture' and its relationship to measurement of intelligence we must go back to the theory of the elect and its sublimation in that of the normal. Quarrels over election were no longer central to the intellectual culture by 1700, but they remained noisy among preachers and congregations throughout the century. England's

---

[1] For an overview, see Roger Smith, *The Fontana History of the Human Sciences* (London: Harper Collins, 1997). On the specific Anglo-French interactions over intelligence in particular, see Ann Jefferson, *Genius in France: An Idea and Its Uses* (Princeton: Princeton University Press, 2015).

main ecclesiastical divide, in this period, now lay between the established church and the nonconformists, and disputes over predestination were conducted mainly within the latter camp. They showed themselves in the differences among its celebrity preachers: between the 'Calvinism' of George Whitefield and 'Arminianism' of John Wesley, each in its modified eighteenth-century form – the first full of fire and brimstone, the second placing value (though not ultimately the decisive one) on the human individual's agency and preparedness.

It was in this historical context that Hartley came up with his attempt to explain psychological phenomena as the product of material causes. His primary illustration of this lay in the 'association of ideas'.[2] This theory, hinted at by Hobbes and elaborated by Locke, says that one idea follows another because they are connected in some way: either by similarity or by contrast. Hartley gave it a materialist and seemingly modern spin, which can only be understood in the light of predestination. Predestination had been a theory about the causes not only of interior status but also of material events. The two discussions had started out as largely separate, and the early seventeenth century's obsession with the first of them meant it had blotted out the second. Hartley's theory forced them into closer proximity, illustrating the historical continuity from divine determinism to the biological variety: his materialism linked the cause of *physical events* in the brain to that of co-located *interior states*.[3] When Priestley later named this theory 'necessarianism' or 'necessitarianism', that was what he meant: the necessity of physiological determinants for psychological phenomena and categories.

By hypothesizing that 'the faculty of thinking' and 'the brain' were materially bonded, Hartley brought Hobbes's metaphysical concept of 'natural necessity' down to an empirical level. It was in evidence, for example, when the brain gets injured. In the conventional Christian view, the body was there to tempt and obstruct the psychological faculties. But for Hartley and then Priestley, body (brain) and mind run – and develop – together: 'as the faculty of thinking in general ripens and comes to maturity with the body, it is also observed to decay with it'.[4] Hartley's

---

[2] On this, see Smith, *The Fontana History*, pp. 251–7; Robert M. Young, 'Association of Ideas', in *Dictionary of the History of Ideas*, 1.111–1.118; David Spadafora, *The Idea of Progress in Eighteenth-Century Britain* (New Haven: Yale University Press, 1990), chapter 4.

[3] Richard C. Allen, *David Hartley on Human Nature* (Albany: State University of New York Press, 1999). On Hartley's later influence see Roger Smith, *The Fontana Norton History*, p. 252ff.

[4] Joseph Priestley, cited in Erwin Hiebert, 'The integration of revealed religion and scientific materialism in the thought of Joseph Priestley', in (eds.) Hiebert, Aaron Ihe and Robert Schofield, *Joseph Priestley: Scientist, Theologian and Metaphysician* (London: Associated University Presses, 1980), p. 39.

materialist account of psychology reformulated a determinism whose terms had previously been exclusively divine ones; he still accepted divine causality, but he identified an additional and equally efficacious tier of it in the earthly, material realm.

Hartley explicitly acknowledges here his debt (minus the materialism) to Malebranche and Leibniz, and their talk of the 'development' of minds as a kind of unfolding. From Leibniz's concept of transcreation (see Chapter 6) Hartley goes on to assert that personhood is a 'material monad'; like a seed, it is an 'elementary infinitesimal body' which 'survive[s] the dissolution of the [physical] body at death', thus restoring the person's interior (elect) identity in immortal form.[5] The psychological aspects of Hartley's materialism came from his desire, like Newton's, to place millenarian religion on a scientific footing. In the triumphant concluding sentence to his *Observations on Man* he warns how the backward and unchanging among us will 'be slain before [Christ's] face, as enemies, at his second coming'.[6] The whole conclusion consists in a grand statement that equates literacy and education with the rescue of the 'inferior orders' from themselves, while seeing the existence of an additional number of unrescuable people as a necessity. This, as we have seen, was a characteristic 'single predestinarian' position. Hartley represents the rescue primarily as that of his intellectual fellows, the threat being that which 'backwardness' poses to their expected day of glory and to the social order generally. The fundamental intra-human divide is maintained precisely by inserting the determinism of the Creator into the 'necessity' of nature while advocating also the need for a correct nurture.

Hartley took Leibniz's idea of a preordained harmony between mind and body and made it compatible with the 'mechanistic' approach to hard science characteristic of the period.[7] Both Leibniz and Malebranche, following Descartes, had confined their own mechanistic explanations to 'corporeal' events alone. Hartley jumps to a psychological application. He remarks that he is acting upon a proposal already made by Newton at the end of the *Principia Mathematica*: that psychological phenomena such as the association of ideas must have a specific location in brain matter, where

---

[5] Allen, *David Hartley*, p. 203.
[6] David Hartley, *Observations on Man, His Frame, His Duty, and His Expectations* (London: Thomas Tegg, 1834), p. 604. On this, see Kara Barr, '"An indissoluble union": mechanism, mortalism, and millenarianism in the eschatology of David Hartley's *Observations on Man*', *History of Religions*, 55/3 (2016).
[7] On these matters, see William Uttal, *Dualism: The Original Sin of Cognitivism* (New York: Psychology Press, 2004); J. C. D. Clark, 'Providence, predestination and progress: or, did the Enlightenment fail?', *North American Conference on British Studies*, 35/4 (2003).

they are triggered by the sensory 'vibrations' of 'very subtle spirit[s]'.[8] (The existence of 'animal spirits', material but so refined as to be undetectable, was the universal sticking plaster physicians had reached for when they needed to explain mental events and their relationship to bodies.)

Like predestination, the theory of a general will applies not only to souls but also to the material realm: causality involves God's 'Will and Purposes', but only at a higher level, because he excludes himself from particular events. On the one hand, it would not have even entered Hartley's head that he could divert causality away from the creator God to corporeal entities and biology that in fact were merely subsequent; on the other, we can see with hindsight that the second causes such as those he described were coming to rival divine first causes in importance, as objects of study. Furthermore, as an anonymous author with ideas close to Hartley's put it, there is a role for human 'Intelligence and Free-Agency', and it now has a developmental emphasis: 'Though man was design'd for that Sort of Happiness which is . . . best adapted to the Nature of his Faculties, yet . . . it plainly appears that this Happiness cannot be obtain'd *immediately* and *at once*; . . . he can make but slow Advances towards his ultimate End.' Anticipating Bonnet and Rousseau exactly, this author stipulates a correct temporal structure: the developing mind must 'from sensible Pleasure . . . be led to the Feeling and Experience of what is Intellectual; and from Intellectual Pleasure to . . . the Pleasures of Religion. . . . He cannot arrive to it but by degrees.' That ultimate end is not only the 'future Happiness of Mankind' but also its 'Interests', which are both 'temporal and eternal' – there being no precise distinction between the two.[9] Primarily the author means salvation, but the principle and possibilities of a complete earthly happiness are envisaged too.

When Priestley takes up the theme, the role for development and for its goals of 'perfection' and 'happiness' becomes clearer. As the millennialist theologian who co-founded the Unitarian church, as the chemist who first isolated oxygen and as one of the political thinkers who in defining 'happiness' to be that of the greatest number inspired Jeremy Bentham – roles that were all of a piece – Priestley is worth looking at in some detail because he stands at a late eighteenth-century crossroads. Three elements from our previous discussions stand out in Priestley: the place of determinism – necessity as 'nature' – in human interiority; the quest for purity;

---

[8] Isaac Newton, *Principia Mathematica*, cited in Hartley, *Observations*, p. 604.
[9] Anon, *An Introduction towards an Essay on the Origin of the Passions* (London: Robert Dodsley, 1741), pp. 5, 29. Italics in original.

and the place of both within wider notions of social and species progress. On the first of these issues, Priestley proposes 'just as much connection between the principles of *sensation* and *thought* and the brain of a man, as ... between the principle of gravitation and the matter of which the earth and the sun are made'.[10]

Acknowledging Hobbes's 'natural necessity' explicitly,[11] he defines this 'necessarianism' or 'scheme of philosophical necessity' as 'a chain of *causes* and *effects*, established by infinite wisdom, and terminating in the greatest good of the whole universe'.[12]

Priestley saw a major antithesis between his own materialist necessarianism and what he decries as 'Calvinism'. In this book I have so far presented these as equivalent versions of determinism, one biological and the other divine, an equivalence which at least one contemporary critic pointed out to him.[13] The reason Priestley saw them as opposites is as follows. Necessity and freedom had not always been in stark contradiction as they tend to be in modern thought. Calvinists had genuinely believed in the human capacity for freedom: it lay precisely in their being free to obey God's dictates, and among these the dictate that had determined their own status. Similarly, Hartley's and Priestley's 'necessity' admitted free will too; one contemporary (in a work which Priestley wrote a preface to) defines the 'rational' person aiming for 'perfection' as 'a necessary agent'.[14] The latter phrase was not a contradiction in terms. What Priestley refuted as the 'Calvinism' of his opponents was in fact only *double* predestination – the doctrine by which God deprives human beings of their own ability to avoid damnation, and which thereby seems to make God himself directly responsible for their sins.

When Priestley rejects this idea of 'absolute ... reprobation', he does so because it sees the cause as lying outside time.[15] The same caveat goes for others of the century's famous educators, who were similarly single predestinarians. It is what is really meant when historians describe Isaac Watts a 'hesitant Calvinist',[16] or Hannah More, despite her attacks on

---

[10] Priestley, *Corruptions: An History of Early Opinions Concerning Jesus Christ*, cited in Schofield, *The Enlightenment of Joseph Priestley: A Study of His Life and Work from 1733 to 1773* (Philadelphia: University of Pennsylvania Press, 1997), p. 227.
[11] Priestley, Preface to Anthony Collins, *A Philosophical Inquiry concerning Human Liberty* (Birmingham: Pearson, 1790).
[12] Priestley, (ed.) John Rutt, *Works* (London: G. Smallfield, 1831), vol. 6, p. 264.
[13] Priestley, *Works*, vol. 6, pp. 252–9.
[14] Collins, *A Philosophical Inquiry* (London: R. Robinson, 1717), p. 57.
[15] Priestley, 'An appeal to the serious and candid professors of Christianity', *Works*, vol. 8, p. 16.
[16] Roland Stromberg, *Religious Liberalism in Eighteenth-Century England* (Oxford: Oxford University Press, 1954), p. 116. See, for example, Isaac Watts, *The Ruin and Recovery of Mankind* (London: Brackstone, 1742), p. 256.

'Calvinism', as 'herself a Calvinist and unaware of it'.[17] As often happens in the history of psychology and theories of interiority generally, the old principle – 'Calvinism' meaning double predestination – was re-characterized as folklore and imputed to the ignorance of the lowest social classes (the curmudgeonly servant Joseph in *Wuthering Heights* is one example). What none of the three had was a 'Pelagian' belief that personal goodness and effort, let alone a cognitive understanding of religion, guaranteed a passage through the pearly gates – at least, not absolutely.

Like Hartley, Priestley positions necessity in second as well as in first nature: that is, as then understood, in what goes on *within* the individual interior as well as in what is determined *for* that individual by God. In preceding centuries 'nature' had been less rule-bound; rather, it had been a demonstration of the fecundity of God's creation. In the eighteenth century, it began to take over the mantle of necessity. In Priestley's terms, this natural necessity could describe not only the workings of the body but also what he calls human 'agency' and moral responsibility. These are now themselves subject to a more formal determinism, a 'uniformity of the laws of nature respecting our minds':[18] in other words, they form a 'mechanism' of a specifically psychological sort, on top of the divinely appointed ontology of 'faculties' and 'operations'. Human access to a knowledge of (divine) primary causes is obtained through cognitive understanding of this natural lawfulness, which must also include an understanding of the lawfulness of the workings of the mind itself.[19] Here, election *is* transitioning into cognitive ability – but without ceasing to be election. Failure of understanding in this cognitive sense leads to 'despondence', 'melancholy' and consequently unbelief, all strong indicators (but no more than that) of damnation.[20]

As for nurture, the need for an extended *preparation* for the second coming, which superseded the mid-seventeenth century's view of the millennium as imminent, informed the demand for an *education* in secular abilities that might underwrite our understandings of religion, of the natural world and of the connection between the two. The cognitive preparation required of the elect subject in receipt of grace would feed

---

[17] M. G. Jones, *Hannah More* (Cambridge: Cambridge University Press, 1952), p. 98.
[18] Priestley, 'The doctrine of divine influence on the human mind', *Works*, vol. 15 (1779/1831), p. 84.
[19] See John G. McEvoy, 'Causes and laws, powers and principles: the metaphysical foundations of Priestley's concept of phlogiston', in (eds.) R. G. W. Anderson and Christopher Lawrence, *Science, Medicine and Dissent: Joseph Priestley* (London: Wellcome Trust, 1987).
[20] Priestley, *Discourse on Various Subjects* (London: J. Johnson, 1787), p. 220. On this topic, see Brooke, 'A sower went forth', in (eds.) Hiebert, Ihe and Schofield, *Joseph Priestley*, p. 42.

into the developmental idea through the secular school curriculum, as we saw in Chapter 3. Not only religious doctrine and moral behaviour but also literacy, general knowledge and even numeracy were taught through the catechism,[21] whose function of assessing interior status became a testing of how far you had progressed towards your goal – a goal that would become increasingly cognitive. Priestley himself wrote an *Essay on a Course of Liberal Education for Active and Civil Life* (1765), which would be the most widely read book on education until Spencer published his 1861 *Essays on Education*.

A second relevant and constant feature of Priestley's work was his search for purity. Education of the sort just described was a means to the purity of heaven-bound elect souls; morals combined with 'intelligence', and both with 'exertion and striving', would be a better marker of purity than the gloomy 'resignation' of 'Calvinists' that might be a token of their own reprobate status.[22] His notion of purity echoes Jansenism, had its contemporary parallel in the Jacobin revolutionaries and also looks forward to the eugenic ideal of purity of descent in Galton.

One indicator of this was Priestley's pioneering isolation of pure oxygen. His interest in it sprang from its role in combustion. The previous century's chemists had assumed the existence of 'phlogiston', a notional substance given off by combustion and causing oxidation; this 'phlogistic putrid effluvium' was supposedly the residue left behind from the attempt at purification, and it thus represented a kind of corruption.[23] Priestley's reluctance to let go of this non-existent phlogiston, which allowed Antoine Lavoisier to establish the identity of oxygen, may have been influenced by the theory of election and its possible corruption by reprobates at communion. The connection may seem stretched, but (as we shall see) Priestley writes about the two theories in the same breath. His key role in the discovery of photosynthesis is also relevant here: the idea of a divine Providence that conjures good out of evil lay at the root of his explanation as to how rotting vegetation, assumed at the time to be the cause of disease by giving off 'bad air', might lead to new growth in which plants supply 'the purest dephlogisticated air'.

Priestley sought also, in his vast historical studies, to retrieve a pure, pristine early Christianity from its subsequent corruption. The

---

[21] See Ian Green, *The Christian's ABC: Catechisms and Catechizing in England c.1530–1740* (Oxford: Clarendon, 1996).
[22] Priestley, *Doctrine of Philosophical Necessity* (London: J. Johnson, 1777), p. 534.
[23] Priestley, *Experiments and Observations relating to Natural Philosophy*, p. 276ff, cited in McEvoy, 'Joseph Priestley, "aerial philosopher"', *Ambix*, 25/3 (1978).

historiographical act situated him as a central figure, in his own estimation, between past and future, in a temporal, progressive account of unfolding Revelation. He himself was part of this linear 'teleology of divine purification';[24] his writings were a stage in 'the progress of the species towards [a] perfection' that was 'the happiness of man, as he advances in intellect' (a text he heads with a quote from Rousseau's *On the Social Contract*).[25]

Purity was important because Priestley, like Newton, Locke, Hartley and so many others before, believed he was living in the End Times. The second coming of Christ was only ever a couple of decades down the line, and the human interior had to be in a state of preparedness, of which purity was one aspect, for the momentous event. The aim was recovery of the prelapsarian state, and for 'our religion [to] be, in all respects, as pure, and as efficacious to promote real goodness of heart and life, as it was in the first'.[26] Notions of purity continued to be important to the rise of the formal disciplines. Priestley's disciple, Benjamin Rush, is one example. Rush would describe how purified, 'dephlogisticated' air 'when taken into the lungs, produces ... [the] serenity of mind' referred to in Genesis 2.7, where God formed man out of the decomposed 'dust of the ground, and breathed into his nostrils the breath of life, and man became a living soul'.[27] A signatory to the Declaration of Independence, he wrote of Priestley as 'the Sir Isaac Newton' of the mind; Rush's image is carried on the seal of the American Psychiatric Association today, as its founding father.

During the peak years of Priestley's experimentation with oxygen, in a period when he was also editing the reprint of Hartley's *Observations*, he was furthermore an enthusiast for the political experimentation of John Wilkes in England as well as for the American Revolution (and later the French), all of which revealed 'the glorious prospect for mankind before us'.[28] He saw the End Times formed by these political events as part of a *natural* linear progress, in which the second coming was to be announced by an intellectual reformation and development of the individual interior – an interior that remained natural even after the individual's physical death. As Leibniz and Bonnet had already suggested, one carries on learning and

---

[24] Colin Wells, *The Devil and Doctor Dwight: Satire and Theology in the Early American Republic* (University of North Carolina Press, 2002), p. 166.
[25] Priestley, 'Essay on the first principles of Government', *Works*, vol. 22, p. 8.
[26] Priestley, 'A free address to Protestant Dissenters on the subject of the Lord's Supper' (1774), *Works*, vol. 21, p. 269.
[27] Benjamin Rush, 'An inquiry into the influence of physical causes upon the faculty', *Medical Inquiries*, 5th ed. (1818), 1:14.
[28] Priestley, *Works*, vol. 2, p. 38.

developing in Paradise. Priestley's materialist science of the mind is accompanied by a bodily chemistry of resurrection and purification: 'Death, with its concomitant putrefaction ... is only a *decomposition*; whatever is decomposed, may be *recomposed* by the being who first composed it; and I doubt not but that ... the same body that dies shall rise again.'[29] In this way he saw his chemical experimentation as 'not ... a business of *air* only ..., but ... [as] diffus[ing] light upon the most *general principles* of natural knowledge'.[30]

This evident interconnectedness appears in a letter of 1771 to a fellow clergyman, where Priestley writes about 'the downfall of Church and State together' as the cataclysmic harbinger of the 'glorious event' of Christ's return. The very next sentence runs (it is his first ever acknowledgement of the topic): 'I have of late been very busy about some experiments on air ... and have discovered ... that process in nature by which air, rendered noxious by breathing, is restored to its former salubrious condition.' And the very next sentence after *that* recommends his own most recent publication on election, in which he had sought to restore the purity of election as 'pure truth', 'pure doctrine'.[31] This run of three sentences constitutes in itself a remarkable association of ideas. He goes on to say that he had been seeking the purity of air that had once obtained in the Garden of Eden. Now he could present this dephlogisticated air in a test tube. The idea of purity versus putrefaction resonates with that of election versus contamination by reprobates. He was, so to speak, on the search for a dephlogisticated mind. It had to leave behind the corruptions it was born with, even if he saw these now not as the product of original sin but as the product of history – that is, of a Christianity that had deviated from its true goal.

The third important element in Priestley's work is the relationship of individual development and its personal goal to social progress and those 'glorious events' that lay ahead. In terms of a psychology of the individual, Priestley has little to add to Hartley. Nor is he out of the ordinary in

---

[29] Priestley, *Disquisitions relating to Matter and Spirit* (London: J. Johnson, 1777), p. 161, cited in John Brooke and Geoffrey Cantor, *Reconstructing Nature: The Engagement of Science and Religion* (Edinburgh: T. and T. Clark, 1998), p. 328.
[30] Priestley, *Experiments and Observations on Different Kinds of Air*, p. 101, cited in Truman Schwartz 'Priestley's materialism', in (eds.) Schwartz and McEvoy, *Motion toward Perfection: The Achievement of Joseph Priestley* (Boston: Skinner House, 1990), p. 112.
[31] Priestley, Letter to Theophilus Lindsey, 23 August 1771, *Works*, vol. 1, part 1, p. 144. The publication referred to is *An Appeal to the Serious and Candid Professors of Christianity* (1770). The manuscript of this letter has not survived, and we are dependent on Rutt, his editor, who sometimes redacted them. Nevertheless, the ideas were clearly jostling each other in Priestley's mind at this point.

relating the developmental idea to that of a broader, social progress. He would have agreed with his German contemporary Gotthold Ephraim Lessing, who maintained: 'That which Education is to the Individual, Revelation is to the [human] Race ... Revelation [is] the Educator of humanity.'[32] Revelation was itself a historical unfolding that occurred in 'stages', observable both from prophecy and by actual political events.[33] The sense of *interiority* as temporally structured, however, seems to play little role in Priestley's thought.

The notion of an individual cognitive ability ('reason') nevertheless contributes to Priestley's account of social and species goals. This is evident from his Unitarian faith, which is particularly important because it connects to the following century's concerns, particularly those of Galton. Unitarianism reduced all three elements of the Trinity to one, and in so doing had made God almost synonymous with reason.[34] It abandoned the notion that Jesus was divine, but it did not abandon all sense of the sacral, since reason was the attainment of 'the human Logos in Christ'.[35] Accordingly, in the human individual's reason, there is 'a capacity for *endless improvement*'.[36] Of course, 'the faculties and operations of the mind necessarily depend upon the state of the body, and particularly that of the brain', but God 'can easily ... continue the same *consciousness* in some other way' after death. Priestley describes this whole process as 'natural', in heaven as on earth. And so when we see him writing of 'natural progress in intellectual improvement', this secular-sounding phrase also signifies a re-sacralization of interiority.[37]

What, then, about *absence* of natural intellectual improvement? 'Incurability' of the intellect – absence of change in its developmental form – shares a common denominator with the reprobate's 'hardness of heart', his inability to receive saving grace. Unchangeability is one of the things which, historically, reprobation offloaded on to idiocy, the latter having previously been curable by Providence. The idea of an interior 'nature' whose definition spans both life and bodily death also creates conditions in which absence of 'improvement' might indicate

---

[32] Gotthold Ephraim Lessing, *The Education of the Human Race* (1778), paras. 1–2.
[33] On this, see Gareth Stedman Jones, 'Millennium and Enlightenment', in (eds.) Kapossy et al., *Markets, Morals, Politics: Jealousy of Trade and the History of Political Thought* (Cambridge MA: Harvard University Press 2018).
[34] See Simon Schaffer, 'Priestley and the politics of spirit', in (eds.) Anderson and Lawrence, *Science, Medicine and Dissent*, p. 45.
[35] Priestley, 'The scriptural doctrine of remission', *Works*, vol. 7, p. 203.
[36] Priestley, 'Institutes of religion', *Works*, vol. 2, p. 58. Italics in original.
[37] Priestley, 'Letters to a philosophical unbeliever', *Works*, vol. 4, p. 318.

a permanent, incurable damnation in *this* life, the earthly one. True, Priestley's benevolent, progressivist belief in the majority status of the elect (shared now even by the otherwise unreconstructed double predestinarians whom he opposed) meant that the reprobate were now few. This belief came from the same greater happiness principle he passed on to Bentham; its converse, however, was the continuing necessity for hell. Without *any* reprobates the whole historical edifice of Christianity would have come tumbling down. Priestley acknowledged its historicity, but hell was still a given.

As the prior condition for enabling psychology to disown its Christian roots and become a rational and godless science, it was not in fact reprobates that had to go. They were simply one passing category which had dominated the discussion for a century or two, and which the underlying anxiety was already replacing with another. What had to go was hell itself. Thinking elites at the start of the nineteenth century would chip away at it more cautiously than at anything else; even Jesus's divinity was easier to abandon, it seems, than the prospect of your body or soul being roasted for eternity. There might be fewer people going there, they might not be there eternally and would get rescued after a bit, and this 'bit' (Priestley surmised) might be a mere five thousand years rather than five million, but it had to exist. There was an alternative evasion, however, which Priestley alongside others also promoted: that reprobate souls at death were instantaneously *annihilated*. In this sense, history was inching closer to the present situation where human beings have taken over responsibility for annihilating by prevention a certain kind of 'developmentally disabled' person, a natural kind upon whom 'suffering' is projected a priori as the justification for doing so.

If cognitive 'idiots' of this kind were being seen in the eighteenth century as more problematic, so was the alarmingly large number of borderline cases: not absolutely determined as unimprovable, but likely to fall by the wayside – especially since their deficiency, as the residue of medieval idiocy, was roughly identifiable with their social status.[38] Priestley is more anxious about this group, alongside his single predestinarian's hope for the possibility of nurturing them. There should be a universal state education whose core purpose would be 'to inspire the people with a sense of their obligations to God and man'; above all, 'the most express provision should be made for the instruction of the lower orders of the people, in

---

[38] See Simon Jarrett, *Those They Called Idiots: The Idea of the Disabled Mind from 1700 to the Present Day* (London: Reaktion Books, 2020).

preference to that of all others' (a state-sponsored street mob had just burnt Priestley's house down).[39] Their children, as well as working all day, needed schools; he approved Robert Raikes and Hannah More, whose non-denominational Sunday Schools taught literacy. Tuition would ensure 'the blessing of them that were ready to perish'. The upshot, echoing Hartley's millennialism, would be that 'the people who were destroyed for lack of knowledge shall celebrate thy name'. Talk of 'destruction' here is not simply rhetorical. Illiteracy and lack of secular knowledge were probable tokens of damnation.

These three preoccupations of Priestley's – necessity, purity, progress – belong in a broader historical framework. As natural representations of present/absent interiority started to take over from theological ones, the discussion about it changed course. Although the original Calvinist and Jansenist obsession with causes was being wrested from theology pure and simple on to a scientific and eventually anti-religious terrain, even while this was happening some form of reprobation with its social connotations remained effectively a fixture until Priestley's death in 1804 and beyond. Only its terms began to change, and gradually. When 'sinners' were replaced by the emerging psychological science's 'idiots', the definition of this second term was no less normative than the first. For Priestley and his contemporaries, reprobation remained the locus of suffering even as it was transitioning into a secular type of cognitive and moral deficiency. Nor was education the only type of external intervention seen as having a role. Human development towards perfectibility still required Providence too, and Christ's return would help it on its way.

Francis Galton and 'Nature versus Nurture'

Priestley influenced the extended scientific circles of the later eighteenth century, notably the Lunar Society and his contemporary Erasmus Darwin, grandfather of Charles and of Francis Galton. In this intellectual patriarch's teleological view of nature and its 'evolution', purity continued to be a developmental goal: 'As life discordant elements arrests, / Rejects the noxious and the pure digests.'[40] However, this world view of Darwin's wavered between optimism and pessimism about whether the goals of development, purity and progress were reachable; the wavering is easily

---

[39] Priestley, 'An appeal to the public on the riots in Birmingham', *Works*, vol. 19, p. 402.
[40] Erasmus Darwin, *The Temple of Nature*, Canto II, section 1.

observed later in his grandson Charles's account of evolution, as well as in what Galton came to see as 'regression' to the mediocrity of the mean.

The pessimism echoes that of earlier writers on predestination. When Charles Darwin began to doubt the Argument from Design for God's existence, he could only start from the intellectual position of the Unitarian faith he had grown up in. Using 'Nature' as the placeholder for God, Darwin bemoaned Its (or His) cruelty and injustice. In other words, he was still seeking a theodicy of sorts. The examples he chose from the natural world were ones that recall the religious world view. The first was the millions of abortions and wasted embryos in nature. Where, Darwin asked, could be the divine plan in that? His question reflects Leibniz's anxiety about the sheer numbers, the millions of reprobates compared with the tiny number of the saved. Another example echoed the medieval iconography of hell, in which a recurring image – constantly cited by Priestley – was the demons pecking at your innards: 'I cannot persuade myself that a beneficent and omnipotent God would have designedly created parasitic wasps with the express intention of their feeding within the living bodies of Caterpillars.' Moreover, such images were easily transposed into psychological terms. The interior hell of Leibniz's unredeemed reprobate points to the supposed interior hell of the nineteenth-century idiot, who has not developed cognitive ability. Why, Darwin asked, on a teleological view, would God create 'idiots'?[41] The argument here continues to hinge on how to justify the existence of evil.

For psychology as such, however, the key figure was Galton. Galton was born, in Priestley's old house, into an intellectual culture that was still socially homogeneous (Priestley's theology was regularly discussed in *The Gentleman's Magazine*), and when the schooling of the middle classes was often provided by nonconformist Dissenters. By the time Galton was active, however, scientific intellectuals were mostly purporting to ignore theology. His 1883 *Inquiries into Human Faculty and Its Development* was his main text on psychology. This was the key work that first reduced a previously tripartite set of influences – predetermination, nurture and a hazily conceived 'nature' midway between them – to the current Groundhog Day debates in which nurture is opposed to a historically created fusion between predetermination and nature. And it was precisely in this context that Galton, as his method for establishing the validity of this new framework, hit on the idea of measuring and comparing the

---

[41] Charles Darwin, letter to Asa Gray, 5 September 1857 (Cambridge: Darwin Correspondence Project).

development of identical twins separated at birth. 'Nature versus nurture' and the measurement of cognitive ability are scientifically and historically interdependent; neither is possible without the other.

In this book Galton continued to invoke the vocabulary of 'necessitarianism' and to identify with it. 'Necessitarians', he says, 'may derive new arguments from the life-histories of twins.' Whereas the psychological element in Hartley's and Priestley's necessity had been biologically determined but still inseparable from God's ultimate causal role, Galton reduced necessitarianism to psychobiology: it was 'science' *in opposition* to 'religion', the latter now redefined exclusively by belief in 'supernatural interference'.[42] Even this, however, still echoes the rational theology of deeply religious men like Leibniz, Bonnet and Priestley, who had equally wanted to sideline the role of the 'supernatural', the miraculous and instantaneous, in favour of something more gradual and developmental.

Alfred Binet and the Mental Age Score

I have suggested already that two traditions rather than one were at work in the nineteenth century, prior to the construction of the formal psychological disciplines: the deeper and more diffuse cultural one launched above all by Bonnet and Rousseau, as well as the more usually cited empirical and scientific tradition that had begun with Locke and Hartley (Priestley's enthusiasm was for both pairs). One of the francophone writers' claims was that a child deprived of communication, not with other humans but specifically with other *adult* humans, would remain a mere reasonless animal, a Cartesian beast-machine. A generation later, during the Revolution, a real-life illustration would appear in the shape of the world-famous Victor, a Wild Boy supposedly raised by wolves, who had emerged from the forests of L'Aveyron. Victor turned out to be incapable of improvement. His optimistic, post-revolutionary psychiatric mentors had to admit in the end that he was a purely static being, on whom the most intensive personalized curriculum could have no effect. His identity was therefore defined by this very failure to develop. He was a continuation of the reprobate category, whose basic interior feature was that their hearts were too set, too 'hardened' to change, marked in their case by the inability to receive saving grace.

If *Emile* was the holy book for the French Revolution's ideas about education, its role in the establishment of modern psychology in France

---

[42] Francis Galton, *Inquiries into Human Faculty* (London: Dent, 1907), p. 169.

was complemented by the increasing influence of the empirical tradition, especially that of Hartley. This was taken up in Hippolyte Taine's widely influential book on intelligence,[43] and culminates in the work of Alfred Binet (1857–1911), inventor of the original version of the IQ test. While Galton has become a controversial figure because of his eugenic preferences, Binet has received a better press. Convention has it that he devised his system of measurement in order to help 'subnormal' children obtain specialist help. And it is true, at least, that he allowed some role for 'nurture' and education in their development, and that the intellectual modesty with which he presented his work contrasts with the bombastic Galton. However, the themes of our previous chapters require us to take a second look.

Whereas Galton tested 'ability' against a ragbag of sensory and physical criteria, Binet tested those of intelligence as we have since come to understand it. Measurable intelligence scores (IQ) began as what he termed Mental Age Scores; in other words, without the developmental idea the IQ or cognitive ability test would have no status. The Metrical Scale of Intelligence announced by Binet and his co-worker Théodore Simon in 1905 simply *was* their Mental Age Score, and was defined by it. It was a 'mental age' test first, and only consequently an intelligence test ('mental age' remains the criterion of competence for legal purposes). It is not the case, as might be assumed, that cognitive ability is the given which marks out differences by age, in the same sense that sensory and physical phenomena are givens. Difference by age, and hence measurement as such, were the given which produced 'intelligence', and in this sense Galton's and Binet's approaches are scarcely comparable.

Binet's immediate prompt was the invitation he received in 1904 to chair the Commission on Abnormal Children set up by France's new left-republican government. These new, markedly anti-clerical rulers (who included several medical men, with a writer on psychology as prime minister)[44] encountered an education system dominated by the religious orders, and abruptly closed thousands of schools in favour of a universal state system. One unarticulated but absolutely necessary by-product of any rule of universality in a social context is the search for inevitable exceptions to it – that is, for that which will enable it to continue presenting itself as universal. Where *development* is the universal, whoever lags behind the

---

[43] Hippolyte Taine, *De l'intelligence* (1870); also Bernard Perez, *L'Enfant de trois à sept ans* (Paris: Alcan, 1886).
[44] See Jack Ellis, *The Physician Legislators of France* (Cambridge: Cambridge University Press, 2011).

norm of developmental performance is the exception, and is usually subject to social as well as conceptual segregation. Such was the case with Binet, who had effectively been tasked with creating a description of the presupposed exceptions.

The existence of age-related deficiency in itself was thus the a priori assumption. Intelligence – its very content, and not just its interpretation – came after. When Binet cast around for criteria, they seem to have been quite random. He took what was historically closest at hand, a loose list of items handed down from medieval faculty psychology via Locke and others (specifically: deficiencies of attention, judgement and abstraction).[45] Another of his possible symptoms of idiocy lay outside this context and was possibly unmeasurable: namely, belief in the supernatural. Binet adhered to the French movement for *laïcité* which was initially associated with primary education, and which was promoted by residual Jansenist and Calvinist elements in the culture whose specific antagonism was to Jesuit belief in the supernatural, rather than to religious belief as a whole.[46] With this in mind he turned playwright for a while, co-authoring Grand-Guignol melodramas, one of them set in a long-stay asylum where the sole perceivable symptom of the inmates' 'idiocy' is their belief that internal change will come about by miracle.[47] Idiocy here amounts to a wrong or outmoded belief about the structuring of the human timeline: to a belief in salvation of the miraculous kind, through penitence rather than through cognitive ability.

This sheds a new historical light on Binet's practical intervention in the French schooling system, namely the setting up of 'special' – that is, segregated – classrooms and schools for 'abnormal' children. It shows the shift from religion to developmental psychology to be a merely incremental one. First, his observation of children's interior status, and of their cognitive ability as such, sprang from motives which originally had to do with preventing contagion. Replaying the conflict between Jansenists and Jesuits, the ideology of segregation that accompanied 'universal' schooling

---

[45] Alfred Binet, *L'Etude experimentale de l'intelligence* (Paris: L'Harmattan, 2004 [1903]); Binet and Theodore Simon, 'Méthodes nouvelles pour le diagnostic du niveau intellectuel des anormaux', *L'Année psychologique*, 11 (1904).
[46] On this, see (ed.) Léo Hamon, *Du jansénisme à la laïcité: le jansénisme et les origines de la déchristianisation* (Paris: Editions de la Maison des Sciences de l'Homme, 1987).
[47] André de Lorde and Alfred Binet, *Les invisibles, tableau dramatique en un acte*, 1912, published in *Le monde illustré, Supplément Pièces de théâtre*, no. 28. See also Agnès Pierron, *Le Grand Guignol: le théâtre des peurs de la belle époque* (Paris: Laffont, 1999); Matthew Wilson Smith, *The Nervous Stage: Nineteenth-Century Neuroscience and the Birth of Modern Theatre* (Oxford: Oxford University Press, 2018).

belonged with the contemporary panic about racial and species degeneration. The same threat to purity hovers around the edges of Binet's mental age testing as it had around the Port Royal schools. In view of the Europe-wide historical context of the rise of eugenics, it is also possible that Binet had been commissioned to codify a formula that would ward off the impure; this was certainly the motive in moves towards segregation in Britain at the start of universal schooling.[48] In this case the concupiscent 'feeble-minded' were to be prevented from associating with the opposite sex and therefore breeding and multiplying. In France, existing church schools had been accused of letting in just about anyone; indeed, the Jesuit educators were accused of being 'socialists'.[49]

Secondly, the control function of the Mental Age Score reinforced the conceptual segregation of childhood in general from adulthood. To fellow republicans seeking to free people's souls from the slavery of religious schooling, Binet issued a warning: do not go from one extreme to the other. Catholics might object to his 'secular educational method' (*l'enseignement laïque*) – that is, of classification by mental age – on the grounds that it lacked a 'moral lesson' of the sort that religion might impart; and they would be right, says Binet. It does not provide such a lesson directly. What is more, it cannot do so. Why? Because children are not fully human. Moral sense – 'altruism, goodness, charity, sympathy, affection, disinterest' – is absent in them, and can only be a *specifically adult outcome* of his preparative method.

Moreover, the adult moral being in this sense is co-extensive with 'rights', says Binet. 'People now talk ceaselessly of the rights of the child', but if 'the purpose is to form free men and women, the method cannot consist in treating the child as a free adult, nor in appealing to its reason when the child has not yet attained the age of reason'.[50] Cognitive ability testing, given its roots in the Mental Age Score, therefore stands in opposition to the very possibility of children's rights. Binet is reminiscent here of Locke and Rousseau, in both of whom the liberation of the child comes at a price. Their work had demonstrated the political, anti-feudal and anti-absolutist principle that adults should not be treated as if they were children but must instead have the freedom to find their own way to God. But if adults are not to be children, then children are not to

---

[48] See George Shuttleworth, *Mental Deficiency in Children: Their Treatment and Training*, 2nd ed. (London: H. K. Lewis, 1900).
[49] Hamon, *Du jansénisme*, p. 174.
[50] Binet, *Les idées modernes sur les enfants* (Paris: Flammarion, 1909), p. 334.

be seen as adults, and a chronologically based 'method' is required to ensure this.

Thirdly, in more narrowly personal terms, Binet's theoretical case just like the Jansenists' was advanced through his own offspring. After an undistinguished early career ending with his traumatic resignation from the Salpêtrière mental hospital, there came a bruised withdrawal into the family circle. This turned out to be the kick-start to Binet's real career. His scientific attention now inevitably focused on just two research subjects: his own children. His observations of Marguerite and Armande Binet formed the entire empirical basis of *The Experimental Study of Intelligence* (1903), on the strength of which came his appointment to the Commission on Abnormal Children and from there the opportunity to invent observation-based developmental norms for the mass individual and for developmental disability in the exceptions. It turned out to be his own personal salvation, and the cue for his going down in history as a founding father of scientific psychology. Piaget, too, only reached international fame and influence with *The Origins of Intelligence in Children* (1936) – a study based on the empirical observation of just three child subjects, Jacqueline, Lucienne and Laurent Piaget. It was the elaboration of these central 'developmentalist' texts that enabled the two men to achieve their own salvation as cognitive beings.

Conclusion

The above are obviously cursory sketches. The burgeoning genre of a popular psychological science, starting with Spencer in England and Taine in France, was not the rational replacement of now enfeebled and marginalized religious beliefs. Rather, a set of teleological beliefs was itself given a new lease of life, casting off the name of religion while continuing not only its social function but also some of its underlying content. Just as without reprobation there cannot be election, so from a developmentalist perspective without the modern compartmentalization of childhood there can be no autonomous, competent adult; and without developmental and intellectual disability, there can be no normal intelligence or moral and emotional maturity.

This book has been about medium- to long-term conceptual shifts within certain fundamental continuities of the past two thousand years. An understanding of it should also enable us to spot the sudden short-term shifts that sometimes take place before our very eyes. Being modern, they are rather too easily looked at from a purely sociological standpoint. Binet's creation of cognitive testing on developmental, age-related grounds was the upshot of an institutional battle, at that very moment, on behalf of the professional body of French psychologists and against that of their psychiatric counterparts: a battle for the right to give a concrete profile to the abstract category of 'the abnormal' and to assume custody of the persons thereby created. Hence such persons had to be not *sick*, but developmentally *slow* and sometimes unimprovable.[51] In other words, the issue seems like one of power relationships among the professions. A similar example is autism. This is a category that sprang from out of the blue a mere century ago but which even within this brief existence has managed to execute a 180-degree turn. When the term was first coined in 1911 it described 'excessive hallucinations and fantasy', but the category was abruptly re-described in the 1970s as the exact opposite, a 'complete lack of an unconscious symbolic life'. In this process it was transferred, in the official rubric, from mental *illness* (schizophrenia) to '*developmental* disorder'[52] – a switch that likewise came about as the result of a victory of epidemiologists over psychoanalysts, in a professional battle typical of the 1970s.

These examples may show us how the act of labelling can be manipulative of human beings, and categorization itself a projection of the categorizer's anxieties. However, the focus on power in this kind of explanation suggests no way of preventing abuse, because it does not question the fundamental premise. That is a job for the historian, and what we learn from the history of psychology is that the ultimate truth of the human essence is something we have made over the course of time, and in time could just as easily make differently.[53]

---

[51] Serge Nicolas et al., 'Sick or slow? On the origins of intelligence as a psychological object', *Intelligence*, 41/5 (2013).
[52] See Bonnie Evans, *The Metamorphosis of Autism* (Manchester: Manchester University Press, 2017).
[53] I am paraphrasing David Graeber, *The Utopia of Rules: On Technology, Stupidity, and the Secret Joys of Bureaucracy* (Brooklyn: Melville House, 2015).

POSTSCRIPT

Further Targets for Historical Research

I have called this book *the* history of a psychological concept, but of course it is absolutely not the whole story. There has been room here for only a handful of pieces in a historical puzzle that must be completed by others. Several other areas for further research spring to mind, to which I have made only passing reference.

The first area that needs attention is the history of political thought, partly because that is the most usual hunting ground for seventeenth- and eighteenth-century conceptual historians. 'Intellectual history' is at present too narrowly defined. It needs to be qualified by the history of psychology as well as vice versa. If it is by now well established that the Enlightenment did not come about in simple diametric opposition to religious belief, the fact is also still overlooked. This caveat applies to more than just Enlightenment thinking *about* man. Modern political thought emanated also from what the thinker believed *himself* to be, qua man: his interior status. And his status in the afterlife would have featured strongly in this self-identity. Certain presuppositions which the eighteenth-century philosopher would have been brought up with were not simply shaken off. He might himself have discarded them as mere vestiges, but what kept on going underneath? The theory of election in Enlightenment texts, on the rare occasions it features, is not simply a dismissible vestige of religion; it is still alive, as part of a transitional phase in the longer-term pattern. A 'vestigial' idea is one thing when seen as such by today's historian, who turns up after the event and is therefore easily tempted to marginalize it, but was quite another thing – despite being a mere vestige even *then* – in an era when elements of election were still lodged semi-consciously in the belief system of the thinker himself. For the eighteenth century mind, what had been jettisoned as conscious belief might nevertheless still be concrete and existential – a fact which no amount of posterity's condescension can alter. The consequences of this for the history of political thought have yet to be probed.

Second is the history of education. As I indicated in Chapter 3, it rarely seems to exhibit any dispute about its own premises. It reifies childhood by having unwittingly always had in mind the *elect* child. I have not examined the German tradition in this book because its place in our topic comes relatively late. Nevertheless, from the late eighteenth century onwards Germany was a leader in education theory, the Prussians having introduced quasi-universal schooling a century in advance of France or Britain. We encountered the seminal theologian Friedrich Schleiermacher (1768–1834) in Chapter 1. As a single predestinarian, he finally dispensed with hell and established the universal possibility of election. And as educational adviser to the Prussian state after its defeat by Napoleon, he established the idea of a universal psychological development as the individual interiorization of social progress and national regeneration. In this duality the normal clearly overlaps with the elect, their common denominator being the capacity for change: 'Humans are beings which carry in themselves the ground for their development from their start to their completion . . ., especially in the life of the spirit (*Geist*) and intellect', and 'where there is no such internal ground, there is no change in the subject, or only change of a mechanical nature'.[1] Absence of change also appears in the educational texts of his better-known contemporary followers such as Herbart and Froebel in the form of 'idiots', 'imbeciles' etc.; these are the exceptions to the universal developmental rule, such a vocabulary now having medical overtones. Schleiermacher also articulated for educationists, a century before Piaget, the theoretical problem of change as one of 'specific [structural] stages' versus 'gradual transition'. Historians of education have the opportunity to promote the academic credibility of their discipline by taking seriously the claims of religion as a founding discourse of modern schooling.

Third comes social history and that of segregated institutions. As we have seen in the course of this book, there are clear links between the ideas of psychological development and of social development, a concept that itself matured over the second millennium and likewise sprang from a distinctly linear conception of time. Over the last two centuries the interior development of individuals has been seen as a function of socioeconomic progress. This assumption might equally be stood on its head: perhaps religious notions of interiority came first, sparking theories of social progress, as the founding sociologist Max Weber already suggested a long time ago. In any

---

[1] Friedrich Schleiermacher, 'Vorlesungen über die Pedagogik', in (ed.) Jens Beljan et al., *Kritische Gesamtausgabe* (1826), vol. 12, translated by Norm Friesen and Karsten Kenklies as *Outlines of the Art of Education* at www.exet.org/schleiermacher.

case, the social history needs to be explored in the light of a partly separate but interrelated conceptual history that does not always proceed at exactly the same rate.[2] One example of the need for a more subtle understanding of this is an existing genre, the history of institutions and the confinement of developmentally disabled people (in British usage, 'with learning disabilities'). This has focused on past ill treatment, largely in order to point a salutary lesson for the treatment of the 'same' people today. However, the very act of doing so reinforces the sense that cognitive ability and lack of it, development and absence of development, are natural, cross-historical kinds.[3] The historian of institutions must search for ways of standing outside this sort of reification. 'Disability' in these senses belongs to an ideology, in the classic sense of that term: that is, to the purview from a historically as well as socially restricted niche.

The fourth area is literature. The novel is seen as the classic literary form representing linear narrative, enhancing the exploration of human interiority. But from its very starting point in the medieval authors such as Chrétien de Troyes and Wolfram von Eschenbach onwards, if any one character type dominates, it is the child or the fool or the foolish child, and his or her journey into maturity. Such novels do not mirror the developmental idea but continually trip it up and subvert the idea that development is a natural kind. So many central characters bend, distort and kick against the sense of linear narrative and of achievable life goals. The obvious example is a comic farrago like Laurence Sterne's *Tristram Shandy* (1767), which sets out quite intentionally to undermine the notion that development is even possible; but it also applies to the more conventional novels of 'personal formation', the so-called *Bildungsroman*. This latter seems to be more a construct of literary theory and a self-justifying outgrowth of the developmental idea itself than an accurate representation of the novels it cites as its classic examples. In the 'personal formation' of their central characters, fiction writers of the genre are often challenging the very thing which the theory says they embody; 'our hero' is often not only a misfit in a spatially hierarchical sense but also, in a temporal sense, a malingerer, who ends up being able to claim only in some very ambiguous sense that they have 'arrived' at their goal.[4] The novel, from its medieval prototypes to its classic nineteenth-century examples, stands as a constant critique rather than a reflection of the developmental idea.

---

[2] See Koselleck, *The Practice of Conceptual History*, pp. 20, 37.
[3] See (ed.) McDonagh, *Intellectual Disability*, Introduction.
[4] See Goodey, 'Victor of Aveyron and the pre-emptive critique of developmental disability in the early modern novel', *Social History of Medicine*, 30/4 (2017).

Index

abstraction, 30, 46, 50, 201
Albertus Magnus, Saint, 49
Ambrose, Saint, 38
Aquinas, Saint Thomas, 68, 93, 99, 119, 179
Aristotle, 25, 34, 44, 49, 50, 101, 157
Arminianism, 61–2, 65, 112, 187
Arnauld, Antoine, 78, 79, 83, 89, 97, 128
attention, 46, 51, 100, 201
Augustine of Hippo, Saint
    concept of time, 39
    homo interior, 10, 21, 29, 38–40
    on holy fools, 54
    the Ages of Man, 56
    The City of God, 39, 71, 92, 100
    The Confessions, 43
autism, 21, 204
Avicenna, 49

Bacon, Sir Francis, 32
Baxter, Richard, 70, 91, 109, 112
Baye, Michel de, 64, 72
Bayle, Pierre, 179
behaviourism, 35, 172
Bellarmine, Cardinal Robert, 62
Bentham, Jeremy, 82, 189, 196
Bergson, Henri, 55
Bérulle, Cardinal Pierre de, 118
Bildungsroman, 207
Binet, Alfred, 77, 186, 199–203
Bonnet, Charles
    definition of psychology, 10
    development as fulfilment of Revelation, 156–65
    on evolution, 140
Bossuet, Jacques-Bénigne, 142
Buddhism, 24
Buffon, Comte de, 151–5
Bunyan, John, 27
Burnet, Gilbert, 122

Calvin, Jean, 103, 123
Calvinism, 60–5, 145, 162, 167, 174, 184, 201
    and Jansenism, 71, 79
    in the eighteenth century, 187, 190–1
    Pascal and, 88, 91, 97, 98, 103
chain of being, 116, 178
Charron, Pierre, 89
children, childhood
    'abnormal', 137, 199–203
    and disability, 23, 41, 155, 206
    and election, 19–20, 113–20, 134
    as incomplete beings, 25, 52, 55, 109, 165, 199, 203
    history of, 70
    punishment and supervision of, 81–3
    rights of, 202
    Rousseau and, 174–6, 184
Chrétien de Troyes, 207
Comenius, Jan, 84
Condillac, Etienne de, 138, 151–3, 156, 162, 168, 170, 171, 174
consciousness, 44, 52, 195
Coustel, Pierre, 80

Darwin, Charles, 198
Darwin, Erasmus, 197
Descartes, René, 80, 88, 115, 188
determinism, 43, 67, 96–7, 135, 149–50
    biological, 198–9
    divine, 62, 63, 88
    divine and biological forms related, 11, 64, 110, 124, 137, 161–2, 187–91
    stadial, 11, 109, 165, 177, 182
developmental disability, 19, 20, 23, 174, 203
    and physical disability, 116
    and reprobation, 42, 52–4, 73, 112, 137, 196
    and social segregation, 84, 107, 206
    Vygotsky on, 137
Diderot, Denis, 179
Duguet, Jacques-Joseph, 130–4, 156

Eberhard, Johann Augustus, 125
economic development, 31, 44, 59, 206
education, 41, 108
  Bonnet on, 159
  Buffon on, 155
  Condillac on, 153, 171
  curricula, religious and secular, 75–8
  Hartley on, 188
  history of, 83–4
  in Jansenist schools, 69–84
  Leibniz on, 123, 126, 150
  Priestley on, 190–2, 195, 196
  Rousseau on, 173, 176, 181
  special, 84, 199–202
election, theory of, 171
  and reprobation, 10, 42, 62, 67, 73, 106–12, 195–6
  and social groups, 105–6
  and the growth of epistemology, 51–2
  and theory of development, 137–65
  as lay sainthood, 40–2, 46
  as source for 'the normal', 19–20, 111–36, 137, 186, 191–2
  Augustine on, 39
  basic principles of, 10, 59–68
  in Pascal, 86–104
  Priestley on, 194, 196
  Rousseau on, 184
  the elect child, 69–84, 171, 206
emotions, the, 13, 16, 30, 34
  maturity of, 17, 19, 23, 28, 55, 105
  Rousseau on, 178, 182, 203
Enlightenment and religious belief, 86, 105, 113, 114, 125, 135–6, 151, 167, 205
Erasmus, Desiderius, 70, 79, 80

Freud, Sigmund, 17, 119
Froebel, Friedrich, 206

Galen, Claudius, 46
Galton, Sir Francis, 111, 186, 192, 197–200
Gerson, Jean, 41
Gomarus, Franciscus, 110

Hall, G. Stanley, 10, 15, 28
Hartley, David, 186–200
Heidegger, Martin, 19
Herbart, Johann Friedrich, 206
Hilton, Walter, 57, 58
Hobbes, Thomas, 14, 87, 142, 187, 190
Hugh of St Victor, 32, 76, 79, 84
Hume, David, 114

Ibn Sina, 49
idiots, imbeciles, 10, 82, 107, 108, 155, 196–7

  and the *literati*, 47
  as legal category, 53–4
  Locke on, 111–13, 145, 147
  Rousseau on, 174–6
Individual, concepts of the, 96, 127, 145, 162, 181, 194
  and interiority, 42–5
  in Augustine, 38–40
information-processing, 50
IQ testing, 77, 199–200
Irenaeus, Saint, 10, 28, 29, 36, 128, 134
Isidore of Seville, Saint, 57
Islam, 26, 27, 32, 35

Jansen, Cornelius, 64
Jansenism, 61–5, 124, 145, 156
  Duguet and, 130–4
  in the eighteenth century, 192, 197
  in the nineteenth century, 201
  Nicole and, 126–30
  Pascal's elaboration of, 85–104
  Rousseau and, 167, 171, 178, 184
  schools and education, 69–84
Jesuitism, 61–6, 87, 123, 127, 201
  Jansenist opposition to, 73, 75, 79, 80, 97, 104
  on freedom and necessity, 122, 129
  Pascal on, 92
Judaism, 26, 27, 32, 37, 61

Lavoisier, Antoine, 192
Leibniz, Gottfried Wilhelm, 164, 188, 198, 199
  and Bonnet, 156–7, 158, 160, 163
  and Condillac, 153
  and Rousseau, 174, 179, 183
  on election and reprobation, 120–6
  preformation of the rational soul, 138–40
Lessing, Gotthold Ephraim, 195
Locke, John, 77, 82, 86, 107, 193, 201
  and Pascal, 91, 103, 104
  and Rousseau, 169, 181, 202
  on election, 42, 106, 111–13, 121, 124, 145
  on idiots, 147, 155
  on the association of ideas, 187
logic, and logical reasoning, 15, 46, 48, 53, 89, 144–5, 177–9
Loyola, Saint Ignatius, 123
Lucretius, 36
Luther, Martin, 89, 123

Malebranche, Nicolas, 106, 121, 124, 134
  and Hartley, 188
  and Pierre Nicole, 126, 129
  and Rousseau, 171, 174, 176, 177, 178, 179, 183
  on children, 117–20
  on preformation, 138–43, 162

Malebranche, Nicolas (cont.)
  on temporal order, 113–17, 125, 131, 147, 152, 160
mental age, concept of, 17, 77, 186, 200, 202
Molina, Luis de, 65
Montaigne, Michel de, 89, 90
Montesquieu, 106, 133, 180
  on election, 135–6, 180
moral imbeciles, 82, 108
More, Hannah, 108, 109, 190, 197

nature
  and developmental stages, 23, 30, 57, 72, 109, 171–3, 177
  as corrupt, 64–6, 72, 104
  as 'dispositional', 118–19, 129
  Buffon on natural history, 153–5
  converging with grace, 10, 20, 79, 113, 151, 166, 178–80
  development as a natural kind, 9, 12–14, 23, 47–8, 104, 169, 207
  Leibniz on natural development, 144–51
  natural causation, 21, 99, 136, 165
  natural law, 45, 118–19, 130, 134, 176, 183
  natural logic, 48–50, 53, 177
  natural religion, 104, 109, 124, 166, 183
  Pascal on, 95–7
  versus nurture, 163, 186, 188, 191, 197–9
necessity, freedom and
  compatibility with nature, 134
  in Augustine, 64
  in Bonnet, 156–7, 160–1
  in Jansenism, 96, 97
  in Jesuitism, 63
  in Leibniz, 122–3, 125, 149
  in Locke, 112–13
  in Rousseau, 98, 174
  theory of necessarianism, 187–91, 199
Nemesius, Bishop, 46
Neoplatonism, 41, 43, 56
Newton, Sir Isaac, 24, 92, 188, 193
Nicole, Pierre, 65, 89, 108, 126–30

Pascal, Blaise, 64, 65, 81
  on development and causation, 95–7
  on human reason, 81, 93–5
  on temporal order, 85–93, 100–4
  on the child-adult distinction, 74
  on the lapse from grace, 74, 83, 97–9
Paul, Saint, 29, 63, 72, 157
Pelagius, 64, 72
Piaget, Jean, 17, 68, 137, 178, 203, 206
Plato, 51, 69
Plotinus, 29, 41
predestination
  of events, 125, 149
  of souls, single and double, 109–11, 123, 133, 136, 142, 190
preformationism
  adapted to psychology, 142–4
  Bonnet on, 156, 161–2
  Buffon and, 153–5
  in biology, 138–40
  Rousseau and, 166, 169
  theoretical basis of, 140–2
Priestley, Joseph, 186–97, 198, 199
psychoanalytic tradition, the, 17, 204
Purgatory, 59

Quintilian, 76, 81, 84

Raikes, Robert, 197
respectability and the normal, 107–8
Richardson, Samuel, 97
Ricoeur, Paul, 19
Rousseau, Jean-Jacques
  and Bonnet, 156
  Discourse on Inequality, 166, 168, 169, 183
  Emile, 11, 63, 73, 77, 85, 166–85
  Julie, 168
  Letters Written from the Mountain, 168
  on development, 138, 153, 164, 169–73
  on happiness, 93, 159
  on psychology and the General Will, 11, 98, 179–83
  On the Social Contract, 181, 185, 193
  The Confessions of Jean-Jacques Rousseau, 171, 184
Rush, Benjamin, 193

Saint-Cyran, Abbé de, 65, 71, 73, 79–83
Schleiermacher, Friedrich, 19, 206
self, concept of the, 33, 87, 101, 102, 103, 170
shamanism, 34–6, 41, 42, 52, 183
Singer, Peter, 53
social progress, 12, 29, 31–3, 55, 80, 102, 106, 117, 127, 130, 134, 185, 194, 206
Spencer, Herbert, 151, 192, 203
Sterne, Laurence, 207
Stoics, the, 28, 32, 56, 67
Sunday School movement, 197
Swammerdam, Jan, 69–84

Taine, Hippolyte, 151, 200, 203
Theory of Mind, 21
time, conceptual models of, 22–33, 35, 38, 44, 67, 86, 95
Turgot, Anne-Robert-Jacques, 12, 102, 185
twin studies, 199

Voltaire, 120, 135, 183
Vygotsky, Lev, 137

Watts, Isaac, 190
Weber, Max, 206
Wesley, John, 108, 161, 187

Whitefield, George, 187
Wild Boy of Aveyron, the, 199
Wilkes, John, 193
William of Ockham, 145
Wolff, Christian, 156, 159

Zanchi, Girolamo, 145

For EU product safety concerns, contact us at Calle de José Abascal, 56–1°, 28003 Madrid, Spain or eugpsr@cambridge.org.

www.ingramcontent.com/pod-product-compliance
Ingram Content Group UK Ltd.
Pitfield, Milton Keynes, MK11 3LW, UK
UKHW022246220326
469255UK00019B/376